Intricate and Simple Things

LEE ZIMMERMAN

# Intricate and Simple Things

## The Poetry of Galway Kinnell

UNIVERSITY OF ILLINOIS PRESS
Urbana and Chicago

Publication of this work was supported in part by a grant
from the Andrew W. Mellon Foundation.

© 1987 by the Board of Trustees of the University of Illinois
Manufactured in the United States of America
C 5 4 3 2 1

*This book is printed on acid-free paper.*

Library of Congress Cataloging-in-Publication Data

Zimmerman, Lee, 1953–
  Intricate and simple things.

  Includes index.
  1. Kinnell, Galway, 1927–      —Criticism and
interpretation.   I. Title.
PS3521.I582Z98   1987      811'.54      86–13237
ISBN 0–252–01375–1 (alk. paper)

*to my mother, Hilda Zimmerman,*
*and*
*in memory of my father, Ralph Zimmerman*

# Contents

# Acknowledgments

Of teachers, colleagues, and friends, first thanks are due to Stephen Yenser, the closest reader of this book as it was getting written. His encouragement was invaluable, and the questions he raised and advice he offered have a lot to do with what I like best here. Those specific responses were very important, but Stephen influenced the book in a more general, and profound, way as well: of that blend of intelligences that, in the act of writing, I imagined as my audience, his was predominant. Of the others I imagined in that audience, I want to especially thank Calvin Bedient and Kenneth Lincoln, who advised and encouraged me on early versions of the manuscript and who demonstrated to me that this kind of work matters. Alison Bahr also provided helpful readings of parts of the manuscript. Ann Lowry Weir and Cynthia Mitchell, my editors, were everywhere patient and helpful. And for typing and other essential help in producing the manuscript I am very grateful to Nora Reyes-Elias and Jeanette Gilkison.

Many people influenced the book in less specific but very important ways. The project was partly conceived in many conversations (not only about literature) with Carolyn Cohen; it was nurtured in the company (and at the home) of Ann Riffe. Discussions with Reed Wilson and Ann Richards about reading and writing poems helped shape my thinking early on. John Engle helped me learn to love poetry, and I also want to thank him for showing me how much fun the terrible pain of writing might be. After the book was mostly complete, Michael Dane Moore and Donna Gregory helped me see some of the implications of my thinking that I could only minimally pursue here; they have inspired what I hope will be future work.

I also thank those people who tried their best to keep me from writing this book; without their distractions and support—moral and immoral—I would have had little to say. José Gutierrez kept insisting I leave my room and join him in savoring the whimsy and woe of other projects than writing. For these other projects, Eric Schroeder made sure I was well provisioned. Cary Franklin tried mightily to convince me to use silly words (he may still think he failed). Greg Belcamino would barge in and try to keep me from finishing even just one more sentence. Zoey Zimmerman, my sister, intimidated (and inspired) me by her artistic energy. And Paul Zimmerman, my brother, never let me forget the batting averages. These people kept faith during bad times, as did Murray Weiler, to whom I am deeply grateful for helping me discover there are things worth saying and some point, after all, in saying them. It feels strange to thank these people for anything that can be put in these few words, for, of course, one cannot do very much justice to the real debts and feelings of gratitude. Doubly strange, then, to thank my parents, who are everywhere in these pages: my father, who though he died long before this book was started, profoundly shaped my thinking and feeling about its central issues; and my mother, who told and tells me things.

Houghton Mifflin Company has granted permission to reprint sections from the following volumes of Galway Kinnell's poetry: *The Avenue Bearing the Initial of Christ into the New World*, copyright 1953, 1954, © 1955, 1958, 1959, 1960, 1961, 1963, 1964, 1970, 1971, 1974 by Galway Kinnell; *Body Rags*, copyright © 1967 by Galway Kinnell; *The Book of Nightmares*, copyright © 1971 by Galway Kinnell; *Mortal Acts, Mortal Words*, copyright © 1980 by Galway Kinnell; *The Past*, copyright © 1985 by Galway Kinnell. Theodore Roethke's "Snake," from *The Collected Poems of Theodore Roethke*, copyright © 1937, 1954, 1957, 1958, 1959, 1960, 1961, 1962, 1963, 1964, 1965, 1966 by Beatrice Roethke, is quoted by permission of Doubleday and Company, Inc. James Merrill's "In Monument Valley," from *Braving the Elements*, copyright © 1972 by James Merrill, is quoted by permission of Atheneum Publishers, Inc. Sylvia Plath's "Ariel," from *The Collected Poems of Sylvia Plath*, edited by Ted Hughes, copyright © 1965 by Ted Hughes, is quoted by permission of Harper and Row Publishers, Inc. Ted Hughes's "That Moment," from *New Selected Poems* by Ted Hughes, copyright © 1971 by Ted Hughes, is quoted by permission of Harper and Row. John Ashbery's "Ode to Bill," from *Self-Portrait in a Convex Mirror,* copyright © 1974 by John Ashbery, is quoted by permission of Viking Penguin, Inc.

I am indebted to the UCLA English Department, whose H. T. Swedenberg Fellowship provided financial help during the writing of much of this book. And I am very grateful to Galway Kinnell for permission to quote from his conversation and for his other help.

# Abbreviations

Citations from Kinnell's works are identified by the following abbreviations:

BL     *Black Light.* Boston: Houghton Mifflin, 1965. The novel was reissued in 1980 by North Point Press, San Francisco.

BN     *The Book of Nightmares.* Boston: Houghton Mifflin, 1971.

BR     *Body Rags.* Boston: Houghton Mifflin, 1968.

FH     *Flower Herding on Mount Monadnock.* Boston: Houghton Mifflin, 1964.

FP     *First Poems.* In *The Avenue Bearing the Initial of Christ into the New World: Poems 1946–64.* Boston: Houghton Mifflin, 1974.

MA     *Mortal Acts, Mortal Words.* Boston: Houghton Mifflin, 1980.

PPD     "Poetry, Personality and Death." *Field* 4 (1971): 56–75.

PPW     "The Poetics of the Physical World." *Iowa Review* 2 (1971): 113–26.

WDS     *Walking Down the Stairs: Selections from Interviews.* Ann Arbor: The University of Michigan Press, 1978.

WIW  "Whitman's Indicative Words" in *Walt Whitman's Autograph Revision of the Analysis of Leaves of Grass*. New York: New York University Press, 1974, 53–63. A slightly revised version of this essay appears in *Walt Whitman: The Measure of His Song*, ed. Dan Campion, Ed Folsam, and Jim Perlman (Minneapolis: Holy Cow! Press, 1981).

WKW  *What a Kingdom It Was*. Boston: Houghton Mifflin, 1960.

FP, WKW, and FH are collected in *The Avenue Bearing the Initial of Christ into the New World: Poems 1946–64*. The collected poems incorporate some slight changes, many of which Kinnell made while reciting the poems to audiences. The collection is my text for the volumes it includes, except where I indicate I am discussing the earlier version of a poem.

I also use the abbreviation SM to refer to Walt Whitman's "Song of Myself," in *Leaves of Grass*, ed. Harold W. Blodgett and Scully Bradley. New York: New York University Press, 1965.

Intricate and Simple Things

# Introduction

Let me glide noiselessly forth;
With the key of softness unlock the locks—with a whisper,
Set ope the doors O Soul.

Tenderly—Be not impatient,
(Strong is your hold O mortal flesh,
Strong is your hold O love.)
    —Walt Whitman, "The Last Invocation"

      It is true
That only flesh dies, and spirit flowers without stop
For men, cows, dung, for all dead things; and it is good, yes—

But an incarnation is in particular flesh
    —Galway Kinnell, "Freedom, New Hampshire"

"If there is one kind of moment from which poetry springs, I would say it's this one," Kinnell once observed in an interview: "When in the presence of the wind, or the night sky, or the sea . . . we are reminded both of the kinship and the separation between ourselves and what is beyond us" (*WDS* 88). There is "a feeling of strangeness and then of terrible kinship" (*WDS* 89), "terrible" because it implies the dissolution of identity, the death of the self, although death too "has two aspects—the extinction, which we fear, and the flowing away into the universe, which we desire" (*WDS* 23). Kinnell's poetic enterprise derives from these two feelings. In ways which this study tries to chart, his writing elaborates—is provoked into being by—the shifting relationships between them. Separation and kinship, multeity and unity, particular flesh and communal spirit—these pairs may at times represent an unresolved conflict, but in the greatest moments of Kinnell's poetry, as in what he calls "the greatest moments of our lives" (*WDS* 97), they are incorporated in a surpassing whole.[1] If he cannot so easily imagine gliding noiselessly forth into this whole as Whitman can, if he glimpses the possibility only in moments, it is because mortal flesh holds on so fiercely. "We do not have to worry about being too consoling," Kinnell knows, "because the reality [of the physical death of the self] is so inconsolable."[2] Like the mock Christ in "The Supper after the Last" (*WKW*), Kinnell has come to prove we are "Intricate and simple things."

Few contemporary poets so consistently mine both sides of an opposition. For Kinnell, as for Blake, whether it indicates conflict or complementarity, "Opposition is true Friendship."[3] But where Blake expressed this opposition by rejecting the dominant literary heritage of his time, Kinnell works within a literary tradition (of which Blake himself is one source). It would not be inaccurate to call this the "Romantic" tradition; like Whitman and Rilke, the most obvious influences, he pursues the Romantic project of finding the self in the world and the world in the self. But it would be inadequate. Good poetry resists easy characterization, but it is Kinnell's particular strength as a writer that the usual labels tell us especially little about his work. Opposition for him pertains not to a rejection of tradition but to his *affinity* with writers who are themselves opposed to each other in important ways. To illustrate this double heritage, I want to place Kinnell in relation to three opposed pairs of literary ancestors. I am not proposing direct *influence* in every case but rather tracing lines of connection, which are pursued more fully in the following chapters. I discuss other connections as well in those chapters (some more directly influential), but focusing initially on these matched, or mismatched, pairs may help clarify the doubleness so essential to Kinnell's writing in general.

The first of these pairs is the most historically immediate. Although T. S. Eliot and William Carlos Williams epitomize opposite impulses in modern American poetry, we need both the abscissa of one and the ordinate of the other against which to plot Kinnell's relation to his century. The connection to Williams is, of course, more overt. "The moment I heard him . . . I felt close to him," Kinnell remembers (*WDS* 93), and it is not hard to see why. As his description of that poetry reading in "For William Carlos Williams"

(*WKW*) suggests, he identified with Williams's anti-academic stance, the immediacy and passion he brought to poetry, in sharp (too sharp) contrast to the "professor / In neat bow tie and enormous tweeds" and other "lovers of literature" who paid "the tribute of their almost total / Inattention" and "then scrammed." Kinnell later realized the arrogance of this early poem, but his link to Williams remained. Frequently taking as his subject matter what he calls "the things and creatures of the world," he follows Williams's theoretical lead in wanting to find "no ideas but in things." This glorification of the local often leads Kinnell to subjects in the American grain—New York's Lower East Side, the civil rights movement, Bruce Pond—and if he is not so rooted as Williams in a single geographic spot (Kinnell's wandering, indeed, constitutes one part of his Americanism), his discovery of value in the local, in "particular flesh," nevertheless aligns him with what Charles Altieri defines as the immanentist tradition: the tradition, deriving from Wordsworth and kept vital by Williams, which emphasizes the mind's *perception* of a sacred presence inhering in the world, rather than, like Coleridge and the symbolist tradition, trying to "redeem the objective by pointing to the ways it is formed and structured in creative acts of consciousness."[4] For Williams and Kinnell, so much depends upon seeing the things and creatures of the world.

To ask what "seeing" means in this context is to begin to explore the ways in which Kinnell's poetry significantly departs from Williams's. "For most of his life," Kinnell observes, Williams "tended to be what I would call 'photographic.' Whitman's adjective enters the thing and feels out some inner quality, while Williams tends to use the straight descriptive word. For example, in his little poem, 'So much depends / upon / a red wheelbarrow . . .' we see the scene but we don't experience it. Without its first line— which is to say without its idea—the poem might not be interesting. Perhaps the Williams dictum, 'No ideas but in things,' in practice actually means, 'No things but in ideas'" (*WDS* 37). Compare the wheelbarrow poem with a poem like "The Porcupine" (to take an extreme instance) to illustrate how "seeing" for Kinnell, as for Whitman, involves a probing below the "photographic" surface to "feel out some inner quality." Williams doesn't seem driven to probe below—or rise above—because he seems to have what he needs right here, effortlessly; Kenneth Rexroth writes, "That's why you [Williams] always had so much to give, because you never wanted anything but what you knew you had already."[5] Kinnell, in contrast, writes not from possession but from deprivation. "I always seem to be floundering," he explains; "My poems are more like the acts of one who is lost" (WDS 38), although they are also the means, he might have added, by which he finds the world again.

The lines of connection to Williams nevertheless remain more direct than those running back to T. S. Eliot. Kinnell has had little to say about Eliot, has certainly never remarked that "I felt close to him"; it might seem odd to link what one critic playfully caricatured as an "Existential Ur-mensch standing there facing me, holding his guts in his hands, his underwear sweat-fetid" with the self-described Anglican and royalist.[6] But the affinity, if submerged, is strong. Unlike Williams, Eliot and Kinnell both hunger for the sacred, feel their distance from it, and chart the strivings of consciousness to contact or be contacted by it—although where Kinnell sees Immanence, a presence dwelling in, or constituted by, the things and creatures and words of this world, Eliot sees Incarnation, the temporary visitation from the other world in this otherwise godforsaken one. As I suggest in my discussion of *The Book of Nightmares*, both poets also take as a central theme the interplay between time and eternity, the intricate and the simple. Many poems touch on such a basic subject, of course, but the structural ramifications of this theme in *Four Quartets* and *Nightmares* make them especially close. I amplify this comparison in my later discussion, but I might point out here that, unlike *Paterson* or the *Cantos*—linear, accumulative, endless—the *Nightmares* and the *Quartets* strive to be perfected wholes. Where Williams's long poem is patterned on the Passaic River, the sequences of Eliot and Kinnell are structured like the Chinese jar in "Burnt Norton" that "Moves perpetually in its stillness"; even as each is a single, "still" whole, a verbally interconnected tapestry, it unfolds in sequence, "moving" in time. In its final section, *Four Quartets* thus figures itself as moving in "consort," as a "dancing together" of its individual words; Kinnell images his poem at the end as a "concert of one / divided among himself."

The split between Eliot and Williams in some ways corresponds to the division between the symbolist and immanentist poetic traditions which, as Altieri shows, trace back to Coleridge and Wordsworth. But whether the mind accommodates itself to the world or reshapes it, whether the eye perceives or half-creates, whether a poet tries "reorienting the subjective consciousness by teaching it ways of attending to its participation in objective laws" or "tries to redeem the objective by pointing to the ways it is formed and structured in creative acts of consciousness" (Altieri 37), a relatively stable reconciliation results. In poetic language, mind and world marry. But rather than opposing Wordsworth and Coleridge to each other, we might oppose both of them to Keats, for whom, as Robert Pinsky argues, language eloigns rather than joins.[7] Language, as a "static, general medium," cannot grasp "the fluid, absolutely particular life of the physical world," Pinsky claims (3), although "the effort to make the gap seem less than absolute has produced some of the most remarkable and moving poetry in the language" (59). Focusing on "Ode to a Nightingale," he shows how, as Keats constructs it, "the situation is inherently, and not temporarily, a quandary: to be a 'sod' or to be 'forlorn'" (55). The poet wants to be "with" the bird but recognizes this implies an "easeful death," the degeneration of self to sod; and language, "the very word" which is inevitably self-conscious, provides the means of retaining his unmerged but "forlorn" being: "Forlorn! the very word is like a bell / To toll me back from thee to my sole self!"

Keats thus works from very different assumptions than Wordsworth and Coleridge about language and the desirability of joining mind and nature. In my discussion of "The Porcupine" and "The Bear" I try to explain in detail how Kinnell writes from both ends of this opposition. Part of my argument focuses on how, discovering parts of himself in those animals, he shares not only Wordsworth's notion that the poem can marry mind and world but also Keats's fear that kinship is often terrible, the obliteration of identity. Kinnell knows that this kinship may extend consciousness, but if his sense of self is not so precarious as Keats's, if he does not feel forced to choose between being a sod and being forlorn, he nevertheless cannot forget that the integrity of the self is threatened by its extension. He knows that, although "it is a death out of which one might hope to be reborn more giving, more alive, more open, more related to the natural life," it is nevertheless "The death of the self I seek" (PPD 74).

The outsidership he frequently cultivates may afford him opportunity to rediscover the world over and over, but if these discoveries enlarge and enliven the self, in the Keatsian tradition they are achieved with what Pinsky calls "a sense of cost, misgiving, difficulty" (59). "Poetry has taken on itself the task of breaking out of the closed ego," Kinnell observes (PPD 64), but as he works at this task, the ego is always, in Richard Howard's phrase, "rigorously *in question.*"[8] In *Mortal Acts, Mortal Words,* the dilemma is formulated in terms which invite a psychoanalytic reading:

> My mother did not want me to be born;
> afterwards, all her life, she needed me to return.
> When this more-than-love flowed toward me, it brought
>     darkness;
> she wanted me as burial earth wants—to heap itself gently
>     upon but also to annihilate—
> and I knew, whenever I felt longings to go back,
> that is what wanting to die is. That is why
>
> dread lives in me,
> dread which comes when what gives life beckons toward death,
> dread which throws through me
> waves
> of utter strangeness, which wash the entire world empty.
>                         ("The Last Hiding Places of Snow")

One need not accept this passage as a strictly literal historical account in order to understand how it suggests that for Kinnell kinship can both extend and extinguish the self, can appear desirable and terrible at once.

Wordsworth and Keats divide over issues which, in more extreme form, divide Whitman and Dickinson. The lines of connection from Kinnell to these American forebears represent the most polarized expression of his double ancestry. The link to Whitman is one of the first qualities anyone reading Kinnell's poetry, essays, or interviews will notice; but his work simultaneously evidences an opposing, if usually covert, bond with Dickinson. With Whitman, we may properly speak of influence rather than mere affinity.

Kinnell's essays and interviews lay bare the premises of his own poetry, and much of what little criticism he has written centers on Whitman. In "The Poetics of the Physical World," Kinnell hails Whitman as the first practitioner of such poetics, as "the first poet in English wholly to discard outward form" (114). He prizes Whitman, not for writing about "the thing which dies" (the true subject of poetry, Kinnell suggests), but rather for refusing to betray his turmoiled love for the world into neat stanzas, for his openness of line and the sense that in the poem all things are possible. Whitman didn't tame the world, he loved it. Implicitly illuminating his own abandonment of formal regularity, Kinnell suggests that Whitman "gave up the attempt to be a poet like the others and followed, rather, his own intimations of a wilder, freer poetry which could not be contained in the old forms. Halfway through his life he discovered the absolutely new" (114). Whitman fulfills—indeed, *defines*—Kinnell's criterion that "in a poem you wish to reach a new place. And that requires pure wandering—that rare condition when you have no external guides at all" (113). (Working with a broad brush here, Kinnell occasionally lapses into overstatement: what syntactic order isn't an external guide?) To Frost's analogy that writing free verse is like playing tennis without a net, Kinnell counters that "the poem is less like a game than like a journey" (114).

Such statements derive from Kinnell's view in this essay that from a historical perspective formal regularity no longer can lay claim to the ontological status it once did. From early English poetry until the nineteenth century, according to Kinnell, rhyme and meter probably "imitated a natural harmony": a regular universe called for poetic regularity. When "that supernatural harmony and that natural order had crumbled," the Romantics and Victorians clung to rhyme and meter to shield themselves from the resultant chaos, and "in this way poetry, along with so many other human endeavors, undertook the conquest of nature" (113). Most nineteenth-century poems in fixed forms thus give off for Kinnell a nostalgic aroma. The implications of this thinking for our century are obvious: "For modern poets—for everyone after Yeats—rhyme and meter, having lost their sacred and natural basis, amount to little more than mechanical aids for writing" (113). (Why does Kinnell exclude Yeats from the blanket condemnation? No one,

after all, saw more chaos in nature, in those salmon falls, those
mackerel-crowded seas, yet none of his verse is free, and most of
it—even when he revels in those crowded seas of generation—is
rhymed.)

This scenario is debatable.[9] But the conclusions Kinnell draws
from it do suggest much about what his formal approach owes to
Whitman. A more fundamental debt emerges in "Whitman's Indicative Words," where, again revealing his own poetic aspirations,
Kinnell describes the communion with the world Whitman achieves
in his language. Whitman's voice is "unmistakably personal, and it
is universal. It is outgoing and attaches itself to the things and creatures of the word [*sic*—an interesting misprint; considering the
phrase is a familiar refrain in his essays, surely he wrote "the things
and creatures of the *world*"[10]]; yet it speaks at the same time of a
life far within" (54). He loved words but "it is obvious what en-
trances Whitman is not words in themselves but the luminous reality. In return for his love, or his carnal knowledge, reality lays its
own words freely and unasked for on his tongue" (56). The East-
ern mysticisms from which Transcendentalism derives emphasize
the non-verbal character of the means by which the self apprehends its own participation in the world, but here Whitman's Transcendentalism is largely a matter of speech:

> An energy flows between Whitman and the thing. He loves the
> thing; he enters it, becomes its voice, and expresses it. But to enter a
> thing is to open oneself to it and let the thing enter oneself, until its
> presence glows within oneself. Therefore, when Whitman speaks for
> a leaf of grass, the grass also speaks for him. The light from heaven
> which shines in Whitman's poetry is often a consequence of these
> loving unions. At the end of "Crossing Brooklyn Ferry" Whitman
> tells the appearances of things, "We use you, and do not cast you
> aside—we plant you permanently within us." (57)

As the diction of these passages suggests, Kinnell, like Whitman,
sees that the bonds uniting self and world are essentially erotic.
Whitman understood that "poetry goes not merely from mind to
mind, but from the whole body to the whole body" (55); Kinnell
thinks that his relationship with Virginia, a real person who becomes a character in *The Book of Nightmares,* is "part illusory,
being purely platonic" (*WDS* 109).

In his poetry, Kinnell invokes Whitman most openly in his longer works, especially "The Avenue Bearing the Initial of Christ into the New World" (*WKW*). That poem seems astonished by all the details it is compelled to include, as if it were seeing them for the first time. Syntactic coordination abounds—that Whitmanesque strategy which, in its refusal to evaluate perception, provides the childlike feel of reality freshly apprehended. For the same reason so does listing and cataloging, although, as Randall Jarrell puts it, anyone who would call some of Whitman's catalogues mere lists "would boil his babies for soap."[11] But, as I argue in my later discussion of "Avenue C," Kinnell's Whitmanesque impulse continually vies with the darker aspect of his vision. In "The Poetics of the Physical World," applauding Whitman's willingness to wander, Kinnell quotes a passage from "Song of Myself," section 46, which ends:

> Long enough have you dream'd contemptible dreams,
> Now I wash the gum from your eyes

Rooted in the immanentist tradition, Whitman, like Kinnell, wants poetry to make us see. But when the gum is washed from their own eyes, the two see the world from very different perspectives. Kinnell sees pain and death, which have an insistent and tragic presence that he wants not to denigrate. Whitman (especially in his earlier work) isn't as troubled by them: "I know I am deathless / . . . I laugh at what you call dissolution" (SM 20). Kinnell sees death inhering in all life, sees "deathwatches" inside of things and "the worms / on his back" that are "already gnawing away" (*BN* 75). What Whitman feels inside of himself "is not chaos or death—it is form, union, plan—it is eternal life—it is Happiness" (SM 50). For Whitman "the smallest sprout shows there is really no death" (SM 6); for Kinnell it shows just the opposite. With ungummed eyes Kinnell sees nightmares, Whitman "the dazzle of light and of every moment" of his life (SM 46). Where for Whitman "It avails not—time or place" ("Crossing Brooklyn Ferry"), for Kinnell nothing avails more than time; "an old man / Can know / A kind of gratefulness / Toward time that kills him," because "Everything he loved was made of it" ("Spindrift" *FH*). Kinnell doesn't directly accuse Whitman of a too-quick-and-easy Tennysonian consolation or of letting his transcendentalism eclipse a proper confrontation with pain and death, but he does feel that Whitman hides his own human effort to accommodate them, to his poetic detriment: "Whitman did not like us to see his troubled side. He wanted us to see him as he wished to be. His confessions of having experienced base emotions are concessions, claims to common humanity, which have a patronizing tone. His poems, therefore, rarely contain struggles of any kind. They begin in the same clarity in which they end. This is often their weakness" (WIW 58).

True, Whitman thinks up some spectacularly nightmarish and bloody images—he relishes the gory details of suicides, amputations, mass slaughter (SM 8,15, 34)—but he is so unfaltering in his presentation that, except for some rare, unguarded moments, he never seems to be struggling to come to terms with these terrors (sometimes they have the feel of just a few more elements in an expansive catalogue that, like a slow child, he doesn't sort out). He presents tragedy—he presents *everything*—but it doesn't truly threaten either his unfazed tone or his loving acceptance of anything the miraculous world can contain. "To die is different from what anyone supposed, and luckier" for him (SM 6), while Kinnell, although he doesn't swerve from death, doesn't feel it is anything like lucky: "When I think there will come a time when I won't experience this world anymore, particularly when I think one day I will leave my children forever, I can hardly bear it" (WDS 91). Again, "we do not have to worry about being too consoling, because the reality is so inconsolable." Here Kinnell's poetics depart from Whitman's, incorporating a truer sense of tragedy.

This difference helps explain why, even when Kinnell sounds most like Whitman, he remains stylistically different in essential ways. Consider, for example, "Vapor Trail Reflected in the Frog Pond," in *Body Rags,* where he parodies Whitman's "I Hear America Singing." Since it is a parody, we might expect it to adopt Whitman's "style" but alter his "content." And to a certain extent it does. Like "I Hear America Singing," it catalogues varied American "carols"; it presents them without direct comment or interpretation, preferring coordination to subordination; it accumulates as many details as it can, in a variety of line lengths and rhythms. But although their ears now may be ungummed, where Whitman hears joyous singing, Kinnell hears cracks, sputs, groans, and curses. Whitman celebrates, Kinnell berates. Whitman himself sings, Kinnell curses, knowing that the common man is less likely to be singing blithely and strongly than he is to be sprawled before a TV, docilely gazing at the commoditization of the human body, unbothered by savage wars.

But this difference in content reflects back and alters the style. Kinnell's parody is only one part of a three-part poem, whose sections relate only obliquely to each other, the stylistic fragmentation matching the troubled content. "I Hear America Singing," in contrast, is stylistically an integrated whole—indeed, it is a single sentence—in accordance with its happier subject matter. This difference disrupts the rhythms as well: Whitman's lines proceed smoothly, they break only after a complete syntactic unit, and the phrases flow together, separated only by commas, never—even when the grammar technically demands it—by stronger punctuation; in *Mortal Acts, Mortal Words* Kinnell's verse will move in this direction, but here, as in most of *Body Rags* and *The Book of Nightmares,* his lines are more jagged, abruptly chopped off. Consider the openings. Whitman introduces his list with a single line, balanced neatly by chiamus ("I hear," "singing," "carols," "I hear") and separated from what it introduces only by a comma. Kinnell, compelled by a less harmonious vision, breaks up his introduction into three lines, separates "I hear" from "America Singing" with "coming over the hills," and makes the transition to the catalogue more abrupt with a colon. Whitman's line beginnings are syntactically the same (the *the*'s provide visual harmony too); Kinnell's anaphora is less regular. Each of Whitman's lines contains one or more unbroken semantic—and syntactic—units, so that each line is a new start, while Kinnell both splits syntactic units ("stabs / the rice") and extends semantic ones beyond a single line ("curses" spreads out over the last three). His poem *is* "Whitmanesque," but his ironic tone and grim subject matter make for a less effusive, jerkier version of what he calls Whitman's "mystic music," a version that, even in less bitter and more accepting poems, typifies his mature work.

I have gone into some detail about how Kinnell both derives and departs from Whitman because this seems to me the central literary relationship in his writing. If here and in later discussions I emphasize the key differences between them, it is because the affinity is more widely acknowledged, and it is the interplay between this affinity and Kinnell's more tragic elements that most distinguishes his verse. I have framed this doubleness here in terms of a dual relationship with Whitman, but another way to express how Kinnell departs from Whitman is to outline how, with quieter steps perhaps, he approaches Dickinson, whom he admires particularly for her descriptions of "those extreme states of feeling," as he puts it, "that nobody else ever uttered, that she herself could barely utter."[12] We might expect to find it hard to square the Dickinson who withdrew to her room with the Kinnell who, like Whitman, often presents himself as roaming about. But where Whitman finds himself at home wherever he wanders, Kinnell, in the beginning of poems especially, is often alone, "unhoused" (*BN* 3). Often he occupies a border zone, a liminal space, some no man's land between two homelands. And often his travels take him to lonely rooms on the road in which he chooses to cloister himself, like an itinerant Dickinson carrying her refuge with her, tortoise-like. Indeed, *The Book of Nightmares* interwines two basic settings—one in which Kinnell is "on the path," physically journeying like Whitman, the other in which he remains holed up in a hotel room, in Dickinsonian seclusion, wrestling like her with "extreme states of feeling."

"What we are dealing with at all times in seeing Dickinson," Suzanne Juhasz observes, "is the initial fact of dislocation—and then the differences, the difficulties, and the strategies to which this relation gave rise."[13] If Kinnell's resultant strategies differ dramatically from hers, if his valves of attention open out into the world instead of, like hers, closing attention off "Like Stone" (303), this "initial fact of dislocation" nevertheless marks a real affinity between them. Whitman's poems, as Kinnell sees them, "rarely contain struggles of any kind. They begin in the same clarity in which they end." Dislocated, Kinnell and Dickinson write poems which *are* struggles, which grope *toward* clarity. The world "beckons" to them but also "baffles" (501). Whitman embraces what is beyond the self, Dickinson battles it, Kinnell does both. Whitman's lines open out, merge with each other, eagerly greet the white space into which they rush. Dickinson's are wary, fight each other off, keep their distance with dashes; they take a tentative step or two out onto the page, then cautiously retreat, afraid to move, for "To stir would be to slip" into a hellish "Pit" (1712). In much of his writing, Kinnell adopts both strategies. His lines race bravely onto the page, the beckoning world, but often break off in mid-phrase, as if suddenly they knew better or were baffled; frequently they snap off barely after they have started, although the poems usually conclude with release, not withdrawal. Combining centripetal and centrifugal energies, Kinnell's verse is impelled by the resultant tension.

Kinnell draws closest to Dickinson in his efforts to "Tell all the Truth" (1129). "Whitman," as he notes, "did not like us to see his troubled side. He wanted us to see him as he wished to be": our most "open" poet is among our most secretive. Where he enjoins us to "Unscrew the locks from the doors! / Unscrew the doors themselves from their jambs!" (SM 24), Dickinson "selects her own Society—/ Then—shuts the Door" (303); but where he for the most part keeps locked up what troubles him, she includes the reader in her Society, tells "all the Truth," shares with us states of mind troubled sometimes to the brink of madness, rehearses in language "those extreme states of feeling that no one else ever uttered." Kinnell too aspires to this sheer but terrible truth-telling, recognizes the poetic necessity of allowing us to see his "troubled side." This resolve to tell all of a difficult truth leads to a rejection of consoling notions of an afterlife. "I don't take at face value the doctrines that suggest some further individual life for a person," Kinnell explains. "The most difficult thing for the human being is the knowledge that he will die. . . . All the theories of personal immortality or personal resurrection or personal reincarnation very likely are the results of wishful thinking" (WDS 97). Dickinson's refusal to quiet herself with this wishful thinking or to find death "lucky," as Whitman does, is a model for Kinnell. When she imagines leaving the world, as Kinnell observes (PPW 124), she does not picture heaven but rather only what she can experience *here*, the buzzing fly; for both poets the world keeps eclipsing whatever may lie beyond. In *The Book of Nightmares* Kinnell dissolves back into "the fingerprint of all things" (68), like Whitman effusing his flesh in eddies into the world at the end of "Song of Myself." But the final lines of *Nightmares* envision another destiny for the poet's flesh:

> On the body,
> on the blued flesh, when it is
> laid out, see if you can find
> the one flea which is laughing.

At the end he invokes not Whitman but Dickinson's buzzing corpsefly.

## CHAPTER 1

# Ambiguous Allegiances:
## *What a Kingdom It Was*

I

"The poetry of Galway Kinnell," Richard Howard writes, "is an Ordeal by Fire. . . . It is fire—in its constant transformations, its endless resurrection—which *is* reality, for Kinnell, as for Heraclitus" (305). But if "fire *is* reality" for both, it is not *all* of reality for Kinnell. Because what is consumed away is equally as real as what consumes it, his poetry is severely unstoical. As opposed to "the orphic pitilessness of Heraclitus," Howard observes, when "Kinnell evokes mortality as a commitment to the fire, there is an unappeasable grief in his 'heart's hell': it is the grief of history, the pain of things happening once and once only, irreversibly" (306). All things are one for Kinnell (the fire), yet since at the same time they happen "once and once only," each is particular. Explaining why he mistrusts similes, he remarks: "I don't think things are often like other things. At some level all things *are* each other, but before that point they are separate entities" (*WDS* 52).

This paradox coils at the heart of Kinnell's writing. His relationship to it varies over the years, he formulates it in renewed terms in each succeeding volume and pursues different implications, but when his first published collection appeared in 1960, he had already found his theme. The poems in *What a Kingdom It Was* unfold with more formal regularity than those in Kinnell's subsequent books, keep their composure even when threatened with the energy that will later break his verse apart, but the unstable paradox that generates that energy remains the central subject. Kinnell moves from separation to kinship, but the kinship remains at once enlivening and terrible. Howard invokes Hopkins as mediator between Heraclitus and Kinnell, but where the burning off of "mortal trash," of "Jack, joke, poor potsherd, patch, matchwood," leaving only a timeless, fleshless residue of "immortal diamond," ignites Hopkins's ecstasy, Kinnell's exhilaration is at least matched in his early work by grief for the mortal trash consumed away. "Away grief's gasping," Hopkins cries out, and "In a flash, at a trumpet crash," it is done.[1] When Kinnell sees "the blue world flashing," he concedes "That only flesh dies, and spirit flowers without stop . . . and it is good"; but because "an incarnation is in particular flesh," when a man dies "he remains dead, / And the few who loved him know this until they die" ("Freedom, New Hampshire").

Whatever communion poems in *What a Kingdom It Was* achieve with the flashing world is predicated on, and incorporates, an initial isolation. In this, the volume is representative of its time. As many critics have pointed out, much poetry of the late fifties and early sixties, of which Lowell's *Life Studies* is perhaps the most remarked-upon example, tries to root in a particular, often isolated, consciousness. Ralph Mills, in the earliest extended discussion of *Kingdom*, offers a typical description of this postmodernism:

> In such poets . . . the pursuit of personal vision often leads toward a precipitous, dizzying boundary where the self stands alone, unaided but for its own resources, before the seemingly tangible earth at hand with its bewildering multiplicity of life, the remoteness of space, the endless rhythms of nature, the turns of night and day, and within, the elusive images of memory and dream, the irrationality and uncertainty of human behavior, the griefs and ecstacies that living accumulates. Here the poet—and Galway Kinnell is certainly of this company—is thrown back upon his own perceptions; his art must be the authoritative testimony to a man's own experience, or it is meaningless.[2]

Responding to Mills, Donald Davie counters that all worthwhile poetry comes from the poet's being thrown back on his own experience.[3] But what is central to Mills's perception is the godlessness of it all. Thrown back on himself, Davie still sees Christ out there. Kinnell doesn't: "When we listen we hear outer space telling us we're a race living for a while on a little planet that will die. As for what lies beyond, we know nothing—our brains are the wrong kind, or are too small, or something" (*WDS* 29). So, Mills suggests, he is left to explore "relentlessly the actualities of his existence to wrest from them what significance for life he can" (67).

Perhaps "wrest" isn't quite accurate, just as in the earlier Mills quotation "seemingly tangible earth" doesn't do justice to Kinnell's sure sense of the physical presence of things. For him, it is a matter less of forcefully wresting meaning from what might be out there than of *opening* himself to a natural world he never truly doubts. This aligns him with those whom Charles Altieri calls the poets of Immanence, who, unlike the confessional poets, find some escape from the potentially solipsistic postmodern dilemma.[4] Turning from Coleridge, who stressed the imagination *projecting* consciousness onto the world, they follow Wordsworth, whose task was *perceiving* a nurturing reality that resides beyond the self and precedes it. How much significance this world yields for Kinnell depends on how completely one does without the other world. If we understand "transcendence" as referring not to a reaching beyond the enclosed ego but rather to a reaching beyond the natural world in which the ego participates, we can say that the central action of *What a Kingdom It Was* is Kinnell's struggle to rid himself of what he calls in "The Supper after the Last" the "Lech for transcendence."

II

In two poems, "First Communion" and "Easter," the rejected "Lech for transcendence" is explicitly Christianity itself. In the former, the boy's insistently materialistic view of church culminates in lines of flat rejection:

> Jesus, it is a disappointing shed
> Where they hang your picture
> And drink juice, and conjure
> Your person into inferior bread.

If the poem consisted merely—or mainly—of such cranky dismissal of Christian ritual, Davie's complaint that the boy's objections are "puerile" and even "mercenary" (18)—that he can't "stand still long enough to understand" what Christianity is all about (17)—might persuade. But the boy *can* stand still, long enough anyway to render a closely observed and delicately written description of the autumn landscape. Far from mercenary, he sees the autumn with a sensitivity that allows the poem's true first communion: "In the wind outside a twig snaps / Like a tiny lid shutting somewhere in the ear." This communion anticipates a future one with a woman, for the real sacred moment in the first section isn't imaged in the eating of the "pastry wafer" but in Uncle Abraham and his woman "Asleep in each other's arms in the haybarn." But the kinship it offers is terrible; the natural world the boy communes with is green and dying, consumed by the Heraclitean fire that created it. Autumn is coming on. The twig is breaking. The boy's room is going out. His true first communion comes in confronting the darkness without the lamp of Jesus.

Although "Easter" finally recoils from the burning world, it does not hide from it in church. As in "First Communion," in this poem Christianity is inadequate—inadequate here to this potentially murderous world where Christ represents our victimization, not our hope. The religion isn't tested directly, but "The disinfected voice of the minister" at the Easter service clearly leaves the townsfolk untouched, undistracted from the mundane, and unconsoled about the gruesome morning news, the rape and drowning of a virgin nurse.

The speaker, like other villagers, at first seems disengaged from both the Easter service and the murder itself. Suggesting the church's abstract remove from the difficulties of earthly life, the flat rhythms and almost cursory rhymes and near rhymes give the first four quatrains a routine, almost bored tone, and the predominantly end-stopped lines truncate any growth of energy and emotion. Then, at the end of stanza 4, it suddenly dawns on the poet that it is not only the nurse and Christ who are subject to death: "A child beside me comforts her doll, / We are dying on the hard wood of the pews." With this realization, his voice stirs, the lines overflow with enjambment, and, as if nature were the right place for surging emotion, the poem, with relief ("at last"), leaves the church:

> Death is everywhere, in the extensive
> Sermon, the outcry of the inaudible
> Prayer, the nickels, the dimes the poor give,
> And outside, at last, in the gusts of April.

By stanza 7, the poem's initial cool detachment, associated with church, has melted, and as the poet apostrophizes and (since his own death has now been broached) identifies with the dead "Virgin lady," the syntax becomes more "passionate" (in Yeats's sense) with the repetition of "can you" and the use of the rhetorical question: "Up through the mud can you see us / Waiting here for you . . . Can you see our hats like a row of flowers?" Glauco Cambon sees that the turnabout from "marked estrangement to involvement" implies "that even in a desecrated world the sacramental values can be restored under the form of human commitment."[5] If this is too optimistic a reading of a poem that ends as starkly as this one, clearly the poet's sympathetic identification with the nurse is meant as a humane contrast to the disinfected irrelevancies of church.

As graceless as the living world may be, the poet won't fantasize about any other one; the nurse's life after death consists of nothing but her corpse journeying downriver. Kinnell's identification with the victim escalates as he projects himself into this journey, and, as Cambon puts it, "he achieves his grand 'largo' effect by encompassing more than three stanzas in one sentence, fluvially sustained through the reviewed 'stations' of the floating body's downstream voyage—until the short clauses at the very end seal the movement in majestic peace" (36).

By the very end, however, this majestic peace has shaded into the peace of resignation:

> Do not, moved by goodbyes, be altogether sorry
>
> That the dream has ended. Turn
> On the dream you lived through the unwavering gaze.
> It is as you thought. The living burn.
> In the floating days may you discover grace.

Whatever sacramental value human commitment can restore won't dissuade the poet from turning on the graceless, burning, dream world. In most of Kinnell's other work we see him turning *to* the burning world, discovering grace not in posthumous floating but in submitting himself to the very Heraclitean fire that he here eschews (in another prayer-like passage a few poems later, in "Alewives Pool," he more typically exhorts himself to "love the burning earth"). As in the very early poem "A Walk in the Country" (*FP*), where the poet isn't enlivened by everything's "shortness" but merely alienated and embittered, we see here that a love for the burning earth must contend with a resistance to it. Many of Kinnell's poems seem generated by this conflict, but few so nakedly express the repulsion and let it stand so unopposed.

And yet, although he here turns on the world, Kinnell remains steadfast in refusing to sweeten his bitterness. He won't return to church, tempting as the Christian promise of resurrection might be. Kinnell knows the nurse won't "rise before dinner," even though it's Easter. Her posthumous existence, those "floating days," is defined by her body (what is "floating") and by worldly time ("days"). There is nowhere to turn *to* after turning *on* this burning world. So as if in compensation for this thematic instability, the verse itself becomes syntactically and rhythmically steadier, the long "fluvially sustained" sentence giving way to more grounded utterances, short and direct, as the lines draw close to a firm iambic base. This verbal steadiness in the face of a spiritual quandary gives the last stanza its prayerful quality—quiet but intense, deprived but composed. Like much of Kinnell's best work, "Easter" burns most brightly just before it dies.

Christ appears twice more in *Kingdom*, most pointedly in "The Supper after the Last," where he is neither hope nor victim but crude shatterer of spiritual illusions, preacher of nothingness. Where "First Communion" and "Easter" struggled against a specifically Christian form of otherworldliness, in this poem the guzzling, mock Christ comes to disabuse us of *any* "Hanker after wings" or "Lech for transcendence." "The Supper after the Last," in fact, culminates a series of six poems, part 3 of *Kingdom*, each driven by the effort to overcome this lechery. Indeed Kinnell himself sees that "about halfway through my first book I ceased to look for that traditional kind of transcendence. Certain poems in the last half of the book are explicit struggles to be rid of such a desire" (*WDS* 24).

"The Schoolhouse," the first of the series, seems not-too-remotely descended from Yeats's "Among School Children." As in the private meditation of that "sixty-year-old smiling public man," we follow the poet's train of thought (both poems use the present tense) as he visits a schoolroom, ponders the vapidity of "modern" education, contemplates the memories evoked by the visit, and finally arrives at some new insight, learns a new "lesson." But where Yeats finally achieves a rhapsodic vision of the unity of the real and the ideal, of the dancer and the dance, of Ledean bodies and soulful Platonic paradigms, Kinnell comes to discredit the ideal realm, to locate paradise here on earth and nowhere else.

When in the first section the poet returns to his old schoolhouse, he is younger than Yeats's sixty years, but like that comfortable old scarecrow, or Wordsworth at Tintern Abbey, he is confronted by the passing of time and his own aging. History creeps pettily along, a "leapfrog through blood," signifying nothing more than "casts of the dice." A sharp sense of the destructive passing of seasons emerges—how a schoolboy once rushed out in spring, how that same boy returns, "Snow-haired in his turn, and plagued by thought, / . . . looking for the dead light." This returnee, the poet himself, once learned "Everything we imagined a man could know" but comes back unsatisfied, looking for something else, some still-unlearned lesson.

In section 2 the poet recalls the isolation and death of a "man of letters," the old schoolmaster, who often walked in his garden, thinking of "Eden and the fallen state." Counterpointing this schoolmaster are some "local tramps" who after his death take refuge in his garden, sprawling "At the foot of the statue of their host . . . which he had called / 'Knowledge,' sometimes 'Death.'" In recalling his teacher's conflation of Knowledge and Death, the poet belies his boyhood belief that he had learned everything a man could know; only in death, or in a perfect, inert statue-state (like Stevens's General Du Puy or the images of Yeats's nuns that "keep a marble or a bronze repose"), does one know it all, possess Knowledge with a capital *K*. Although the statue's one gesture "seems to beckon" from the other world, it "remains obscure" to the living—it too breaks hearts. We may eat from the tree of Knowledge, but what we know in life remains marginal: when one tramp eats an apple, another hollers, "'Hey now Porky, gie's the core'"; Porky replies, "'Wise up . . . they ain't gonna *be* a core.'"

The dead schoolmaster's musing on "Eden and the fallen state" makes the education of modern schoolchildren—taught by "innocents"—look pathetic by comparison. Just as Yeats is told that students learn "To study reading-books and histories, / To cut and sew, be neat in everything / In the best modern way," Kinnell hears of modern schoolchildren

> Soaking up civics and vacant events
> From innocents who sponge periodicals
> And squeeze that out again in chalky gray
> Across the blackboards of the modern day.

Those last two lines, cut and sewn to make a technically perfect and perfectly facile heroic couplet, themselves are as vacant and colorless as that modern classroom, as innocent in their unviolated iambic pentameter as those modern teachers. Kinnell imagines the schoolkids, passively soaking up intellectual mush, would "Rake their skulls if they found out we returned / By free choice to this house of the dead, / And stand here wondering what he could have learned." Aware now of not having been taught everything a man could know, he searches for what the schoolmaster learned, "His eyes great pupils and his fishhook teeth / Sunk in the apple of knowledge or death."

Yeats's poem never does return to the long schoolroom. Its closure derives from the rhetoric of its last stanza rather than from a sense of structural completion, and it ends firmly suspended between this world and the other (Yeats manages this paradox of "firm suspension" with a conclusion that is at once an unanswered question and, implicitly, an unambiguous declaration). In contrast, "The Schoolhouse," after a meditation stirred by its initial scene, returns to its beginnings. Kinnell comes back around to the start, having now learned a lesson:

> I think the first inkling of the lesson
>
> Was when we watched him from the apple wrest
> Something that put the notion in his brain
> The earth was coming to its beautifulest
> And would be just like paradise again
> The day he died from it.

This lesson, the Stevensian one that death is the mother of beauty, seems to be what Kinnell sought when he first returned to the schoolhouse "plagued by thought." Not, like Yeats, rhapsodically suspended between two worlds but calmly planted in this one, the poet responds to his teacher's death with composure, quietly asserting his loyalty to the earthly realm; after the teacher's death, "The flames went out / in the blue mantles; he waved us to the night— / And we are here, under the starlight."

We are here, that is, and nowhere else. Whatever other world we imagine is just projection, for the schoolmaster's final existential lesson shows that what is order from one point of view is chaos from another: "I / Remember he taught us the stars disperse / In wild flight, though constellated to the eye." This astronomically sound teaching may thwart transcendental aspirations, but it also implies a world of possibilities; perpetually expanding into virgin space, into the unimaginable void, the universe itself has a lot to learn, as Whitman also knew:

> I open my scuttle at night and see the far-sprinkled systems,
> And all I see multiplied as high as I can cipher edge but the rim
> of the farther systems.
>
> Wider and wider they spread, expanding, always expanding,
> Outward and outward and forever outward.

(SM 45)

Where Stephen Crane is so overwhelmed by the unfathomable, unpatterned dimensions of godless space that he sees men only as "lice which were caused to cling to a whirling, fire-smitten, ice-locked, disease-stricken, space-lost bulb" ("The Blue Hotel"), Kinnell here affirms human life in spite of his daunting, intergalactic perspective. Steering between Whitman's exuberance and Crane's morbidity, the last lines of "The Schoolhouse" express humility in the face of a mysterious cosmos, the dignity of the poet in the face of his own smallness, and a reverent acceptance of the "uncoiling," dying world:

> And now I can see the night in its course,
> The slow sky uncoiling in exploding forms,
> The stars that flee it riding free in its arms.

Like "The Schoolhouse," "The Descent" juxtaposes events from the speaker's past to his present meditations. Relying on narrative to shape and sustain the discourse, both poems evince their ideas

25

only in their things, although the latter adheres even more strictly to Williams's pithy dictum. Indeed, Kinnell here out-"Things" Williams, whose "The Descent" exemplifies part of what Kinnell might mean when he says, "The Williams dictum . . . in practice actually means 'No things but in ideas'" (*WDS* 37). Williams's poem begins very abstractly, descending from some unspecific realm, not rising up from particulars (its opening, in fact, sounds something like the opening of the *Four Quartets*):

> The descent beckons
>     as the ascent beckoned.
>         Memory is a kind
> of accomplishment,
>     a sort of renewal
>         even
> an initiation, since the spaces it opens are new places
>     inhabited by hordes
>         heretofore unrealized.

"Things" do eventually stir in the poem, but they never crystallize into specificity, and so the poem's bardic conclusion seems more a return to the original, tenuous abstraction than an idea that has sprouted up from particulars. Kinnell's poem, partly because of its narrative base, sticks closer to things—so much of its effect depends upon a dying mountain climber, a flight of jackdaws, a dead crow.

Where a poem like "Seven Streams of Nevis" gets along by the opposition between melodrama and meditation, "The Descent" is impelled by the interplay between ascension and descent, the way down, as it usually does for Kinnell, finally subsuming the way up. The first of its four parts begins with a "Lech for transcendence" as the belaying group of mountaineers, which includes the poet, "must have seemed / Some crazy earthworm headed for paradise," or, racing for the crest, "an ascension of crows." But every uprising in this section is answered by a downfall. The sun rises, but the moon sets. Jan reaches the crest first but dies, "Sprawled on the shellbursts of his heart." The first motion in the section is mountain climbing, the last Jan's body sliding down.

The events in part 1 call to the poet's mind in the second part a boyhood memory about another death, a shotgunned crow in

Seekonk Woods. Like the first, this section opens on high ground, Indian Hill, but where the poem starts with climbing, this section begins with the boy "buried like a quail / In the grass and shadows." This identification with birds helps explain the boy's impulsive, tender act when, after a shotgun blast, the skyward escape of two crows is countered by a third's thumping to the ground: "I scooped it up, splashed across the ford, / And lit out—I must have run half a day / Before I reached Holy Spring." Prefiguring the outcome of later struggles, at the heart of this section lies the boy's confusion of the way up and the way down, his affinity for the way down based on ingenuous physical observation:

> (Anyway,
>
> I thought it was holy. No one
> Had told me heaven is overhead.
> I only knew people look down
> When they pray.)

He doesn't challenge heaven's existence, but locates it underground, in traditionally hellish regions (just as in "Seven Streams" Kinnell places heaven "In the heart's hell"). Just after he himself had been "buried like a quail," he buries the crow, supposing he is sending him off to heaven, which will be "'way this side of China, for sure.'"

With section 3 the poem shifts from the narration of the twin descents to a meditation upon them. Kinnell first half-heartedly repudiates and then implicitly reaffirms his boyhood notion about where heaven is:

> Heaven is in light, overhead,
> I have it by heart. Yet the dead
> Silting the darkness do not ask
> For burials elsewhere than the dusk.
> They lie where nothing but the moon can rise,
> And make no claims, though they had promises.

The implicitness falls away in the anti-Christian stridency of those last two lines (the heroic couplet stands out sharply in this otherwise loosely accentual context) and we see how Kinnell, grown up now, focuses not so much on a fantasized subterranean paradise as on the physical reality of bodily burial. The bold assertions modulate in the section's final stanza to a summarizing image. No longer declaiming outright that the dead don't rise, Kinnell presents us with graveside milkweed whose life cycle recapitulates the undulations of the poem: the weeds "Climb from the dead as if in flight," but their ascension is cut short in ignominious blooming, and they fall back to the graves from which they sprang, "Strange, homing lamps, that go out seed by seed."

The poem's final section returns to Seekonk Woods, where on Easter an adult Kinnell has come looking for Indian Hill. He seeks the holiness he felt when he baptized and buried the crow, but Indian Hill is now bulldozed. It is an Easter without Christ: the only cross around is a TV antenna; the only rising is by a flight of jackdaws, "Seized by some thaumaturgic thirst." Although those "earth-birds" lech for transcendence here, their ascent, like the mountaineers' and the milkweed's, is finally unmiraculous. It is countered by a single visionary bird who

> Dodged through the flock again and burst
> Eastward alone, sinking across the trees
> On the world-curve of its wings.

After this descent, the poem once again turns from narration to meditation, from the past tense to a more immediate present:

> So it is,
>
> Mirrored in duskfloods, the fisherbird
> Stands in a desolate sky
> Feeding at its own heart.

With this fisherbird and, more explicitly, in the ensuing sentence, "In the cry / *Eloi! Eloi!* flesh was made word," Christ finally appears in the poem, bringing into focus a series of crucifixion images planted earlier. But he doesn't come to redeem us. Rather, as Mills puts it, "His cry articulates the agony of every living being, of all who feel the torment of mortality. . . . Kinnell sees Christ as the exemplary sufferer in whose speech, passion, and death the pain of others is embodied, manifested as the supreme, heart-rending instance of man's 'thaumaturgic thirst' for immortality—and its defeat" (82).

And yet, there is more than mere agony and defeat at the end of this poem. Our "thaumaturgic thirst" may go unquenched, but we don't go entirely without nourishment, for the bird, after all, is "Feeding at its own heart." Kinnell borrows this image of heart eating from a Stephen Crane poem (with which he introduces his essay "Poetry, Personality, and Death") in which heartfood is both bitter *and* good:

> In the desert
> I saw a creature, naked, bestial,
> Who squatting upon the ground,
> Held his heart in his hands,
> And ate of it.
> I said, "Is it good, friend?"
> "It is bitter—bitter," he answered;
> "But I like it
> Because it is bitter,
> And because it is my heart."

In Christ's agony there is also *poetical* nourishment as "flesh was made word." This transubstantiation isn't the Christian miracle but the poetic one. Later in his career, Kinnell elaborates: "Since words form in the poet's throat muscles, they can be said to come out of his very flesh. And since the reader's throat muscles also have to form the words, the words enter the reader's very flesh. Poetry goes not merely from mind to mind, but from the whole body to the whole body" (WIW 55). Thus, without muting the suffering of defeated transcendentalism, indeed by confronting it, "The Descent" offers up value and authenticity in poetry and in our good, bitter hearts. And this agonized authenticity provides true communion. The real meaning of Christ's cry echoes both within our individual bodies—in our blood and bones—and outside them, in the branches (alliterated *b*'s insist on the connection), in the not-altogether-desolate night:

> In the cry
> *Eloi*! *Eloi*! flesh was made word:
> We hear it in wind catching in the branches.
> In lost blood breaking a night through the bones.

The anti-transcendental preoccupations of this third part of *What a Kingdom It Was* culminate in its final two poems, "Freedom, New Hampshire" and "The Supper after the Last." Stylistically, however, these poems move in opposite directions. In "Freedom, New Hampshire," the most overtly autobiographical poem in the volume, we hear a forerunner of the voice—at once intimate and bardic—that we hear in parts of *The Book of Nightmares* and *Mortal Acts, Mortal Words,* while the voice in "The Supper after the Last" is mysterious and charged not with intimacy but with a weird, abrasive surrealism. The more personal voice of "Freedom" probably characterizes most of Kinnell's best subsequent work, but that voice will operate in a freewheeling, associative structure that he introduces in "Supper." "It is from this poem," Kinnell wrote, "that I want to make a fresh start . . . I mean towards a poem without scaffolding or occasion, that progresses through images to a point where I can make a statement on a major subject."[6] Mills interprets this new start as toward "the creation of a poetry which relies less and less upon logical or narrative structure, upon the presentation of external events . . . but which develops around a highly suggestive grouping of images whose source is inward experience, memory, dream, or vision" (82–83).

Chief among these images is the bawdy wild man as Christ. This Christ, as Mills puts it, "apparently has been robbed by His suffering and death of the illusions of His teaching, His promises at the Last Supper," and thus his message is "mortality without reprieve. This supper has nothing sacred or life-renewing about it; plainly it is a feast of sheer annihilation" (84).

The poem thus is stridently untender. In a blunt parody of the Gospel, this guzzler of a Savior indeed comes "not to bring peace, but a sword," not to proffer eternal life, but to preach nothingness:

I came not to astonish
But to destroy you. Your
Jug of cool water? Your
Hanker after wings? Your
Lech for transcendence?
I came to prove you are
Intricate and simple things
As you are, created
In the image of nothing,
Taught of the creator

By your images in dirt—
As mine, for which you set
A chair in the sunshine,
Mocking me with water!

For once, Kinnell's heightened sense of death doesn't yield a complementary heightened sense of life. In the final section, thus, we aren't brought close to the quick of life, to what he calls in "Alewives Pool" the "pulse" of the "burning earth"; instead, the scene begins to dissolve:

The witnesses back off; the scene begins to float in water;
Far out in that mirage the Saviour sits whispering to the world,
Becoming a mirage. The dog turns into a smear on the sand.
The cat grows taller and taller as it flees into space.

Underscoring the Saviour's message of doom, even the scene out of which he preaches to us evaporates to mirage. He continues to dampen our "Lech for transcendence," his voice itself dying, a mere whisper drifting from a nebulous "hot shine." No matter how we "struggle from flesh into wings," those wings "live gripping the contours of the dirt," our burial place that, shadow-like, is always with us, getting in the last word, in our lives and in the poem:

I cut to your measure the creeping piece of darkness
That haunts you in the dirt. Step into light—
I make you over. I breed the shape of your grave in the dirt.

Burial has the last word too (and the first) in "Freedom, New Hampshire." At the moment when Kinnell might most want to hanker after the other world—the poem is an elegy for his brother—he is most adamant about death's finality:

But an incarnation is in particular flesh
And the dust that is swirled into a shape
And crumbles and is swirled again had but one shape
That was this man. When he is dead the grass
Heals what he suffered, but he remains dead,
And the few who loved him know this until they die.
                    For my brother, 1925–1957

Kinnell does not regard this finality with equanimity. He is adamantly "unwise," full of, as one interviewer sees it, "a kind of belligerence, that is both rebellious and regretful" (*WDS* 96). "The unwillingness of the acceptance," Kinnell explains, "is mostly due to the fact that it's an elegy for my brother, who died when he was thirty-two. You can't 'accept' someone else's death, least of all that of someone who died young" (*WDS* 96). And yet, from the poet's "rebellious and regretful" conclusion a light shines over "Freedom, New Hampshire" and bathes its details with sacredness. In "Supper," because things are ephemeral they evaporate; here they glow with meaning. *Because* things are particular, they endear themselves to us. Kinnell comes not merely to destroy us but to show how that destruction transforms our lives: "That we last only for a time, that everyone and everything around us lasts only for a time, that we know this, radiates a thrilling, tragic light on all our loves, all our relationships, even on those moments when the world, through its poetry, becomes almost capable of spurning time and death" (PPW 125).

From his earliest poetry, this haunting sense that "we last only for a time" has brought Kinnell not to morbidity or nihilism but to that "thrilling, tragic" attachment to the things of this world. In "Island of Night" (*FP*) he dreams of time's destructive power, of "a beautiful island / Surrounded by an abrasive river"; soon the island is "all rubbed into river and / gone forever." He awakes "Into the river of darkness around us" that will soon rub *us* out, and—as a result of this awareness—"love happened." In "The Feast" (also from *First Poems*) Kinnell concludes, "If love had not smiled we would never grieve," but the transitive property applies; surely, if we had not grieved, love would never have smiled.

"Freedom, New Hampshire" is comprised mostly of Kinnell's memories of a summer he and his brother, Derry, spent on a farm there. An awareness of the eternal cycles of birth and death infuses these memories; indeed, the poem seems ignited by the rubbing together of life and death, of beauty and ephemerality. The title evokes limitlessness and the first section establishes that we are in a child's world, but from the start, it is death that lingers in memory:

> We came to visit the cow
> Dying of fever,

Towle said it was already
Shovelled under, in a secret
Burial-place in the woods.

Young Galway and Derry "prowled through the woods / Weeks,"
looking for the grave—fascinated by death? unreconciled? Inescapably drawn, in any case. The section carefully keeps a balance.
A cow dies, but its grave nourishes a patch of greenery. The boys
shovel dung, the last step in a cycle, but that too helps make a
green place. At first they remain at a remove from the cyclic activity—they arrive too late for the cow's death and never do find
the grave—but this shoveling of dung soon implicates them, fore-
shadowing Derry's own return to dust. Kinnell establishes in this
first section a prosody that reflects his dual response to the natural
cycles. Death leads to life, yes, and "spirit flowers without stop,"
and in that sense unity prevails; but this oneness is balanced (in the
end, overbalanced) by the haunting claims of the individual: every
death is the absolute end of some bit of "particular flesh." The
verse thus plays wholeness against division; the sentences are often
long, grammatically sprawling unities constituted by many broken,
irregular, unpredictably particular lines.

Extending this prosodic strategy, the first eight lines of section 2,
each rhythmically distinct, comprise a single sentence. Responding
to the poem's first image—a dying cow—Kinnell here remembers a
cow skull he and Derry found. But, still keeping the balance, he
then recounts the birth of a calf. The cow simultaneously chews
millet and gives birth, takes in and gives out, and doubleness prevails also in the calf's young life: "It was sopping with darkness,"
but also "it was sunburned"; it "drank at the milk of light," but
when they "got it balanced on its legs, it went wobbling / Towards
the night." Galway and Derry, themselves having helped haul the
calf from the darkness, are once again implicated in the life cycle,
and Derry's death is thus again presaged. "Walking home in darkness," they too are wobbling toward the night, full of youth and
summer but, inadvertently perhaps, anticipating summer's passing:

We saw the July moon looking on Freedom New Hampshire,
We smelled the fall in the air, it was the summer,
We thought, Oh this is but the summer!

33

The prosodic interplay between unity and particularity escalates again in the third section, whose forty-eight irregular lines, with the help of a rambling syntax and a few semicolons, add up to a single sentence. A meandering, dreamy section results, that, as it trips from one memory to the next, is seductive and nostalgic but very much caught in the flow of time. Like the first two sections, this one starts with an image that suggests both birth and death:

> Once I saw the moon
> Drift into the sky like a bright
> Pregnancy pared
> From a goddess who thought
> To be beautiful she must keep slender—
> Cut loose, and drifting up there
> To happen by itself—
> And waning in lost labor.

And once again, the boys are soon implicated—"we lost our labor / Too"—lazily drifting, parentless (as far as the poem goes) as the moon. They themselves became the agents of time the destroyer and provider, crushing flies with which they nourished baby meadowlarks, while in turn dusk came upon them as they "skirled out" their hearts on "toilet- / papered combs," "dandruffed / Harps" that sounded—it all links up—like flies. Night fell, but, evening the scales,

> the stars
> Made small flashes in the sky,
> Like mica flashing in rocks
>
> On the chokecherried Ledge
> Where bees I stepped on once
> Hit us from behind like a shotgun,
> And where we could see
> Windowpanes in Freedom flash
> And Loon Lake and Winnipesaukee
> Flash in the sun
> And the blue world flashing.

Section 3 builds toward this climactic passage of Heraclitean burning. But even as matter flashes into light, Kinnell keeps us grounded in the substantiality of his language; the transformation incorporates the things of the world, is only made possible by them. The five repetitions of forms of "flash" (which phonetically incorporates "ash" and semantically anticipates it) insist on that word as a physical *presence* (a thing of this world in its own right), and the palpable presence of other sounds (other "things") is emphasized by end rhyme ("shotgun"/"sun," "see"/"Winnipesaukee"), assonance ("sky / Like mica"), consonance ("small flashes," "blue world flashing"), and heavy alliteration ("Freedom flash," "Loon Lake," "where we"/"Windowpanes"/"Winnipesaukee").

With the final section, as the syntactic units get shorter and more sharply defined and the images cease to run together, we are plucked out of the dreamy train of summery memories. Instead, Kinnell presents three moments of remembered communion with the physical world, three moments when the self connected with the outside—eyeballs with the sky, fingernails with the air, blood with the surf. Having ridden memory to the point of connection with the changing earth, the poem itself enacts the passing of time and shifts into the present tense. From this vantage point in the present, Kinnell briefly glances back at the various elements of the remembered summer, but now with a more self-conscious sense of mortality. Grass can now be "green for a man" (green because a man is buried underneath) as well as for the cow or the dung that children will think of. The bull calf they "Dragged from the darkness" now "breaks up again" there. The larks they fed have "long since crashed for good in the grass." This brief review appears as an unsorted list, and then Kinnell breaks it off. He realizes that although "The mind may sort it out and give it names," this naming is itself conditional: "When a man dies he dies trying to say without slurring / The abruptly decaying sounds."

The poem ends granting that "It is true / That only flesh dies." But that "only" is robbed of any power to console by the final stanza, quoted above, which insists that "an incarnation is in particular flesh" and swears Kinnell's first loyalty to particular incarnations. In this sense, he sees the Heraclitean fire as a tragic burning (unlike Hopkins, for whom "flash" rhymes with "mortal trash," rather than "particular flesh"). Later in his career, Kinnell comes closer to James Merrill's complex but comforting proposition that "nothing either lasts or ends,"[7] but here his sense of temporariness is fierce, and his heart brims with what Howard calls "the grief of history, the pain of things happening once and once only, irreversibly" (306).

Kinnell has written that the best poems don't escape personality but go through it to reach beyond the self. Commenting on some contemporary work, he concludes: "The selflessness in these passages is the result of entering one's own pain and coming out on the other side, no longer only James Wright or John Logan, but all men. The voice is a particular recognizable voice; at the same time it mysteriously sheds personality and becomes simply the voice of a creature on earth speaking" (PPD 67). This assumption and shedding of personality occurs at the end of "Freedom, New Hampshire," and it accounts for the authentically bardic tone. We respond to the phrase "this man" by thinking of Derry and all the details of that remembered summer but also by substituting "any man." Derry *is* both only Derry and any man. The poem's last gesture—"For my brother, 1925–1957"—is toward particularity, but by then we realize Kinnell has been both elegizing and, as he put it, trying to "teach" (*WDS* 42).

III

The poems in part 3 of *What a Kingdom It Was* I have been discussing are engaged in a struggle against the "Lech for transcendence." But it is one thing to forego this lech, another to actually make do with what is left. So even as Kinnell keeps turning to this world, he is feeling out the resultant joys and difficulties. Several poems in the first two parts of the volume—less structurally complex than those that follow but thematically presupposing them—undertake this exploration. Left only with earthly life, Kinnell strives in these poems to open himself to it as fully as he can, to burst the grape of experience on his tongue, bearing the melancholy and relishing the delight. All poets, perhaps, want some kind of "opening"—to the Muse, or the unconscious, or nature—but few pursue it with Kinnell's *dual* sense of why it is at once enlivening and difficult, why it both extends and extinguishes the self: "And to open oneself to the rhythm of reality, the whole rhythm of being born and dying, while it is awful, since it means facing your terror of death, it is also glorious, for then you are one with the creation, the cosmos."[8] When Howard patronizes what he calls

Kinnell's "superstition of openness as, in itself, a Good Thing" (317), he temporarily underestimates that, to the extent openness is a Good Thing for Kinnell, it's also a Hard Thing and a Sad Thing and a Dark Terrifying Thing.

"First Song," the initial poem of *What a Kingdom It Was*, introduces this ambivalence and begins to characterize what Kinnell means by "opening." It starts off already plunged into time's flow, the first phrase ("Then it was dusk") casually locating what follows in chronological relation to what has passed: the poem's world is bounded—is constituted—by time, as if one couldn't *but* start *in medias res*. The other two stanzas thus straightaway locate themselves by means of temporal relationship ("*Soon* their sound was pleasant," "It was *now* fine music" [my italics]). Night falls but is balanced by growing awareness. The first line offers both waxing ("the small boy") and waning ("dusk"), and soon these merge into one movement ("Dark was growing tall," "the towering Illinois twilight"). The boy is small, at an early stage in the life cycle, but like the boys in "Freedom, New Hampshire" (whose "Buzzing and skirling on toilet- / papered combs" is anticipated by his cornstalk scraping), he has been working with dung, the final stage.

The heart of the poem is its final image, the boy scraping on his makeshift violin:

> And into dark in spite of a shoulder's ache
> A boy's hunched body loved out of a stalk
> The first song of his happiness, and the song woke
> His heart to the darkness and into the sadness of joy.

His awakening to the inseparability of sadness and joy, of life and death, seems catalyzed by the presence of time in the poem—nightfall, the boy's own weariness—but, more directly, this awakening results from "the song," which surely originates in the "darkness" it evokes. Here, in the first poem of his first major book, his own first song, is the seed of Kinnell's aesthetic: art opens us to the darkness and springs from it. "Darkness" comes to mean many things, but in this poem already we can see that it incorporates for Kinnell the kinship between humans and animals, between boys (and their scraping) and frogs (and their croaking): "It was now fine music the frogs and the boys / Did in the towering Illinois twilight make."

The image of these musical frogs harks back to D. H. Lawrence's "River Roses" ("and simmering / Frogs were singing"), a poem which seems to have influenced "First Song" in other ways as well. Both short poems, set at twilight, achieve a murmuring, summery atmosphere, where what Mills calls the "strident realities" of opening to the darkness "are softened, almost sentimentalized, by pleasant details" (68). Lawrence's poem lulls with seductive rhymes (based on humming sounds and sibilance) and "First Song," too, leans heavily on tightly patterned rhyme (indeed, in no other Kinnell poem does rhyme seem quite so integral) made first of soft sounds (liquids and nasals) and then, as night falls, of the harder *k* sound. The effect in both poems, heightened by the heavy internal rhyme, is nostalgic, yet neither shies from death or physicality. "River Roses," according to Kinnell, moves us "far into mystery . . . into worship of sexuality itself" (*WDS* 54) and, like "First Song," expresses the kinship between human and animal: "We whispered: 'No one knows us / Let it be as the snake disposes / Here in this simmering marsh.'"

A few poems later we see the boy discovering more about what the darkness contains. Frogs and boys may be in the same boat, but so are wolves and boys: in "To Christ Our Lord" the boy confronts not his capacity for song but his predatoriness. Mills suggests that the tension in that poem results from "the sharp discrepancy between what Jesus represents for the boy and the very different acts which existence seems to force on him" (69). Kinnell glances at one way of resolving that discrepancy between Christian love and brutal natural law by taking as his title the dedication of Hopkins's "The Windhover," a poem in which love and death are fused in the single image of Christ as a bird of prey who saves by destroying. Hopkins is happy giving himself over to "the mastery of the thing," but in doing so he does not have to contend with conflicting impulses within his own mortal breast. Kinnell's boy's heart also stirs for a bird, but he eats that bird for dinner.

The initial juxtaposition lays out the dilemma. The image of wolves hunting elk is set against the image of a woman basting a bird—the victim of man's hunting, crucified over the coals, at Christmas, presumably a time of love and peace. The boy wonders, "is it fitting / To eat this creature killed on the wing?" but Kinnell's characters are inevitably at cross-purposes, and the conflicting claims meet head on:

> He had not wanted to shoot. The sound
> Of wings beating into the hushed air
> Had stirred his love, and his fingers
> Froze in his gloves, and he wondered,
> Famishing, could he fire? Then he fired.

The boy repudiates this killing as a "wicked act" and sees that the grace before dinner hypocritically praises it, but at the same time he accepts what he has done:

> There had been nothing to do but surrender,
> To kill and to eat; he ate as he had killed, with wonder.

Like Hopkins, the boy surrenders to a brutal force, but for the Jesuit this brutality embodies both the externalized, overwhelming power of salvation ("a billion / Times told lovelier, and more dangerous") and the violence of the crucifixion that must precede the resurrection; for Kinnell it remains an aspect of his own terrible kinship with the creatures of the earth: the boy was "Famishing," and so he killed and ate a bird.

Had the poem stopped here, it would have appeared complete. The boy's eating of the bird finishes the main action, and his surrender is as close as the poem comes to laying aside its original discrepancy and accepting, as Mills puts it, "the tragic mixture of love and death inherent in creation" (70). But instead Kinnell ends more mysteriously:

> At night on snowshoes on the drifting field
> He wondered again, for whom had love stirred?
> The stars glittered on the snow and nothing answered.
> Then the Swan spread her wings, cross of the cold north,
> The pattern and mirror of the acts of earth.

The setting of this scene suggests the boy's unrigidified, "drifting" understanding of the universe (untracked snowfields occur frequently in Kinnell's work, usually indicating this state of maximum openness). And on this "drifting field" things which once seemed established are thrown into question. The boy's query is at first puzzling: "wondered again" seems to link it back to the previous stanza ("he ate as he had killed, with wonder"), but where that earlier "wonder" (a noun) means "astonishment" and perhaps "admiration," here (a verb) it means "put the question." And the question itself also puzzles, for we have already been told that it was "The sound / Of wings beating into the hushed air" that had "stirred his love"—stirred it, the implication is, for the bird, just as Hopkins's heart "stirred for a bird."

For whom else *could* love have stirred? Perhaps the shifting blankness of snow, eclipsing the landscape, sets the boy to wondering if the world is there at all, if what might have stirred his love is only his own projected image of the bird ("for whom did love *really* stir, the bird or myself?"). Or perhaps love could have stirred for all of creation, represented by the bird, and since it is Christmas, the boy is wondering about a creator ("for whom did love stir, the bird or the universe that created it?"). In any case, there is something primal about the question: is anything out there? what? And at first it seems the boy is quite alone, for "nothing answered." Then, as if in answer, the Swan (Cygnus) appears in the sky, but it proves an ambiguous answer at best. It is paradoxically both the "pattern" (the source) and the "mirror" (the reflection) of earthly life: Being originates both internally and externally, in the mind and in the world; a constellation consists, after all, both of objectively "real" stars and of the arrangement imposed on them by consciousness. (Likewise, part of the poem's rhyme pattern is submerged—the penultimate syllable in the fourth line of each stanza rhymes with the last one in the first line—potentially present but needing to be picked out, like a constellation.) Ambiguous as it is, the sudden appearance of the Swan ("spread her wings" gives it an active presence) has the feel of a revelation. And as the "cross of the cold north," it catches up the previous crucifixion imagery and aptly summarizes much of what the boy has learned about sacrifice and acceptance.

In "To Christ Our Lord" Kinnell begins to take stock of the "darkness" he evokes in "First Song." The two senses of the attendant "wonder" adumbrate the central tension in his work, but if in *Kingdom* "admiration" sometimes outweighs "put the question" (by *Body Rags* the verb will gain ascendancy, as the hunter in "The Bear" is left to spend his day "wandering, wondering," although even there both meanings pertain), it remains far from unalloyed. "Easter," as I have suggested, seems overcome by the brutality darkness can contain, just as in "A Walk in the Country" (*FP*) joy is entirely eclipsed by sadness. Even a poem like "Lilacs," which mocks a withdrawal from the darkness, implicitly demonstrates Kinnell's wariness at entering into it. The first stanza, whose "flaming imagery," according to Cambon, is "reminiscent of Van Gogh's paintings" and "makes 'Lilacs' a truly expressionist poem" (33), establishes the park as a place of darkness and burning, of sex and decay and rank and rampant sensuousness where, like the heavily enjambed lines, everything flows into everything else:

> The wind climbed with a laggard pace
> Up the green hill, and meeting the sun there
> Disappeared like warmed wax
> Into the ground. Down on the south slope
> A bitch stretched, and swaths of fierce lilacs
> Opened huge furnaces of scent.

In the second stanza, Kinnell sets up a straw man, or straw woman, who "betook herself into the park." The mocking tone of "betook" indicates her primness, but it also suggests the bluntness of Kinnell's approach here. With "Her dry legs crackling in darkness," *of course* it was all too much for her when "Summer slopped at her knees" and she caught "The hot scent of herself beating herself / Out of closets in the well-governed flesh." Predictably, she retreats back

> To the narrow parlor, where tea and dry supper
> Would be laid, and a spoon would arrange
> The leaves on the bottom of her china dream.

The dichotomy is extreme. Outside: the sloppy summer, vitality, openness, intensity, energy, chaos, sex, death—the blazing wildness of nature. Inside: narrowness, dryness, vapidity, arrangement, containment, civilization—a "china dream." Kinnell deals out the choices and takes sides, but by focusing exclusively on the straw woman's retreat, he doesn't himself have to wade into the sloppiness. By polarizing things so neatly, he can remain aloof from the woman's difficulty, as if staying out in the park were as easy as pie. Had he been more personally involved in the poem, the inevitable conflicts would have made it more interesting. Kinnell's appraisal of Robert Bly's "The Busy Man Speaks" might have been made of "Lilacs": "Speaking in his own voice, the voice of a complicated individual, he would have been forced to be lucid regarding his own ambiguous allegiances" (PPD 58).

Appearing eleven years after "Lilacs," this comment reflects a good deal about Kinnell's poetic development in that time, but even in *Kingdom* he often speaks "in his own voice." "Freedom, New Hampshire" is autobiography, and "To Christ Our Lord," although it retains the third person, doesn't simplify the "ambiguous allegiances" of a "complicated individual." Neither does "Alewives Pool," also structured by the tension between and resolution of those conflicting allegiances. Like "Sailing to Byzantium," this poem begins with the once-again "wondering" and "stirred" poet deeply troubled about the passing of time:

> We lay on the grass and heard
> The world burning on the pulse of April,
> And were so shaken and stirred, so cut, we wondered
> Which things will we forget
> And which remember always?

As if searching for an answer, he goes down to the Alewives Pool (his version of Yeats's darkly teeming "mackerel crowded seas"), "Where herring driven by lust from the seas / Came swarming until the pond would spill." Confronted with this generative profusion, like Yeats's, his thoughts turn to age. But Yeats's meditation on the aged man, that "paltry thing," appeals entirely to soul. Kinnell's dying woman has in mind not the singing of her soul but memories of her bodily life—wearing "frills" (versus Yeats's "tatter" of "mortal dress"), laughing, dancing, crying.

Instead of sailing off to Byzantium to be gathered into the artifice of eternity, Kinnell returns to the Alewives Pool. The birds there (with whom the poet has earlier been linked) are full of exhilarated vitality, are "astonished / By the passion of their song," in sharp contrast to Yeats's cold form "of hammered gold and gold enamelling" and its indifferent singing. Yeats wants "God's holy fire" to burn off his mortal part, just as Hopkins has the Heraclitean fire burn off those parts of himself which are "Jack, joke, poor potsherd, patch, matchwood"; the same fire makes Kinnell rejoice in his mortal part to the point of ecstasy.

Both Yeats and Kinnell begin stymied by time. But where Yeats responds by wanting out of nature (his golden bird, of course, can nevertheless only sing of time, of "what is past, or passing, or to come"), Kinnell comes to experience the blossoming of the astonishing, passionate natural life within himself that binds him to creation. This ecstasy suffuses the end of the poem, where elements of the first section are reincorporated, now raised to a higher pitch, simultaneously rounding off the poem and suggesting a newness of perception, underscored by the shift into the present tense. This higher pitch results partly from the higher concentration of alliteration, consonance, and assonance, and partly from the emergence of a steadier, almost iambic rhythm. As the poem modulates from bardic prayer to the challenging imperative of the final line, Kinnell turns directly toward the reader—the poem is no longer merely overheard—and incorporates us into his blazing, blossoming vision:

> Now by the trembling water let death and birth
> Flow through our selves as through the April grass—
> The sudden summer this air flames forth
> Makes us again into its blossomers—
> Stand on the pulse and love the burning earth.

This conflation of blossoming and flaming governs much of Kinnell's early poetry. Indeed, in *First Poems* he can already exclaim, "And grass, grass, blossom through my feet in flames" ("In the Glade at Dusk"). As this line suggests, it is not merely the image of the burning world that Kinnell claims this early; he also implicates *himself* in all that burning. "It is an easier thing," Howard supposes, "merely to report the world in conflagration without insisting on an engagement of identity, without being rigorously *in question*" (309). If Kinnell does not seem "*in question*" in poems like "Lilacs," starting from "In the Glade," his poetry is nevertheless increasingly an effort both to see the world on fire and to engage his identity to the conflagration—to stand on the pulse and love the burning earth as it enlivens and destroys.

In "First Song," it was his song which woke the boy's heart to "the darkness"—or to "the burning," Kinnell might have written—but by "Leaping Falls," the focus on this power of song—on poetry—has widened to include the power of even "unpoetic" uses of speech. The starting point of this poem is a familiar one in Kinnell's work—a journey through unmarked snow into the unknown. There is no trail to follow (except a deer trail), no human signs to mediate. But although the poet sheers eccentrically across the snow "into outer space," he has been to this country before. He is tracking the "forgotten journey of a child," as if to recapture the perceptual immediacy of a boyhood journey through this unmarked place. His depressed frame of mind isn't presented as directly as, say, Wordsworth's when he returns to Tintern Abbey, but like Wordsworth, Kinnell here feels the discrepancy between his sprightlier past and the frozen, devitalized present, figured in the landscape: the once downrushing "Leaping Falls," "Routing from ledge to ledge," now are "draped / Without motion or sound, / Icicles fastened in stories / To stillness and rock"; and "Underneath, / A heap of icicles, broken, / Lay dead blue on the snow." Cambon's analysis suggests how the movement of the verse conveys this contrast between past and present: "The 'downrush' of the cascade comes through by virtue of the headlong movement of syntax, which encompasses in one sentence the twelve lines of the first two stanzas. The next two stanzas offset this dynamic picture by presenting the falls frozen," a description "enhanced by the breakup of discourse into brittle short clauses, like icicles: 'Cold was through and through, / Noiseless, Nothing / Except clouds at my nostrils / Moved'" (31–32).

With those clouds, the poet's breath—his own not-yet-extinguished power—enters into the scene, and at the poem's crux, he uses it to speak: "Then I uttered a word, / Simply a bleak word / Slid from the lips." Disrupting the frozen stasis, the vibrations of this utterance set the scene in motion:

> A topmost icicle came loose
> And fell, and struck another
> With a bell-like sound, and
> Another, and the falls
> Leapt at their ledges, ringing
> Down the rocks and on each other

Like an outbreak of bells
That rings and ceases.

Keeping pace with this new motion, the verse returns to the "head-long movement" of the first two stanzas—the single sentence of stanza 5 spills over to stanza 6 and ceases only when the ringing does—and the language itself, "distinct yet expanding, icy yet intense" as Howard put it (310), mimics the cascading icicles.

By this falling, catalyzed by language, the poet seems to recapture something of the fluidity of childhood. The *word*, half beckoned by the frozen world itself, now opposes the deathly fixity of that world. True, this word precipitates a fall, but it is a fall that issues in beauty, the "bell-like sound." The silence returns, but where, before the uttered word, underneath the falls "A heap of icicles, broken, / Lay dead blue on the snow," by the poem's end, "A twigfire of icicles burned pale blue." What was once a fragmented heap is now an ordered twigfire; what once lay dead blue now burns pale blue. Although the silence returns, the landscape thus suggests a condition very different from the earlier fixity. The final image, combining fire and ice, indicates a resolution of contraries has been achieved (indeed, the title itself draws together rising and falling), just as Wordsworth comes to feel, in the presence that dwells both in the landscape and in his own mind, a reconciliation of consciousness and nature. The essential reconciliation in "Leaping Falls" is of life and death, figured in the burning icicles of the final line. The frozen world is simultaneously released into life and sent melting by flame into extinction. As a song once woke the heart to darkness, here a word wakes it to burning.

IV

*What a Kingdom It Was* concludes with a long poem of immigrant life on New York's Lower East Side, "The Avenue Bearing the Initial of Christ into the New World." Mills treats this work together with those in *Flower Herding on Mount Monadnock* rather than as part of *Kingdom* because he accurately assesses that "The Supper after the Last" brings "a course of thematic exploration to an end": having exposed the "hopeless falsity of those longings for eternity," Kinnell has prepared "as the ground for his future writing certain limitations of existence within which his poems must be created." He thus "takes a new grasp on the world at hand, on his life here and now in all of its immediacy or engages himself with the particulars of other lives" (102). If incarnations are in particular flesh, Kinnell in "Avenue C" begins to render those particularities more particularly than he has so far.

In a recapitulation of Kinnell's earlier renouncement, the Christian god has already been discredited, reduced to a duplicitous insect—

> A child lay in the flames.
> It was not the plan. Abraham
> Stood in terror at the duplicity.
> Isaac whom he loved lay in the flames.
> The Lord turned away washing
> His hands without soap and water
> Like a common housefly

—or, "a held breath," denied existence altogether. The title evokes Christ, not to suggest possibilities of redemption, but as an analogue to the irrevocably suffering immigrants (and the exterminated Jews of Europe). For them, the new world is flaming, but without ecstasy. As Isaac burns, they suffer, but—possessed by a will to live that, against all odds, affirms life anyway—"They survive like cedars on a cliff, roots / Hooked in any crevice they can find."

In certain respects, "Avenue C" is the most Whitmanesque of Kinnell's poems. It is built by "accumulation and expansion, not by compression," as Cambon points out, in a Whitmanesque endeavor to "seize the throbbing and shrill variety of New York life" (31). Like much of Whitman's work, it extends out to incorporate every detail it can reach with a narrative mobility and omniscience that establishes both the poet's intimacy with, and bardic remove from, all he surveys. Kinnell puts it that "much of Whitman's poetry is devoted to celebrating ordinary sights and sounds and in this respect the 'Avenue C' poem probably does follow Whitman." But he immediately qualifies the comparison: "But in my poem time and progress appear as enemies, as they never do in Whitman" (WDS 88). Both poets take America as their theme, but Kinnell knows that for many the promised land didn't keep its promise. This knowledge darkens "Avenue C" and tempers whatever celebrationalism it might want to share with Whitman, whose flirtation with death it finds exasperating:

> Maybe it is as the poet said,
> And the soul turns to thee
> O vast and well-veiled Death
> And the body gratefully nestles close to thee—
>
> I think of Isaac reading Whitman in Chicago,
> The week before he died, coming across
> Such a passage and muttering, Oi!
> What shit!

As I have suggested in my introduction, although Kinnell often surveys the same territory as Whitman, he often views it from a more tragic perspective. And this less harmonious vision reflects stylistically even in the poem's most "Whitmanesque" passages. Section 1, for example, contains many details, as if, like Whitman, Kinnell wanted to offer them up for their own astonishing sake. But the lines are so loaded with metaphors and (relatively rare) similes that they end up presenting the poet's imagination at least as much as they do the sights and sounds of the city. This duality checks whatever impulse the passage might have to blurt out "Listen to *that*!"—to sound more overwhelmed by affection for its details, more like "Song of Myself," section 26, which also presents, although without much interpretive metaphor, the sounds of a city. Since Whitman hears these sounds "running together, combined, fused or following," he contains them in a single long sentence (ll. 3–14) and never (not even when he hears the sound of "disjointed friendship") breaks up syntactic units. Thriving on separation, Kinnell's catalogue flows less smoothly, plays against itself. The lineation fragments sentences and smaller syntactic units, at its most extreme splitting subjects from verbs ("A broom / Swishes"), verbs from objects ("a woman throws open / Her window"), and even dismembering hyphenations ("A propane- / gassed bus"). Each observation, moreover, is confined to its own sentence, and the rhythm hesitates and falters. We are not swept up in headlong movement, as in Whitman. "Song of Myself" is a longer poem than "Avenue C," but since in Kinnell's poem "time and progress appear as enemies, as they never do in Whitman," it seems more conflicted about pushing forward, proceeds at a much slower clip.

Section 2 of the "Avenue C" poem seems perhaps even more Whitmanesque than section 1, more extreme in its thirst for detail. But even as Kinnell gushes forth with all those names, he considers what will come of them. When Whitman presents a list of names—"Kanuck, Tuckahoe, Congressman, Cuff" (SM 6)—he does it without comment, too swept up by generosity to wonder ironically about their futures. For him, the Americans these names represent are equal ("I receive them the same"), virtually interchangeable—that's the point. Kinnell uses the same rhetorical strategy, the list, to render the Jewish children, and their various destinies, syntactically equal; but once again uneasy with the notion of a unifying Oversoul, he renders those destinies semantically disparate:

> A dozen children troop after him, barbels flying,
> In skullcaps. They are Reuben, Simeon, Levi, Judah, Issachar,
>     Zebulun, Benjamin, Dan, Naphtali, Gad, Asher.
> With the help of the Lord they will one day become
> Courtiers, thugs, rulers, rabbis, asses, adders, wrestlers,
>     bakers, poets, cartpushers, infantrymen.

The counterpoint between syntactic sameness and semantic disparity (courtiers and thugs, asses and adders, bankers and cartpushers) makes the list as much an ironic commentary on a problematic promised land as a Whitmanesque glorification of detail. Whitman's lists do sometimes contain disparities, but finally the sweep of his rhetoric democratically levels them: Tuckahoe and Congressman are incorporated into a transcendental whole with little regard for what distinguishes them, while courtier and thug remain distinct. The fire may unify the latter two, but at that point they are no longer particular, no longer courtier and thug. They become the fire itself.

The tension in "Avenue C" results from this counterpoint of sameness and disparity, but it is a tension which informs certain passages only; it does not structure the poem as a whole. Constructed by "accumulation and expansion," the poem lacks the sense of development that characterizes Kinnell's later long poems, as if it were treading water, rather than swimming for parts unknown. (The many published excerpts thus largely retain their effect). This too connects to Whitman, whose poems, according to Kinnell, "rarely contain struggles of any kind. They begin in the same clarity in which they end" (WIW 58). Kinnell faults "When Lilacs Last in the Dooryard Bloom'd" because "the grief is too thoroughly consoled before the first line is uttered." But, uncharacteristically, the hard work likewise seems to have been done before "Avenue C" opens; the stoic acceptance seems already struggled for and won, and the poem contains little sustained drama (little, that is, of what a long poem seems especially suited for). (We have perhaps seen this preliminary struggle in the preceding poems—this one concludes the volume—although this doesn't really compensate for its absence *here*.) It too begins in the same clarity with which it ends; the final section achieves strong closure and reaches an elegiac pitch, but rather than *arriving* at a resolution, it merely intensifies what has been in the poem all along. The conclusion occurs at an appropriate time, but not an inevitable one, as if, although the loss of accumulated detail would diminish the impact, Kinnell would have been *capable* of saying these lines at any previous point in the poem—or at the start.

"Avenue C" can remain relatively free of struggle, perhaps, because, as closely observed as it is, the poet himself stands apart: his own being is not at stake in what he surveys. Only in the final section does the first person—plural—occur, and by then we cannot feel that the poet himself is, as Howard put it, "*in question.*" The very scope of his vision belies limitation; the immigrants may "survive like cedars on a cliff," but the poet surveys so much he must stand atop that cliff. One thinks again of Kinnell's critique of Bly's "The Busy Man Speaks": "Speaking in his own voice, the voice of a complicated individual, he would have been forced to be lucid regarding his own ambiguous allegiances." Appearing at about the same time as *The Book of Nightmares*, this remark reflects one way that later long poem surpasses "Avenue C," and it pinpoints Kinnell's challenge at the end of his first book. He had, as Mills said, prepared "as the ground for his future writing certain limitations of existence within which his poems must be created." Next, he had to learn to "speak in his own voice" more consistently, to engage his identity within those limitations, to dance to his own first song.

## CHAPTER 2

# Knocking on the Instants:
## *Flower Herding on Mount Monadnock*

I

As the self and its "ambiguous allegiances" approach the foreground of his writing, Kinnell's poems begin to turn inward— not in retreat from the world, but rather in an attempt to get "be- yond personality by going through it" (PPD 65): "When you go deep enough within yourself, deeper than the level of 'personality,' you are suddenly outside yourself, everywhere" (*WDS* 6). But "if we are willing to face the worst in ourselves," he knows, "we also have to accept the risk . . . that probing into one's wretchedness may just dig up more wretchedness" (PPD 67); and certainly as Kinnell matures as a poet, his willingness to run the risk increases. *Flower Herding on Mount Monadnock* is an important step down into the self, but it is only a step.

By the end of *What a Kingdom It Was*, there can be no other starting point *but* the particular flesh of the self. That volume es- tablished the conditions of the "pursuit of personal vision," Mills described, that "often leads toward a precipitous, dizzying bound- ary where the self stands alone"; but *Flower Herding* begins the pursuit itself, the rediscovery of what may lie beyond the boundary. Thomas Kinsella puts it that "everywhere in modern writing the stress is on personal visions of the world, in which the basic things are worked out repeatedly as though for the first time."[1] Kinsella's countryman Seamus Heaney admires how his father and grand- father could cut turf but laments, "I've no spade to follow men like them." The old ways of digging are unavailable. But a pen can re- place a spade; through poetry one can go "down and down / For the good turf" of the self:

Between my finger and my thumb
The squat pen rests.
I'll dig with it.
              ("Digging")

Like Kinnell, Heaney sees poetry as a "revelation of the self to the self," a dig that by penetrating the individual psyche can "let down a shaft into real life" and thus escape the enclosed ego.[2]

Thrown back on themselves, however, Kinsella and Heaney still must reckon with the influence of their native place; Ireland can be rooted in or run from, but like Faulkner's South, it's always *there*, a cultural force inevitably shaping consciousness. Similarly, when Lowell moves beyond the Alps of his Catholic period, the terra firma he comes down to (and perhaps doesn't dig beneath) is his own history, a specific "place" with 91 Revere Street as its capitol. This is a more private territory, perhaps, than Ireland, but Lowell sees that everyone has a private history leaning on his present, that "We are all dealers in used furniture."[3]

Unlike Lowell and the Irishmen, when Kinnell is thrown back on himself, he retains no inevitable, primitive association with a specific native place (this is not to suggest of course that the poetry isn't, in a more general sense, shaped by cultural and historical forces). Heaney may lack a spade, but "The cold smell of potato mould, the squelch and slap / Of soggy peat" can still awaken in his head "Through living roots"; Kinnell counts himself among those "who have no roots but the shifts of our pain" ("The River That Is East"). And yet, if part 1 of *Flower Herding* thus roams from New York to Calcutta to Japan, the poems in part 2 do seem to "come home" to the natural world. Although the analogy must remain tentative between that world, with its eternal cycles, and places like Boston, Dublin, or even the Irish countryside, which are intimately bound with human history, nature nevertheless functions for Kinnell roughly as those other places do for Lowell and Heaney—as the "given" context of his working out the basic things "as though for the first time."

In working out these things without consistently specific historical coordinates, Kinnell's verse here is closer to Yves Bonnefoy's, whose *On the Motion and Immobility of Douve* he translated in the early sixties, as he was writing his second book.[4] Kinnell stresses this connection: "[Translation] is a way of getting really close, under the skin of a poem you admire. When you translate a poet, you invite or dare that poet to influence you. In my case I think you can see Bonnefoy in *Flower Herding*" (*WDS* 13). Douve *is* a "resinous heath" (9), but it marks no mapable location; it might be anywhere, a different manner of place than the Toner's bog of Heaney's "Digging." In *Douve*, as in *Flower Herding*, we are thus unmoored, adrift in the river of time. Kinnell sees that what roots we have are shifty and identifies with "processions of debris like floating lamps" that go out, drifting on "The immaculate stream, heavy, and swinging home again" ("The River That Is East"); Bonnefoy whispers:

> Be still for it is true we are the most
> Shapeless of night's gravitating roots,
> Washed matter turning again to the old
> Resounding archetypes whose fire has withered.
>
> (99)

The epigraph to *Douve*, from Hegel, also expresses the premise of *Flower Herding*: "But the life of the spirit is not frightened at death and does not keep itself pure of it. It endures death and maintains itself in it." Life maintains itself in death: the puzzle is partially solved by Kinnell's view that "there is another kind of glory in our lives which derives precisely from our inability to enter that paradise or to experience eternity" (PPW 125). This view echoes Rilke, but also the postwar existentialism that influenced Bonnefoy. (Orestes, in Sartre's *The Flies*: "Human life begins on the far side of despair."[5]) He too knows that

> If it is to appear, the deep light needs
> A ravaged soil cracking with night.
> It is from the dark wood that the flame will leap.
>
> . . . . . . . . . . . . . . .
>
> You will have to go through death to live,
>
> (61)

This conception of death also guides Kinnell's translation. Where Bonnefoy writes, "Vraiment je fus heureuse / A ce point de mourir" (82), another translator, Anthony Rudolf, has "Truly I was happy / *To the point of dying*";[6] Kinnell here makes death a condition of the poet's joy, rather than a measure of it: "Truly I was happy / *At this moment of dying*" (83) (my italics in both). (Kinnell's reading of "I Heard a Fly Buzz When I Died" helps gloss: he agrees with Stan Rubin that in Dickinson's poem "the moment of death is the moment of increased life"; the poem reveals "the heightened feeling she would have for the world when she left it" [*WDS* 23]). When Bonnefoy writes of a stone, "Elle porte la présence de la mort," Kinnell departs from the rather neutral "It bears death's presence" (Rudolf's choice) and offers a more emotionally laden phrase, "Death shines from it," a change justified by the images of light which directly follow. The lines epitomize both Kinnell's predilection as a translator and the glory both poets see radiating from death:

> Regarde, diras-tu, cette pierre:
> Elle porte la présence de la mort.
> Lampe secrète c'est elle qui brûle sous nos gestes,
> Ainsi marchons-nous éclaires. (102)

> Look, you will say, at this stone:
> Death shines from it.
> Secret lamp it is this that burns under our steps,
> Thus we walk lighted. (103)

If we walk in light, for neither poet is this the light of Christian heaven; dying into life has a very different implication here. Sarah Lawall's analysis of Bonnefoy's *Words in Stone* characterizes the difference: "The quest for an earthen Grail leads Bonnefoy to see this world as a 'true place,' a 'here and now' that must be recognized for itself and not as the threshold of things to come. . . . [T]he wished-for Eden is not just across the threshold, but is the threshold itself."[7] Sustaining the Romantic tradition, both poets remove paradise to earth. But if Kinnell and Bonnefoy undertake similar projects, their means reveal very different poetic temperaments. The Frenchman "writes a metaphysical poetry," as Lawall puts it (xi), leading his readers "into a closed, almost hermetic poetic world" (xii); the American wants, as much as possible, to usher the physical world into his writing, to achieve what Neruda calls an "impure poetry," worn "with the hand's obligations, as by acids, steeped in sweat and in smoke, smelling of lilies and urine."[8] (Neruda remains Kinnell's favorite non-English poet [*WDS* 51].)

Bonnefoy's is a "clear, depersonalized voice" (xi), uttering "essentialized language" (xv); Kinnell, like Heaney, values a poet's "speaking in his own voice" (PPD 58). The difference derives in part from a basic distinction Bonnefoy himself notes between English and French, and between their literatures:

> The greatness and richness of English poetry come from service to . . . liberty, as if offering it at every moment the entire range of its possibilites, so that any given word can open up a world, a "brave new world" to our perception. With French poetry it is a very different matter. Generally, with this more cautious, more self-contained kind of poetry, it is a fact that the words seem to state what they denote only to exclude immediately, from the poem's field of reference, whatever else is not denoted. The poet's statements do not set out to describe external reality but are a way of shutting himself in with certain selected precepts in a simplified, more circumscribed world. . . . A more coherent world of intelligible essences is substituted for the real world.[9]

Thus, "The linguistic structure of French poetry is 'Platonic' while that of Shakespeare's English is a sort of passionate Aristotelianism," and "English poetry . . . can be represented by a mirror, French by a sphere" (42).

Bonnefoy calls for a criticism—and perhaps a poetry—to bridge the gap, and like Kinnell's his work certainly lines up against Plato as it "celebrates his perpetual awareness of an unfinished, unstable reality" (Lawall xvi). But in its depersonalized voice, in its etherealized treatment of even salamanders, *Douve* remains essentially French. In important ways, *Flower Herding* has more in common with some of its American contemporaries. As Charles Molesworth suggests about the volume, "Regarding it as the barometer of other, larger currents at work in American poetry in the sixties, it clearly stands with Bly's *Silence in the Snowy Fields* (1964) and Wright's *The Branch Will Not Break* (1963). These three books can be seen as developments away from the ironic mode practiced and perfected by, among others, Ransom, Tate, Nemerov, and Wilbur, and toward a poetic mode first announced by Theodore Roethke as early as 1950."[10]

Certainly Bly and Wright in those works share Kinnell's postmodern sense of having to "work out the basic things as though for the first time" from the starting point of the isolated, stripped-down self. And unlike Lowell or Plath, they share his Words-worthian vision that the natural world, too, is "given," the inevi-table, potentially redeeming context of human life. The prototypical poem from these three books presents the poet, alone in nature, intuiting and meditating on some correlation between the scene and his internal state (a realization that occurs in an abandoned plunge into experience, rather than in the controlled, civil rapprochement with it achieved by writers, like Richard Wilbur, of what Lowell called "cooked" poetry). The three works form a cluster of blos-soms—barbed by the twentieth century—on a tree first planted by Wordsworth:

> On Man, on Nature, and on Human Life
> Musing in Solitude, I oft perceive
> Fair trains of imagery before me rise,
> Accompanied by feelings of delight
> Pure, or with no unpleasing sadness mixed;
> And I am conscious of affecting thoughts
> And dear remembrances, whose presence soothes
> Or elevates the Mind, intent to weigh
> The good and evil of our mortal state.[11]

In *Silence in the Snowy Fields* Bly's mind is perhaps more easily soothed and elevated than Kinnell's, his delight less mixed with "unpleasing sadness." Both write from what Ekbert Faas calls "the conviction that our human life is embedded in the larger life around us," but *Flower Herding* lacks what Faas sees as *Silence*'s confi-dence "that despite death, it will continue there."[12] Death does preoccupy Bly, and occasionally its unexpected appearance does produce a chill. "Poem in Three Parts," for example, begins san-guinely—"Oh, on an early morning I think I shall live forever!"— but the last lines undermine this cheer, intimating what eternal life costs in terms of human identity: "we shall sit at the foot of a plant, / And live forever, like the dust." More frequently, however, Bly con-centrates on the soothing participation in the life beyond himself rather than these intimations of "unpleasing sadness." As the price of that participation, death cannot be forgotten, but it can be imagined as an unmixed blessing: "we move to the death we love" ("With Pale Women in Maryland") and find "A home in dark grass /

And nourishment in death" ("A Home in Dark Grass"). Since for Kinnell "death has two aspects—the extinction, which we fear, and the flowing away into the universe, which we desire" (WDS 23), death's blessing remains mixed in *Flower Herding*, the poems more consistently double-edged. Her bones make him aware of a lover's "beautiful degree of reality," but they call to mind more than beauty:

> I think of a few bones
> Floating on a river at night,
> The starlight blowing in place on the water,
> The river leaning like a wave towards the emptiness.
> ("Poem of Night")

Bly can escape such conflict, perhaps, because his identity is less engaged in the poems. When the claims of one's bit of particular flesh are minimized, you can flow away into the universe without regret; death becomes more loveable. Thus Kinnell's telling critique of Bly's first two books:

> Though he speaks in the first person about intimate feelings, the self has somehow been erased. The "I" is not any particular person, a man like the rest of us, who has sweated, cursed, loathed himself, hated, envied, been coldhearted, mean, frightened, unforgiving, ambitious, and so on. Rather it is a person of total mental health, an ideal "I" who has more in common with the ancient Chinese poets than with anyone alive in the United States today. This would be a blessing for all of us if Bly had really succeeded in "transcending" personality in his poetry. But I think he has not. He simply has not dealt with it. (PPD 56–57)

Kinnell finds Bly's later writings more affecting, for they "go beyond personality by going through it," and later in that essay he praises James Wright's "The Life" for the same reason. But Wright seems to have begun "speaking in his own voice" earlier than that poem, as early in fact as *The Branch Will Not Break*. Unlike the early Bly's, Wright's "I" *is* "a man like the rest of us, who has sweated, cursed, loathed himself" and so on. But it is an "I" like Bly's and Kinnell's, who nevertheless often senses its life "embedded in the larger life around us." Many of the poems in *Branch*, as in *Flower Herding*, thus cleave to a single moment of immersion in this sensation. Each instant carries the potential communion, each grain of sand holds a world, "Each moment of time is a mountain" ("Today I Was So Happy, So I Made this Poem"). Feeling part of a larger life depends on feeling prey to the natural cycles of that life—thus "the death we love." But at these moments Wright, more often than Kinnell, allows death to remain *merely* loveable, stripped of its threat to identity. His cheerful confidence in a benevolent nature sometimes eclipses an awareness of its destructive power, so that grief no longer troubles him. Like the jay he spies jumping on a branch, he "abandon[s] himself / To entire delight," for he knows "That the branch will not break" ("Two Hangovers"). In such a mood he writes, "I see that it is impossible to die" ("Today I Was So Happy").

Ultimately, however, *Branch* is most interesting for its "ambiguous allegiances." Because of the particularity of Wright's "I"—the attempt to go through personality, not around it—death often isn't so impossible or so utterly loveable and nourishing. "Entire delight" doesn't for long keep pure of "unpleasing sadness." As "the evening darkens and comes on," the poet may suddenly, sharply feel that "I have wasted my life" ("Lying in a Hammock at William Duffy's Farm in Pine Island, Minnesota"). Waste is possible only if our connection to the life around us is tenuous and potentially severed, if everything might not turn out OK; maybe the branch *will* break. It seems to have broken in some poems, especially early in the volume. In "A Message Hidden in an Empty Wine Bottle that I Threw into a Gully of Maple Trees One Night at an Indecent Hour" (how images of desolation proliferate wildly in this title!), Wright's loneliness rivals Lowell's in "Skunk Hour." When he writes

> The unwashed shadows
> Of blast furnaces from Moundsville, West Virginia,
> Are sneaking across the pits of strip mines
> To steal grapes
> In heaven.
> Nobody else knows I am here.
> All right.
> Come out, come out, I am dying.
> I am growing old,

Lowell, in his own indecent hour, isn't far away:

> A car radio bleats,
> "Love, O careless Love. . . ." I hear
> my ill-spirit sob in each blood cell,
> as if my hand were at its throat. . . .
> I myself am hell;
> nobody's here—
>
> ("Skunk Hour")

And just as, at the conclusion, Lowell's desperate detachment is mysteriously, tentatively relieved by the unflappable skunks, making do any way they can, Wright's forlorn call, "Come out, come out, I am dying," is strangely, ambiguously answered in the poem's last lines: "An owl rises / From the cutter bar / Of a hayrake." Wright's desolate times come early in *Branch*. By the end, he has moved beyond the self into sometimes entirely delightful contact with the world, but he attains this "blessing" only by going *through* personality. Only by living his dark, indecent hour can he overcome his dread of death, his "fear of harvests," and open to the dying life around him. "Once, / I was afraid of dying," he writes, "But now" he tries "to keep still" and listen to insects "sampling the fresh dew that gathers slowly / In empty snail shells / and in the secret shelters of sparrow feathers fallen on the earth" ("I Was Afraid of Dying").

## II

If Kinnell reserves his most indecent hours for *Body Rags* and *The Book of Nightmares*, if in these later volumes he is more unabashedly "a man like the rest of us, who has sweated, cursed, loathed himself," etc., it is nevertheless in *Flower Herding on Mount Monadnock* that he begins this "going through personality." If we sense his struggle to take the self as a subject, it is because his poems remain spurred into being by a preoccupation with mortality, with the sheer, ultimately ungraspable fact that this footprint, this flower, this woman is here now and soon won't be: if, as Kinnell writes, "the subject of the poem is the thing which dies" (PPW 125), the self is a hard subject to choose.

In *Body Rags* he recalls his brother's claim that " 'the bonfire / you kindle can light the great sky—' " although " 'to make it burn /

you have to throw yourself in . . .'" ("Another Night in the Ruins"). The enlivening possibilities of self-immolation are close to the surface in the second part of *Flower Herding*, but the first part, composed largely of cityscapes, concentrates more on pain and ugliness. Having forsworn the illusion of any other world, Kinnell tries to incorporate into his poetry the disillusionment of this one.

The first three poems, trailing in the wake of "Avenue C," set us squarely in a New York City of failed hopes, the territory mapped by the longer poem. In "The River That Is East," everything is fallen, faded, spent; all the images in the first section tell the story of enervation: "Buoys begin clanging like churches / And peter out," tugs are "Sunk to the gunwhales," the "Jamaica Local crawls" over the Williamsburg Bridge, which "hangs facedown from its strings," and the gulls are "dangling limp red hands." The speaker isn't taken in by "illusory suns" that reflect in puddles or the reflection of the entire scene in the river, "the chaos of illusions" which, like the long, ten-line sentence, blends together a hodgepodge of images.

The boy in the second section also watches the river flow by, but he doesn't see the garbage. Instead he spies the *Isle de France* and wonders "if in some stateroom / There is not a sick-hearted heiress sitting / Drink in hand, saying to herself his name." Like the famous American dreamers the stanza invokes, he goes "baying after the immaterial." But the poem soon undermines this baying. On their deathbeds (at their moments of truth) Kane recalls Rosebud, Gatsby "his days digging clams in Little Girl Bay"; they and the rest die "Thinking of the Huck Finns of themselves," thinking, that is, of the fulfillment the material world offers (it is Huck Finn the junior existentialist here, who relies on his own experience—of nature and of justice—not, like Tom Sawyer, on make-believe).

Section 4 returns to the speaker's own undazzled view of the river's flux. Like Huck, he eschews fantasy, but the East River is less happy than the Mississippi. The material world saddens as well as satisfies. We are sure only of the "onflowing river" (even our vantage point, the shore, "is mist beneath us"), and our future, if we can glimpse it at all, is "a vague scummed thing." Without Grail hunting, we have nothing but ourselves, "We who have no roots but the shifts of our pain, / No flowering but our own strange lives." The natural world, at this point, offers no terrible and glorious kinship—only the river, which Kinnell invests with a gloomy, emblematic significance:

> What is this river but the one
> Which drags the things we love,
> Processions of debris like floating lamps,
> Towards the radiance in which they go out?

But no generalizing will finally suffice. Even this interpretation of the river's meaning is undermined, as Kinnell surprisingly answers his own rhetorical question: "No, it is the River that is East" (no, it is merely the East River—not an existential emblem). He ends, thus, with just this cruddy, material river, seen at just this passing moment:

>                                   —river
> On which a door locked to the water floats,
> A window sash paned with brown water, a whisky crate,
> Barrel staves, sun spokes, feathers of the birds,
> A breadcrust, a rat, spittle, butts, and peels,
> The immaculate stream, heavy, and swinging home again.

If Jane Taylor's view that Kinnell here "achieved an affectionate understanding of the external and internal materials of the experience" seems too cheerful,[13] certainly his reaction to the drifting waste contrasts with the solipsistic dejection Whitman experiences ("I perceive I have not really understood any thing, not a single object, and that no man ever can"), wending along Paumanok's debris-strewn shore, identifying with "Chaff, straw, splinters of wood, weeds, and the sea-gluton, / Scum, scales from shining rocks, leaves of salt-lettuce, left by the tide" ("As I Ebb'd With the Ocean of Life"). Kinnell conveys neither dejection nor precisely affection, but a resolute acceptance, like Bonnefoy's toward the "washed matter" in the passage I quoted earlier. Untainted by the immaterial—in this sense "immaculate" *because* of its debris—the East River is all we have, the image of our "strange lives," rootless but offering the only "flowering" possible.

Kinnell turns to one such strange life in "The Homecoming of Emma Lazarus." Near death, she doubts her earlier optimism about the New World. "Facing the Old World the Green Lady [the Statue of Liberty] whispers, 'Eden!'"—whispers, in effect, "Give me your tired, your poor"—but a disabused Emma is no longer so blithe about the prospects of Europe's wretched human refuse. Once she wanted to embrace all the world, but now Kinnell describes her relinquishing and rejecting: "Her arm lies along the bench, her hand / Hangs over the edge as if she has just let something drop. . . . Her shoulder shrugs as though / To drive away birds which, anyway, weren't intending / To alight." Unlike Emma, the poet can *still* embrace the new world, even stripped of its promise; though Eden is repudiated, like "The River That Is East" the poem ends with a gesture of generosity and surrender:

> In the Harbor the conscript bugler
> Blows the old vow of acceptance into the night—
> It fades, and the wounds of all we had accepted open.

Because "pain and death" are "the very elements" of Kinnell's poetics (PPW 119), many of the poems in part 1 of *Flower Herding* likewise blow this vow of acceptance. Cued by those urban leavings in the East River, they look hard at the modern city—New York and Calcutta—in an effort just to see the waste land without recoiling, not to raise a jeremiad. Kinnell registers the waste without resorting to the immaterial, becoming a "hapless / Witness" ("For Denise Levertov") like the Bengal poet in "Calcutta Visits." That poet looks from his window on the corrupted city, a place with no patience for illusions—"'No like, dance'" a whore announces, "collapsing on the carpet, 'Fookey!'" His sick-hearted city pains the Bengal poet, but it is a necessary pain, for "It is his pain, by the love that asks no way out."

In "Room of Return" Kinnell himself looks out the window at the underside of New York. He spies ocean liners on the river but, unlike the boy in "The River That Is East," doesn't daydream of lonely heiresses in staterooms. Rather, his thoughts skip to the alley cat who sneaks up for some cream to wash down a rat. The whole poem is a sentence fragment; mired like the poet who looks and listens from the window but does not leave the room, it goes nowhere. But at least Kinnell, like the Bengal poet, looks out of the window. In "For Denise Levertov," an insulted Levertov, reciting poems in "utter, gently uttered / Solitude," doesn't look through the window and see the bum outside—"his liquored eye, / The mowed cornfield of his gawk." Had she glanced up, maybe the "hapless / Witness" would have stirred in her breast. And maybe, if she had written about subjects instead of "objects of faith" ("Buildings, rocks, birds, oranges"), her solitude would have been less utter. Witnessing haplessly, Kinnell provisionally contacts the pain-ridden world; he more than merely *looks* out the window. In "To a Child in Calcutta," because he is out in the street among the pimps, whores, and beggars, he meets a child and for a moment becomes a "strange father." But the street people are as much his kin as the innocent babe; the waste land mirrors part of himself. In Calcutta again:

> I heard a voice in the distance,
> I looked up, far away,
> There at the beginning of the world
>
> I could make out a beggar,
> Down the long street he was calling *Galway*!
> I started towards him and began calling *Galway*!
> ("Doppelgänger")

In "Under the Williamsburg Bridge" Kinnell begins to haplessly witness painful evidence in the world of creatures other than humans. He sees a black gull "Killing the ceremony of the dove" and "Tearing for life at my bones," stark observations in which we still hear the resolve not to be insulated or distracted, the "old vow of acceptance." Amid the decaying cityscape, he sees "an old spider wrapping a fly in spittle-strings"—a horrific truth of nature even as the "great and wondrous sun" shining on the scene is a happy one. The insect's demise isn't evil design so much as disinterested natural process; Kinnell grudgingly accepts what appalls Frost.

This distinction underlies the mixture of admiration and criticism in "For Robert Frost." Kinnell admires Frost's sometime willingness to look closely at the design of darkness, to venture "into the pathless wood"—

> He had outwalked the farthest city light,
> And there, clinging to the perfect trees,
> A last leaf. What was it?
> What was that whiteness?—white, uncertain—
> The night too dark to know.

—and in an interview he praises some of Frost's work for "making sudden frightening probes into the unsayable" (*WDS* 65). But Kinnell also sees that Frost sometimes kept his acquaintance with the night from developing into intimacy. We all have promises to keep, but there is something uncourageous about his retreat:

> He turned. *Love,*
> *Love of things, duty,* he said,
> And made his way back to the shelter
> No longer sheltering him, the house
> Where everything real was turning to words.

Words here replace reality (he would "seal the lips / Of his sorrow with the *mot juste*"), and thus Frost's loquacity, on which the poem opens, is more than a peccadillo. Why *does* Frost talk so much, Kinnell asks? To make up for "some long period of solitude"? (Kinnell, for whom solitude is to be nurtured, not compensated for, cannot condone this.) Or, more likely, "is talk distracting from something worse?"—death? the appalling design of darkness? darkness without even design? If, as Kinnell maintains, meter and rhyme keep an awareness of nature and death (and life) at bay, talk can too—especially for a man who, for all his forays into the darkness, Kinnell (almost self-righteously) sees as "not fully convinced he was dying."

### III

In part 2 of *Flower Herding,* Kinnell himself outwalks the city lights. After the rootlessness of the earlier poems, he comes home to what operates for him as his native place—the natural world. Indeed, such rural landscapes as we find in these poems literally had been his home for awhile: "When I was about twenty-two I spent six months in Vermont without once sleeping under a roof. . . . Mostly I lived out in the woods, where I walked, swam, wrote, read, and lazed around."[14] Other people aren't mentioned in this catalogue, and the speaker in these poems does move for the most part in extraordinary isolation; other humans just don't impinge much here (far less often than, say, in *Walden*). "It *is* necessary to accept the loneliness," Kinnell remarks, "to lose one's dread of it. Without the loneliness there can be no poetry" (*WDS* 11). Solitude, then, establishes the condition in which the poet can start the dig into the self and thereby reach beyond. As Molesworth observes about *Flower Herding*, "It is only when Kinnell escapes the city for the country that the possibilities of mortality become positive rather than negative" (229). Like the cityscapes, the nature poems struggle against a hanker after wings (sometimes dramatizing this struggle more directly, they are generally more interesting), but they also manifest the *enlivening* prospects of such forbearance. Ceasing to bay after the immaterial may open wounds, but it also opens the channels (the wounds may *be* the channels) through which the poet finds the world.

I have suggested that several poems in *What a Kingdom It Was*, refusing the "Lech for transcendence," also draw on the enlivening unity of life and death. But the key poems in *Flower Herding* do this with a far greater sense of the poet's experience at a discrete instant; like Wright, for whom "Each moment of time is a mountain," Kinnell shares Emerson's belief that "the universe is represented in an atom, in a moment of time" ("The Over-Soul"). "Last Spring," while itself not one of the "moment" poems, describes their starting point: after a winter of lying still and dreaming, of losing grip "On the things of the world" and "Settling for their glitter," the poet is awakened by the spring sun. Its "Swath of reality started going over / The room daily, like a cleaning woman"; after the spring cleaning, what remains is solitude, "And time to walk / Head bobbing out front like a pigeon's / Knocking on the instants to let me in." Launched by this tercet, the poems in part 2 of *Flower Herding*, pointedly written in the present tense, catch one or another of the instants opening to Kinnell's knock. Mills describes how many of the poems thus "adhere closely to the lineaments of a specific experience; rather than enlarging on it as some previous pieces do, they attempt to seize it through a literal correctness" (105–6).

"In Fields of Summer," "On Hardscrabble Mountain," and "Cells Breathe in the Emptiness" adhere closest to the details of the poet's experience and to his awareness of his life as just one of many ongoing natural processes. This awareness leads to a sometimes frightening intimation (less frightening here than in *Body Rags*) of life deeper than consciousness, not exclusive of it. In participating in the natural goings on, however, he retains his distinguishing identity—like Koisimi, who, gazing at the landscape and hearing the wind, cries *"it is me,"* but also *"It is not me"* ("Koisimi Buddhist of Altitudes"). (Recall Kinnell's distrust of similes: "I don't think things are often like other things. At some level all things *are* each other, but before that point they are separate entities" [*WDS* 52].) "It is me," however, goes virtually unanswered in "In Fields of Summer." Of all the moments that open to Kinnell's knock, this is the least ruffled by any pangs of mortality. The poet's body shares in the joyful proceedings of the organic world—the sun rising, the goldenrod blooming, the lark bursting up "all dew." Life shines equally, and gloriously, in the goldenrod and the poet and the grass. Although an "old crane" makes an appearance and "The rumble of bumblebees keeps deepening," the predominant movement is skywards: "The sun rises," the poet's life "shines up," "A phoebe flutters up, / A lark bursts up all dew." The poem ends with these birds, a cheerful conclusion quite unlike that of Bly's "Poem in Three Parts," where the initial glorious communion ("joyful flesh") is subverted by the final foreboding simile (Bly will "live forever, like the dust").

Usually, Kinnell too takes such a darker turn, as in "Cells Breathe in the Emptiness." The first of its two sections, virtually a photographic negative of the beginning of "In Fields of Summer," offers another list of observations of nature, but the thrill is gone. "The sun rises, / The goldenrod blooms, / My own life is adrift in my body," has become

> The flowers turn to husks
> And the great trees suddenly die
> And rocks and old weasel bones lose
> The little life they had.

The title announces this "emptiness," but it tells us, too, that the emptiness isn't entirely so, for in it "cells breathe." In the second section, thus, the still air is invaded by "the sound of the teeth / Of one of those sloppy green cabbageworms / Eating his route through a cabbage." The sound arises from a compost heap—a graveyard, but also a source of nourishment for the worm; the emptiness is filled by the sound of destructive and creative organic cycles. The final image, too, rhymes with the end of "In Fields of Summer." In the earlier poem, "A phoebe flutters up, / A lark bursts up all dew." In this one, "A butterfly blooms on a buttercup, / From the junk-pile flames up a junco." Both moments thrill, but the overtone of transience in "dew" is amplified in "junkpile" and "flames," adding the downward tug of mortality to all the pretty upwardness.

The poet, however, isn't an active character in the poem. His own body participates in the shining life in "In Fields of Summer," but not (except by implication) in life's destructive process in "Cells Breathe." "On Hardscrabble Mountain" includes him directly in this process (although its use of the past tense—the only poem in part 2 to do so—still keeps some distance). It begins with the poet "stretched out on the mountain," himself a part of the winterscape. But his kinship soon turns potentially deadly:

> I waked with a start,
> The sun had crawled off me,
> I was shivering in thick blue shadows,
> Sap had stuck me to the spruce boughs.

I sense that this image of sticking to the boughs figures visually what Kinnell is perhaps reticent to express openly—an impulse to have done with consciousness and merge with the elements, like Bonnefoy, who is more direct: "'I love blinding myself, surrendering myself to the earth. I love no longer knowing what cold teeth possess me'" (109). But, like Keats abruptly bidding adieu to the seductive nightingale, Kinnell unsticks himself from the boughs and heads down the mountain. In response to the more immediate presence death has assumed for him in the poem, he starts to pray—not to "god," but

> to a bear just shutting his eyes,
> To a skunk dozing off,
> To a marmot with yellow belly,
> To a dog-faced hedgehog,
> To a dormouse with a paunch and large eyes like leaves or
> wings.

A prayer is an act of communion *and* a recognition of need; his pantheistic outpouring suggests both the poet's provisional participation in the life around him (he too dozes off) *and* his separation. "[I]t is me"; "It is not me."

Donald Davie has chided Kinnell for wanting "to experience the transcendent without paying the entrance fee, for instance, in the currency of humility" (20). But, leaving aside the question of whether "the transcendent" is a fair term to describe what Kinnell wants to experience, humility seems precisely the poet's condition in "On Hardscrabble Mountain," if by humility we mean an awed sense of one's limitation, of one's smallness in the face of Being— even if it manifests itself in a skunk. Kinnell's *tone* is not timid, but how much humbler can you get than praying to a dog-faced hedgehog? Kinnell's prayers do, however, go out also to larger entities, especially in "On Frozen Fields," which builds toward a mysterious expression of the need for forgiveness. The poem has barely begun, with a description of the speaker and his companion happily walking arm in arm, when it pulls up abruptly and breaks into the concluding prayer:

> You in whose ultimate madness we live,
> You flinging yourself out into the emptiness,
> You—like us—great an instant,
>
> O only universe we know, forgive us.

Kinnell takes a cosmic perspective, but it offers no solace. He doesn't flinch from the troubling astrophysical facts: the universe, still expanding outward from the original Big Bang, *is* literally flinging itself out into the emptiness. And like the sun (and the meteors and Northern Lights in the first section), everything in it *is* burning itself out. Astronomers think that eventually either all the suns will cool and the universe will go dark or everything will collapse back into the center and blend together again. In either case, *this* particular universe will come to an end. It, like us, is dying, is bound by time, is "great an instant."

Although in "On Frozen Fields" Kinnell has company as he knocks upon the instant, usually when an instant opens to his knock what he finds is anything but another person. Even in "On Frozen Fields" the lover exists only by implication in "we" and by the presence of an arm. Of all the "moment" poems in *Flower Herding,* only in "Poem of Night" is another person really important. This is a love poem, although it is typical of Kinnell's sensibility that human contact occurs here between two bodies, or between the life that is "adrift" in bodies (as in "In Fields of Summer"). Lying in bed, he apprehends the woman solely as a material, indeed anatomical, presence (he feels "Slopes, falls, lumps of sight," "Lashes," "Lips," "The bones' smile," "Zygoma, maxillary, turbinate"), and he senses her in fragments: "A cheekbone, / A curved piece of brow, / A pale eyelid / Float in the dark." But soon, we begin to understand Kinnell's concentration on her body:

> Hardly touching, I hold
> What I can only think of
> As some deepest of memories in my arms,
> Not mine, but as if the life in me
> Were slowly remembering what it is.

As Mills observes, Kinnell "perceives a portion of his own existence embodied in the contours of her familiar form; her self has been so deeply bound up with his for a time that in holding her body in his arms he feels he is embracing something fundamental to his own nature" (107).

Fundamental to *everyone's* nature, we might add. Some readers dismiss Kinnell as "primitive," an enemy of consciousness, and certainly in this volume when he breaks out of the "enclosed ego" to reach another human being, her consciousness remains off stage. She is defined by her slopes and falls, not her awareness—as if she could be anybody. Indeed, in *Mortal Acts, Mortal Words,* he will acknowledge that "It is good for strangers / of a few nights to love each other / . . . and merge in natural rapture" ("Flying Home"). Taken as a whole, however, Kinnell's writing doesn't oppose the corporal and the conscious. He seeks, rather, their common ground. In "Poetry, Personality and Death" he quotes an "odd little poem" by Lawrence in which the poet wishes he could snuggle with a woman "and really take delight in her / without having to make . . . the mental effort of making her acquaintance" (72). But Kinnell understands even Lawrence knew that a "union deeper than personality . . . is not to be had that way. As with poetry, so with love: it is necessary to go through the personality to reach beyond it. Short of a swan descending from heaven, the great moments of sexual love are not between strangers, but between those who know and care for each other, and who then pass beyond each other, becoming nameless creatures enacting the primal sexuality of all life" (72).

If "Poem of Night" reaches beyond the self by passing through the poet's own experience, it would have been more complete had we glimpsed the lovers first knowing and caring for each other. But Kinnell's gift isn't for catching others' personalities; he creates no cast of characters to rival poets with a more social bent, like Merrill or even Yeats. We know other people in Kinnell's work mostly by indirection, by the shapes they trace on his consciousness, by the stuttersteps the otherwise "enclosed ego" takes toward the world.

In any case, even in "Poem of Night" the physical kinship doesn't exclude his awareness. If, as Kinnell has it, "the body makes love possible" (*WDS* 112), it also makes the death of love inevitable. "You lie here now in your physicalness, / This beautiful degree of reality," the poet affirms, yet the poem concludes not with joy but with a sense of the transience of this beauty. The night of intimacy ends. The day, a "raft that breaks up," affords no sense of renewal. Zygoma, maxillary, and turbinate now evoke a very different response:

> I think of a few bones
> Floating on a river at night,
> The starlight blowing in place on the water,
> The river leaning like a wave towards the emptiness.

These lines, successively straining closer to the blankness beyond the margin, themselves ripple toward the emptiness. Where the conclusion of "On Frozen Fields" shifts from "you," the entropic universe, to "us," this ending begins with the poet and then departs from him, the changing focus portending his own eventual extinction.

In both of these conclusions the word "emptiness" is asked to bear considerable weight. This is a key word in what Cary Nelson has called Kinnell's "vocabulary for visionary evacuation."[15] He suggests that the context for this vocabulary in *What a Kingdom It Was* is "inescapably theological," while in *Flower Herding* "the same vocabulary begins to function as its own justification; it becomes a ritualized, necessary signature for any poetic utterance. . . . Words like 'emptiness,' 'nothingness,' and 'darkness' accompany a host of gestures toward loss and self-extinction." In later works, where each gesture toward extinction finds its own customized verbal accompaniment, Kinnell resorts less often to this vocabulary. But if its use sounds ritualistic in *Flower Herding,* the ritual is rarely hollow; these words are usually justified by more than their own presence—partly because, while the images often suggest the cosmic, they seem also to retain traces of the microcosmic, of Kinnell's own biography. Occasionally, he acknowledges this link, if only tacitly. In the title poem, an adult vision of the sky as a "nothingness" follows (and, we seem asked to suppose, derives from) an earlier void: after his birth, the poet discloses, "It was eight days before the doctor / Would scare my mother with me." Whether or not this awful tale is literally true, even the suggestion of a biographical source saves "nothingness" from empty ritual.

When Kinnell's "vocabulary for visionary evacuation" in *Flower Herding* isn't linked to his past, it usually arises from and comments on a specific dramatic scene in the present (in contrast to Merwin, who Nelson claims uses the same vocabulary "to evoke a sense of romantic mystery" [66] and whose poems from *The Moving Target* on are more tenuously located). In "Middle of the Way," for instance, the ritualistic use of the key term "darkness" is more evocative than hollow. Indeed, the title itself begins to establish the resonances of this word. Echoing the opening of *The Inferno,* it signals an imminent descent (like Dante, Kinnell is lost in the woods), although Kinnell's going down is more like Eliot's, who is also "in the middle way" before he enters the dark in "East Coker" (section 5). Kinnell's darkness is first a physical condition, an element of a dramatic scene, not (as in Eliot) a mystic one. Lying in the woods at night, he participates in the scene (*"it is me"*) and simultaneously feels isolated from it (*"It is not me"*): "I love the earth, and always / In its darkness I am a stranger." He doesn't, however, feel forced to choose between being a "sod" (merged but unconscious) and being "forlorn" (conscious but alien), as Keats does.[16] Rather, awareness and oblivion remain in equipoise; lying on the earth Kinnell is at home *and* a stranger, a paradox that again recalls "East Coker"—"And where you are is where you are not."

The poem's second section takes the form of a prose journal. This is the outer world, not the inner one—day, not night. In an unmystical mood, Kinnell structures his log by clock time as he treks through the snowy forest, climbs a mountain, eventually loses the trail, looks for it awhile, and at 7:30 P.M. makes camp in a snow field, not yet having found the trail. His account of these events evinces his double relation to the darkness. By losing the trail, he leaves the finite, historical, daylight world. But, joined spatially to the unbounded wildness (off the trail), he nevertheless maintains his temporal bearings by keeping track of clock time, and thus he retains the rational, ordering functions of consciousness. Temporally "at home," spatially a "stranger," he is both in and out of history (as Eliot is momentarily "in and out of time" in "The Dry Salvages").

In the final section, which returns to meditation and verse, the elements of the scene begin to dissolve as "The coals go out," and "The last smoke weaves up / Losing itself in the stars." And the poet's presence too is tenuous. He thinks of the non-being implicit in his own existence, of the worm in his heart "That has spun the heart about itself" and will one day "break free into the beautiful black sky," joining him entirely with the darkness. But he doesn't blink away this threat to flesh:

> I leave my eyes open,
> I lie here and forget our life,
> All I see is we float out
> Into the emptiness, among the great stars,
> On this little vessel without lights.

Our planet itself has "lost the trail," or, rather, there never really was a trail to follow. We lean "in any direction, which is the way" ("Koisimi Buddist of Altitudes"). Urging you to travel your own road, Whitman hopes to help you keep your eyes open—"Now I wash the gum from your eyes"—but expects you will then see "the dazzle of the light and of every moment of your life" (SM 46); Kinnell, with ungummed eyes, sees how few lights there are, whichever way we lean. But this darkness doesn't evoke mere absence: just as vacancy becomes plenitude for Eliot, "emptiness" here is a space for filling—an invitation to addition rather than the void left by subtraction. The poem concludes with Kinnell (for the moment, comfortably) in the middle, loyal to both day and night, light and dark, consciousness and body. Opposites become complements in the final stanza, at once confessional and sacerdotal, of two worlds and—resounding with "I know"—ringing with certitude:

> I know that I love the day,
> The sun on the mountain, the Pacific
> Shiny and accomplishing itself in breakers,
> But I know I live half alive in the world,
> I know half my life belongs to the wild darkness.

Davie has reproached Kinnell for the "self-contradiction" of wanting transcendence without humility or of declaring for the world of appearances but also trying to "bash his way through by main force into the transcendent, the absolute" (20–21)—as if what we wanted from our poets was the pure metal of unmixed motives. By this criterion he could have dismissed "Middle of the Way" as a lowly alloy. But instead, to illustrate a poet who "thrashes about in manifest self-contradiction" Davie picks on "Spindrift," the first of two extended "moment" poems that end *Flower Herding*.[17] Actually, this seven-sectioned poem presents a sequence of moments—first a view of a beach and then a series of more narrowly focused perceptions of the scene, reflections upon it, and memories aroused by it. Whether or not in these moments the poet thrashes about in self-contradiction each reader may judge, but, as in "Middle of the Way," the scene does provoke a series of double responses from Kinnell.

As the poet regards the beach in section 1, his catalogue of sights first centers on remnants—a "tree thrown up / From the sea," "old / Horseshoe crabs, broken skates, / Sand dollars, sea horses"—as if existence were essentially a destructive affair. But then, after commenting on that destruction, he looks

> At chunks of sea-mud still quivering,
> At the light as it glints off the water
> And the billion facets of the sand,
> At the soft, mystical shine the wind
> Blows over the dunes as they creep.

The scene thus encompasses images of motion as well as stillness, animation as well as dilapidation. The original disorder is countered by the later lines' neat initial assonance; the dark mood is offset by the lighter one that suggests, in the "soft, mystical shine," a realm beyond the scene itself.

In section 2 this doubleness surfaces immediately in the "bitter, beloved sea" ("stable sameness and ceaseless change," as Mills puts it [109], sustainer and destroyer). Kinnell tells himself to "Pluck sacred / Shells from the icy surf" and "Lift one to the sun," but even as the shells, "Fans of gold light," sustain the light imagery of section 1, since the lifting is "a sign you accept to go / As bid, to the shrine of the dead," the earlier destruction is also recalled. Like the previous one, however, this section ends with an unfathomable "shine" that suggests perhaps death isn't final: holding the shell (literally a corpse) up to the sun, the poet tells himself to "See the lost life within / Alive again in the fate-shine." (Kinnell later dropped the lines, minimizing this conciliatory note in the newer version.)

Next, Kinnell considers a "little bleached root." Its life was a temporary aberration; "Brittle, cold, practically weightless," it has now assumed its true form:

> If anything is dead, it is,
> This castout worn
> To the lost grip it always essentially was.

But, once again, Kinnell pivots. Although it has "lost hold / It at least keeps the wild / Shape of what it held." While remaining a constant reminder of loss, it thus also becomes a paradoxical memento of constancy, "one of the earth's / Wandering icons of 'to have.'" (The possibility of eternal possession has by this point accumulated an explicitly religious vocabulary—"mystical," "sacred," "shrine," "icon"; later "pilgrim" joins the list.)

Pursuing this paradox, Kinnell returns in section 4 to the doubleness of the "bitter, beloved sea," listening to its power (its ruinous potential) but also its "inexhaustible freshness." Then, the sound of a wave crashing in "overlapping thunders going away down the beach" unifies these opposing aspects; that single sound "is the most we know of time" *and* "it is our undermusic of eternity." Time and eternity coincide in the wave's crash, or, rather, it is through the wave's crash that we can know them together. That such knowledge is rooted in sensory experience illuminates Kinnell's epistemology here, and it also undermines the flirtation with the immaterial incipient in the guardedly upbeat endings of the previous sections. This section concludes not with mystical shining or optimistic iconography but with time and eternity—"to lose" and "to have"—held in balance.

In section 6 this balance is finally figured in terms of the poet's own being:

> Across gull tracks
> And wind ripples in the sand
> The wind seethes. My footprints
> Slogging for the absolute
> Already begin vanishing.

Stressing the poet's "Slogging for the absolute," Davie sees Kinnell approaching the position that "the perceivable and perishing world of the creatures" is "all the good he will find" (20) but then here recoiling from it. And we *have* seen Kinnell in this poem drawn to the absolute; even in this section he holds the death-defying shell. If he were never tempted, however, settling for the perishable world would seem too easy. By dramatizing the struggle, the difficulty of watching those footprints evanesce, Kinnell both authenticates whatever success he manages to have and keeps the focus on what is after all his true subject: the self *in search of* the world.

In perhaps his most significant emendation for *The Avenue Bearing the Initial of Christ into the New World,* Kinnell eliminated the concluding three lines of "Spindrift." Originally, the poem ended poised between an allegiance to the perishable world and an attraction to whatever might not perish. "What does he really love," Kinnell asks, "That old man," walking "in the ungodly / Rasp and cackle of old flesh?" From the physical standpoint time uses us badly. But complaint to time then gives way to gratitude and identification:

> Nobody likes to die
> But an old man
> Can know
> A kind of gratefulness
> Towards time that kills him,
> Everything he loved was made of it.

Such an unadorned declaration bears the authority of plain speech. But these lines, despite their obvious closural force, aren't the last ones in the original version. Three lines follow:

> In the end
> What is he but the scallop shell
> Shining with time like any pilgrim?

Implying man's lost life can, like the shell's, come "Alive again in the fate-shine," this question qualifies the gratefulness just preceding. Although it anticipates the old man's physical death—he will become just a skeleton, a shell—it points beyond the finality of that death and thus compromises Kinnell's pledge of allegiance to the world of appearances. Dropping these three lines (and the lines in section 2 to which they refer) achieves a conclusion less perfectly balanced, more perfectly grateful. Like James Merrill in "The Book of Ephraim," Kinnell here begins setting himself against time and comes around to realize that he *is* time.

The consequences of such a constitution, however, are invariably more grief-ridden for Kinnell. For Merrill, time may be our adversary as well as our nom de plume ("X"), but in his essentially comic vision when time appears as a dragon it is slain by the knight-artist ("Q"), and when it sneaks into the house in the guise of a burglar, it takes nothing of value, "or nothing we recall" ("Z"). Death is finally more bearable when you can chat with your deceased chums at the Ouija board. Both poets favor elegy, but the dragon's bite in Kinnell's work produces a harder-to-bind wound, losses aren't so gracefully recouped, and the death of the self looms more menacingly.[18] The title poem from *Flower Herding* illustrates. Like "Spindrift," it represents a series of moments—perception, sensation, memory, contemplation—experienced this time as the poet hikes on a mountain. One moment simply follows the next without interpretive or narrative connection, as if no other arrangement but chronology structured the poem. But as though pattern were embedded in the scene itself, this series of moments tells a story: the poet's close observation of the forest gradually awakens in him an awareness of the mortality inherent in Being.

In the first three sections, the poet appears to operate in a prelapsarian state. Not perhaps as frankly Edenic as Spenser's Garden of Adonis (which Merrill evokes in "Ephraim"), at first the New Hampshire hillside is, as Kinnell experiences it, nonetheless innocent of time and trouble. If the poet has had some nightmares, he laughs these off and anticipates the new morning. Dawn breaks but does not yet release the landscape into the temporal flow; rather, the scene is nearly crystallized: "The song of the whippoorwill stops / And the dimension of depth seizes everything." What bird song continues does not disrupt this stasis: the song of a peabody bird "enters the leaves, and comes out little changed"; "The air is so still" that as they recede "The love songs of birds do not get any fainter." Even when the poet inadvertently demonstrates the movement of his consciousness through time, he outwardly points to what he supposes is inviolable: "The last memory I have / Is of a flower which cannot be touched."

But time his troubler is. In section 5 the birds' songs become elegies, although at first Kinnell finds in them "something joyous." He imagines the birds are "Caught up in a formal delight," even though he now recognizes "the mourning dove whistles of despair." Although he persists for awhile in hearing joy and delight, more ominous matters thus have now crept into the poem. He lapses from grace to grief:

> But at last in the thousand elegies
> The dead rise in our hearts,
> On the brink of our happiness we stop
> Like someone on a drunk starting to weep.

From this point on, images of violability and loss proliferate. The poet had been climbing, but now he kneels at a pool and thinks he sees bacteria beneath his reflection, performing (we gather) their catabolic rites. Literally they are munching moss, but his face is not immune; self-reflection is figured as the dissolution of the self:

> My face sees me,
> The water stirs, the face,
> Looking preoccupied,
> Gets knocked from its bones.

He perceives the forest now, not as a place of stillness and permanence, but as a place of fallings and disintegrations, a "shaken

paradise." The wind blows and "last night's rain / Comes splatter-
ing from the leaves"; a waterfall "Breaks into beads halfway down."
However much we strain skyward, death has the last word:

> I know
> The birds fly off
> But the hug of the earth wraps
> With moss their graves and the giant boulders.

The poem culminates in an epiphany, but rather than glimpsing
the far side of mortality, the unifying darkness into which each
dying thing may dissolve, Kinnell is seized by an entrancing awareness of evanescence itself. He discovers a flower (now one which
*can* be touched) whose blossoms "claim to float in the Empyrean,"
but, as it did to the skyward-winging birds, earth has the final say;
like the poet's own, the flower's "appeal to heaven breaks off." As
Bonnefoy regards Douve—"each instant I see you being born,
Douve, / Each instant dying" (9)—so Kinnell regards the flower: its
life and death are inseparable, simultaneous, defined by each other.
The flourish of pyrotechnic imagery may catch this doubleness, but
finally Kinnell, like Bonnefoy, can only quietly state the sheer fact
of what Howard calls "the death that is being, the being that is
death" (314):

> In the forest I discover a flower.
>
> The invisible life of the thing
> Goes up in flames that are invisible
> Like cellophane burning in the sunlight.
>
> It burns up. Its drift is to be nothing.
>
> In its covertness it has a way
> Of uttering itself in place of itself,
> Its blossoms claim to float in the Empyrean,
>
> A wrathful presence on the blur of the ground.
>
> The appeal to heaven breaks off.
> The petals begin to fall, in self-forgiveness.
> It is a flower. On this mountainside it is dying.

Nothing else to say.

## CHAPTER 3

# Romanticism in the Rag-and-Bone Shop: *Body Rags*

## I

With the pared-down sentences that conclude *Flower Herding on Mount Monadnock*, Kinnell had risked writing himself into a corner. "It is a flower. On this mountainside it is dying." After the sometimes frenetic slogging for and away from the absolute, these sound like last words. What else to say along these lines, the chief lines along which Kinnell's poetic gift had run? In *Body Rags*, his third book of poems, he confronts this impasse, not by cultivating new concerns, but by personalizing the old ones to an extent that the verse is transfigured. "It is dying" is not yet "I am dying," and so the poet's voice, at least, lives on.

But even leaving aside questions of "personality," *Body Rags* directly addresses the problem of surviving the blazing vision of the first two books of poetry. Writing of this third, Richard Howard notes its concern with mere survival: "After the fire, then, a still small voice. Humbled, reduced, but reduced in the sense of *intensified*, concentrated rather than diminished, life, having passed through what Arnold called 'the gradual furnace of the world,' life for Galway Kinnell becomes a matter of sacred vestiges, remnants, husks" (314). As he points out, merely the titles themselves comprise a catalogue of leftovers: "Another Night in the Ruins," "The Fossils," "One Who Used to Beat His Way," "The Last River," "Testament of the Thief," and so on. If all that outlasted the fires, though, were remnants and husks, *Body Rags* would remain a rather ossified work. But, on the contrary, its essential quality is its *vitality*. If a pile of ashes remains, well, something stirs there; look closely—flies buzz around the kitchen midden. Whatever sacred vestiges may lie about, what really survives is, like the poet, stubbornly alive. "Lost Loves" begins after the fire, "On ashes of old volcanoes," but the next two words—"I lie"—reassert the abiding life of the poet. "The Poem" presents a field of bones, but after eight lines—action:

> we hunt
> the wild hummingbird
> who once lived nesting in these
> pokeweed-sprouting, pismired
> ribcages dumped down all over the place.

An historical interpretation of this kind of vitality is articulated by Ted Hughes, another poet of survival:

> Popa, and several other writers one can think of, having cut their losses and cut the whole hopelessness of that civilization off, have somehow managed to invest their hopes in something deeper than what you lose if civilization disappears completely and in a way it's obviously a pervasive and deep feeling that civilization has now disappeared completely. If it's still here it's still here by grace of pure inertia and chance and if the whole thing has essentially vanished one had better have one's spirit invested in something that will not vanish. And this is a shifting of your foundation to completely new Holy Ground, a new divinity, one that won't be under the rubble when the churches collapse.[1]

One denizen of this new Ground is Hughes's own *Crow*. Embodying some vitalistic essence, some irreducible precipitate of Life, the bird is ugly as sin but able to walk away from whatever catastrophes the world can cook up—and he's always hungry. When "the pistol muzzle oozing blue vapour / Was lifted away" and "the only face left in the world / Lay broken" and "the trees closed forever / And the streets closed forever / And the body lay on the gravel / Of the abandoned world," then "Crow had to start searching for something to eat" ("That Moment"). When the serpent invaded the garden, man and woman and even God went all to pieces,

> But Crow only peered.
> Then took a step or two forward,

79

Grabbed this creature by the slackskin nape,

Beat the hell out of it, and ate it.
　　　　　("A Horrible Religious Error")

In "A Disaster" a word-monster destroys the world, leaving only "a brittle desert / Dazzling with the bones of earth's people / Where Crow walked and mused." Thus, as Hughes explains, the book evokes "a complete abolition of everything that's been up to this point and Crow is what manages to drag himself out of it in fairly good morale" (207).

How does Crow manage this? Hughes speaks of an "irruption, from the deeper resources, of enraged energy," of tapping the "elemental power circuit of the Universe." But he cautions:

Once the contact has been made—it becomes difficult to control. Something from beyond ordinary human activity enters. When the wise men know how to create rituals and dogma, the energy can be contained. When the old ritual and dogma have lost credit and disintegrated, and no new ones have been formed, the energy cannot be contained, and so its effect is destructive—and that is why force of any kind frightens our rationalist, humanist style of outlook. In the old world God and divine power were invoked at any cost—life seemed worthless without them. In the present world we dare not invoke them—we wouldn't know how to use them or stop them destroying us. (200)

But what exactly is the nature of the risk here? Hughes (a bit boastfully) implies that he has tried to invoke and harness the power, but he seems not to have been driven berserk. Do people go crazy—or literally get destroyed—from writing poems? Hughes's analogy to "energy" in an "elemental power circuit" inevitably conjures up Faustian devils in the form of nuclear fears: of some *actual* elemental energy sources it is all too true that "once the contact has been made—it becomes difficult to control." Indeed, the "complete abolition" that Crow "manages to drag himself out of" often suggests the aftermath of nuclear war. But as applied to writing poetry, the "contact" with "something beyond ordinary human activity" probably refers to a probing beneath ordinary consciousness, beneath "our rationalist, humanist style of outlook." While acknowledging the potentially divine aspect of the powers, Kinnell frames the issue more directly in these psychological terms: "Many people feel one shouldn't poke under the surface—that one shouldn't tempt the gods or invite trouble, that one should be content to live with his taboos unchallenged, with his repressions and politenesses unquestioned; that just as the highest virtue in the state is law and order, so the highest virtue of poetry is formality and morality—or if immorality, then in the voice of a *persona*—and on the whole cheerful, or at least ironic, good humor" (PPD 67).

What, then, are the risks of poking under the surface? Doesn't psychological common sense tell us that the more we know about ourselves the better? Well, our soberer poets keep warning us not to know too much too soon. For every Whitman who exhorts "Unscrew the locks from the doors! / Unscrew the doors themselves from their jambs!" (SM 24), a Dickinson cautions "Tell all the Truth but tell it slant— / Success in Circuit lies" (1129), or an Eliot admonishes "human kind / Cannot bear very much reality" ("Burnt Norton"), although these truths and realities aren't merely psychological. The danger Hughes may have in mind is the possibility of being overcome by what you dig up. The id *does* have an energetic, amoral, potentially destructive aspect, and if Mr. Hyde gets out perhaps nothing short of Dr. Jekyll's death will stop him (Kinnell suggests that Hyde is so dangerous precisely because he was denied for so long, that the story is "a true myth of repression and its consequences" [PPD 70]). Hughes and Kinnell both fall subject to attacks from those who fear this possibility, especially its political implications. The bird in "Hawk Roosting," Hughes tells us, "is accused of being a fascist . . . the symbol of some horrible totalitarian dictator" (199). Davie proposes that it was Kinnell's sort of Promethianism "that was drowning Vietnamese hamlets in a sea of fire" (14), and he links Kinnell's so-called titanism to Charles Manson (22).

Such nervous political worries cannot be summarily dismissed. Better poets than Kinnell or Hughes have embraced fascism, and many poets *do* have lapses of sanity, although self-destruction is more common than genocide. But nothing suggests an inevitable connection between probing the unconscious and going crazy. Poking around *may* conceivably pose a risk, but—as in Kinnell's reading of the Jekyll and Hyde story—so may *not* poking around.

Certainly one imagines that artists, like Kinnell and Bly, who denounced the Vietnam War were more interested in contacting the unconscious than were President Johnson and General Westmoreland. And if writing can exacerbate existing psychological disturbance in some cases, certainly in these and many others, it can offer a way of sorting out the difficulty, a provisional antidote.

Neither Hughes nor Kinnell has literally gone mad or perpetrated mass murder. But there is another, less severe, danger. If we probably won't be overcome by monsters from the id, there is no guarantee that self-exploration will prove in any way ameliorating. Crow embodies a primitive aspect of the self—he is *real*—but there is little else to recommend him. Kinnell praises James Dickey for courageously searching out and exposing a difficult but important part of himself in "The Firebombing," but he also sees that by resorting to a persona "Dickey does not accept the risk of this search, the risk that in finding reality we may find only death; that we may find no source of transfiguration, only regret and despair" (PPD 60): "If we are willing to face the worst in ourselves, we also have to accept the risk I have mentioned that probing into one's own wretchedness one may just dig up more wretchedness" (PPD 67). If Kinnell exaggerates the possibilities—and it is hard to imagine so entirely "wretched" a being surviving past infancy, much less fostering any poetic impulses—perhaps it is because this danger strikes home for him. He recalls a poetry recital where, after he read "certain poems that exposed my own wretchedness," a woman from the audience handed him a "poem" she had just composed:

> Galway Kinnell
> Why
> Are you in love with blood?
> What
> Dark part of your soul
> Glories so
> To wallow in gore?

". . . Depravity . . . Exhalt in ugliness" and so on. It ends, "You / are a sickness" (PPD 67–68). Kinnell laughed but kept the verse as a reminder: "It *is* a risk; it is possible we will go on to the end feeding, with less and less relish, on the bitter flesh of our heart.

The worst is that we ourselves may be the last to know that this is how we spent our life" (PPD 62).

This second risk points to a third. If, exploring the self, contacting some primal energy, one doesn't like what turns up, why continue the search? Why write? As his above remarks suggest, Kinnell did possess a looming sense of his own "wretchedness," a wretchedness exposed by writing poems. And yet, his debt to poetry was as extreme; wondering if his early efforts at formal verse were ill-advised, he realizes: "I will never know, and in any event, it is not possible for me to regret a travail which released in me so much energy and excitement, to which I gave myself so entirely, and which saved me."[2] By persisting in the very kind of writing that may render writing itself merely pointless or bitter, Kinnell runs the real risk of losing the thing which "saved" him.

The risk of writing poems which tap the "elemental power circuit" or "poke under the surface," then, must be seriously reckoned with, although it is perhaps a less heroic—or less dramatic—one than Hughes implies. But I suspect that the frequent allusions to "risk" in poets like Hughes and Kinnell often have to do rather with "difficulty." Metaphors which rely on acts of speech like "invoke" or on simple physical operations like poking, probing, and digging convey a false sense of ease: just grab a shovel and heave to it. But if it is hard to vacate personal consciousness, as Eliot wants to do in *Four Quartets,* we must also overcome considerable resistance in order to reach beneath it. " 'Be it life or death, we crave only reality,' " Kinnell seconds Thoreau's maxim (PPD 67), but this view is incomplete. Freud proposes that we crave a flight from reality as well. The unconscious is unconscious precisely because one part of us prefers it that way: we *want* to remain unaware and thus actively repress, to avoid shame or fear or conflict or, as Norman O. Brown interprets Freud, the prospect of our own death. Truths may emerge quite spontaneously in dreams, but the truth they tell is slant. Kinnell takes issue with Eliot's use of a persona in "Prufrock" because "it functions like the Freudian dream, fictionalizing what one does not want to know is real" (PPD 58). Perhaps when Hughes complains that "in our present world we dare not invoke" the "divine power," he also means that we scarcely know how.

In any case, Hughes's willingness to try this invocation and Kinnell's to "tempt the gods or invite trouble"—despite the risks and the difficulty—testify to an authentic and powerful vitality. Yet for both, this vitality spawns a poetry of violence, brutality, and death. Describing Hughes as "our first poet of the will to live," Calvin Bedient explains this paradox: "The will to live might seem the first and healthiest of subjects; in fact, it is almost the last and most morbid. Men come to it after the other subjects have failed. It is the last stop—waterless, exposed—before nothingness. Civilization blows off, love and utopia evaporate, the interest the human mind takes in its own creations washes out, and there, its incisors bared, stands life, daring you to praise it."[3] A praise commensurate with such desperate conditions won't sound as pure as Rilke praising the world to the Angel. *Crow* and *Body Rags* are by no means artless, but theirs is an art of indelicacy. Both draw on a Neanderthal power, as if merely remaining alive left little energy for nuance or lyricism. Rilke's gentle words of praise float toward us through rarefied space; those of Hughes and Kinnell make their way through noisome, excremental clouds. The body in its least appealing aspects is everywhere, and sometimes gore becomes just another routine element of the landscape. "Crow's Account of the Battle," Bedient has it, "slings blood and anguish like a clown slinging pies" (101). Kinnell sometimes resorts to innards if nothing else comes to mind, the way early Yeats resorted to Druids.

Kinnell is still very much the nature poet, but he has moved beyond pastoralism. Just as Yeats deserts circus animals for "the foul rag-and-bone shop of the heart," Kinnell gives up flower herding for body rags. Although it intends not to repudiate the difficulty of its participation in natural process, much of his earlier work has a prettiness—butterflies blooming on buttercups, juncos flaming up from junkpiles, larks bursting up all dew—that this third volume strips away. The ugliness and squalor of the earlier city poems have spread to the outlands; everywhere we find "the naked dirty reality" ("The Fly").

Here at the nub of things, though, diversity seems superfluous— enough of a struggle simply to *be* there. If further distinctions don't much matter, particular words sometimes won't either. To a lesser degree, Bedient's characterization of *Crow* also describes *Body Rags:* the style "is slung out like hash. At this stage of case-hardened disillusion, so Hughes seems to say, words will all taste the same anyhow" (114).

Bedient designates this style as "the croak of nihilism itself": "To keep death from drawing a black line and adding every effort up to zero is . . . the whole sum of life" for Hughes—"It is all a struggle against debit; the credit side is a blank" (101). Here is where Hughes and Kinnell part company. The best Crow can hope for is to survive in "fairly good morale." But for all that it annihilates and appalls, life in *Body Rags* still retains possibilities for ecstatic self-transfiguration. To survive is to be born again. After a night of terror, Kinnell's crow, unlike Hughes's, heralds a morning of re-newed possibilities:

> and above me
> a wild crow crying '*yaw yaw yaw*'
> from a branch nothing cried from ever in my life.
> ("How Many Nights")

Remnants are strewn about the volume, but they evidence life transfigured. Although loves get lost, the poet can still "rejoice / that everything changes, that / we go from life / into life" ("Lost Loves").

On the back cover of *Crow* Hughes peers coldly out, against a darkened background, half in shadow, the mouth—the entire face—set grimly, cast in iron, the one eye not in shadow boring in on us in defiance or challenge, keeping us, keeping everything, at bay. He's wearing a leather jacket. On the back of *Body Rags* we see Kinnell against whiteness, in profile. The eye is just closed, the mouth half opened in a smile, the countenance relaxed; he looks absorbed in some pleasant fragrance. He cuts a rough-hewn figure, but we seem privy to an unguarded moment (in profile, and with closed eye, he appears unaware of us), almost an intimate one. This striking contrast in photographs reflects Hughes's steely nihilism and Kinnell's Adamic sense that survival can be ecstatic renewal—that life's incisors aren't always bared—but it also epitomizes the other basic distinction between the two volumes. In keeping with the defensiveness of his photo, Hughes's poems deflect attention away from their creator; like Eliot or Pound, he works for a stylis-tic impersonality. As in his picture, Kinnell allows himself to be observed in his poems (his modernist master here is Yeats, who wanted the reader to "feel the presence of a man thinking and feeling"[4]). Kinnell's poems thus are more directly about himself than are Hughes's. *Crow* gives us myth or denuded folktale or Disney cartoons;[5] *Body Rags* continues and intensifies the exploration of the self.

When it is explicitly the self that is at stake, nihilism becomes less tenable. But in a violent world where Hughes's kind of nihilism will always tempt, placing the self in question may require some preliminary measures. As Kinnell pushes beyond *Flower Herding,* his explorations take him to more elemental, more terrifying places, to rag-and-bone shops more foul than ever, but his first foray into these regions is accomplished in the third person. Between *Flower Herding* (1964) and *Body Rags* (1968) comes his only novel, *Black Light* (1966). It is as if Kinnell wasn't yet ready to broach—in his true voice, in poetry—the "wretchedness" he was bringing to light, so he eased his way in with a story about someone else.

In *Black Light* Kinnell first discovers the will to live that carries him through to his later poetry. An old opium smoker advises Jamshid, the protagonist, that "to be alive is all that matters";[6] later he witnesses this for himself:

> Kneeling at the girl's bedside, he heard the huge, passionate gasps of her body clamoring for air. It gasped with the ruthless will of an infant sucking at the breast. It was funny, he thought, how at night a person clings savagely to a life that, in the daytime, he only wants to throw away. (107)

A later passage is even more reminiscent of *Crow:*

> The noise of the snores seemed to grow louder. It was as if the sounds had slid over some last edge of the human world. The room filled with deep, throaty noises of animal suffering. A breath gurgled like a new baby as it went in, and death-rattled as it went out. There arose a great seething, tearing, sucking noise, of an enormous mouth gobbling compulsively at life itself. (110)

Admittedly, this is more like what Bedient calls "the will not to die" (101) than the will to live. And the novel does come closer than *Body Rags* to *Crow*'s position that staying alive is its own meager reward. Jamshid opens to the darkness, but the compensations remain muted and tentative.

Shrugging off his "horrid moods" in "To J. H. Reynolds, Esq.," Keats abandons verse and takes refuge in prose. In *Black Light,* Kinnell reverses things. Or rather, perhaps because prose may be imagined as offering some protection, it is a safer way to begin journeying into what Keats sees as our bloody bourne, to look, as he puts it, "into the core / Of an eternal fierce destruction" without losing sanity or abandoning the search. Although Merrill doffs "The shoe of prose" because "In verse the feet went bare" ("The Book of Ephraim," "A"), that shoe can sometimes let us get used to territory too rough at first for unshod feet (even "Ephraim" started as a novel). Thus, for example, Lowell's "91 Revere Street" paves the way for the painfully autobiographical poems later in *Life Studies.*

But even as *Black Light* prepares for *Body Rags,* it surpasses it in the finish of its language. No hash slinging here. Howard offers this comparison: "His poetry has . . . a jagged aphoristic thrust without much patience for rhythmic consecution or, after the first poems, for regularity of rhyme. The prose, on the other hand, is heavy with hypnotic cadences, and likely to be the vehicle for a more evidently 'poetic' manner than Kinnell will permit himself in his verse" (307). The novel, then, is more densely textured and "perfected" than much of *Body Rags,* less "streaked / with erasures" ("The Poem"). Every detail is positioned so precisely that *Black Light* yields to sentence-by-sentence explication far more readily than the poems. Perhaps too readily. Plot and characterization are as condensed as the language. If, as Howard claims, the poetry "is not a body of work susceptible of too intent a formal scrutiny" (307), the novel may add up all *too* neatly—or rather, such neatness would cloy if in other respects *Black Light* more closely resembled a regular novel. But, recognizing that, as a foreigner, he couldn't provide a deep understanding of Iran's social fabric—of "the inner workings of that ancient, complex, tradition-ruled, abruptly modernizing country" (115)—Kinnell intends *Black Light* less as a novel than as a fable. Some narratives give back life's complexity; some more overtly try to teach. Among the latter, fables by nature simplify, straighten, neaten up.

Not that the narrative events themselves in *Black Light* are any-thing like well groomed. One of its chief lessons is that "there are worse fates than getting dirty" (33), and the catalyzing act is an appalling murder (after plunging the garden shears into the mullah's chest, Jamshid found that "by opening and shutting them slightly, making little silent snips down in the dead heart, he was able to loosen them" [14]). This aligns *Black Light* with other contempo-rary fictions that center around a murder committed by a spiritually journeying protagonist. In James Dickey's *Deliverance*—more clearly a novelistic work—Ed Gentry, like Jamshid, encounters the darker, hidden side of himself and the world (the way killing unites slayer and slain also links the novel to "The Bear"). The unex-pected suddenness of Jamshid's action and the matter-of-fact tone of its narration recall the pivotal scene in Flannery O'Conner's *Wise Blood,* where Hazel Motes runs over his double, although Motes's turnabout—from professed existentialism (but how com-ically he lacks any gift for sinning!) to a severe form of Christian-ity—is the very anithesis of Kinnell's carpet mender's. Indeed, *Wise Blood* offers a closer counterpart to Jamshid in Enoch Emory and his pathetic, curiously moving devolution into Gonga the Gorilla.

Among such novels, Camus's *The Stranger* is *Black Light*'s clos-est relative. On the river, Dickey's Ed encounters something primi-tive and essential, terrifying and enlivening, but back in the city, he starts believing the big lie. The river gets dammed up, and the bodies are buried for good. The prose flattens out. The novel's en-ergy is sapped. Meursault, like Jamshid, doesn't take refuge. Al-though he starts at loose ends and finishes in confinement—revers-ing the flow of external events in *Black Light* (Jamshid doesn't literally start in jail, but his clockwork life in Meshed is as im-prisoning)—his final realization makes him spiritually free: "I'd acted thus, and I hadn't acted otherwise; I hadn't done *x*, whereas I had done *y* or *z*. And what did that mean? . . . Nothing, nothing had the least importance."[7] Jamshid approaches the same brink: "'I've learned one thing in my life,'" Effat, a truth-telling pros-titute, tells him: "'It's that nothing matters.' 'Nothing?' said Jam-shid. '*Nothing?*' Effat smiled broadly. 'Nothing at all'" (106).

Mersault's imminent execution liberates him, just as death did his mother: "With death so near, Mother must have felt like some-one on the brink of freedom, ready to start life all over again. No one, no one in the world had any right to weep for her. And I, too, felt ready to start life over again" (154). Similarly, Jamshid is liberated only after two frenzied suicide attempts; after trying to drink poison (the bottle turns out to contain only dried face powder), he runs out in the street: "He kept running until he came to the gate, that passage back to the world. He wished only to throw himself at a policeman and beg him to shoot him on the spot. But he could not see a policeman. He stopped and looked about. As he stood there a man walked past him and continued to walk through the gate and out the other side. Jamshid was astonished. The gate was not guarded. He was free" (110). At the last, he apprehends that "the world was dark" (112), just as Meursault, at the very end, feels "the benign indifference of the universe" (154). Such realizations make both murderers existential communicants. Though "the world was dark," Jamshid knows that "we who inhabit it are also dark" (112): "Wasn't he kin to those filthy, dark beings which, in his shop in Meshed, he had so desperately tried to hide and do away with?" (111). Meursault, too, recognizes his kin: "To feel it [the universe] so like myself, indeed, so brotherly, made me realize that I'd been happy, and that I was happy still" (154).

We believe that Meursault had always been happy, because—although he's sometimes maddeningly daft, sometimes unaccountably unfeeling—from early on, his narrative conveys a sheer (although passive) pleasure in existence. Even his claim that he "never cared for Sundays" (25) is tacitly belied by the care with which he describes his day, the delight he obviously derives from watching out his window as the afternoon unfolds. His lyrical outpouring at the end (the very opposite of *Deliverance*'s final verbal cooling) doesn't exactly climax a journey; rather it signals a heightened awareness of where he has always been (he never does regret the murder).

Jamshid's final insight, in contrast, culminates his complete turnabout. And, as I've suggested, this reversal and its significance are portrayed with fatalistic, almost diagrammatic directness. One easily traces the arc of Jamshid's education. Self-righteous, ordered, and conventionally religious, he starts off filling gaps (he is a carpet mender, but the gaps aren't just in wool)—restoring, in fact, the head of a woven bird of paradise. Evading the knowledge that all things, including carpets, fade, he is nervously bent on repairing "a gap through which darkness was visible" (1), hoping that "this gap, too, like so many others would be healed for good." Geometric order calms him and he won't stand for its dissolution: "The sun patch, touching the base of the wall, now started to diverge upward. Soon it would creep over the border of the geometrical and turn into chaos. This was the sign it was time to close shop" (1). He does have prophetic, disturbing visions of chaos; the bird of paradise he is restoring "suddenly seemed peculiarly unreal, as if he had woven only the absence of a head. He felt a strange dread. In the last few weeks there had been other moments when a thing, when he glanced at it, would blur and become a dark tear in reality" (1). But he dreads and flees these visions, taking refuge from them—and from the "gloom, noise, filth and commerce" of the bazaar, the "suffocating maze"—in the mosque, with its "harmonious mass of minarets" decorated with "hieratic calligraphy," a "rectangular space" which offers "ordered calm" (3). Even here, though, his refuge isn't secure. Washing in the pool, "he saw in the ripples an image of himself, and even though he shut his eyes he could not keep from seeing himself torn to pieces" (3). Something is clearly amiss, but at this point Jamshid still tries to ignore it. He clings to God, polygons, and constellations and can't stand, though he is haunted by, vanishings and unconstellated skies. He is not, in chapter 1, a Kinnellian hero.

In life, people sometimes manage to sustain self-righteous escapes. In fables, there is no evading the darkness. Jamshid's own dark energy erupts, with redoubled power perhaps from all the denial, when he plunges his shears into the mullah's breast. Almost immediately he is reborn. Although he hadn't cared for children, now "he experienced an almost giddy sympathy with these creatures who ran so freely in the sunlight" (16). Walking down a familiar lane, "now he saw it as the street of his childhood" (16). He recalls how, as a boy, he and his friend Varoosh had set off on a voyage of discovery, only to return the next day, and "he experienced intense regret": "Of all the adventures they had dreamed of, he, Jamshid, had not dared taste even one" (21). His senses come alive as if awakening from a long sleep. Fleeing Meshed, retracing the same road he and Varoosh had taken, he sets off on a real journey, a kind of descendental pilgrimage into the "gloom, noise, filth, and commerce" he had always agoraphobically avoided. In *What a*

*Kingdom It Was,* "the song woke / his heart to the darkness."
Here, murder does.

Wandering in the desert, Jamshid is befriended by an outlaw
who becomes his mentor, Ali of the Good Ears (as in *The Stranger,*
knowledge is grounded in the senses), from whom he learns "there
are worse fates than getting dirty" (33); soon, sleeping on the
ground, he is no longer "tempted to borrow the carpet to put between himself and the earth" (46). Just as his imminent execution
triggers Meursault's review of his life, not until Jamshid notices
that his own arm smells like Ali's corpse does he recall the painful
memories of his dead wife, their courtship and marriage. He has
only the most dubious notion of where he is headed, but he knows
precisely where he has been: "He had spent all those years in
Meshed weaving closed the gaps, as if he had thought that if you
perfected a surface what it was laid upon no longer had to be reckoned with. Now that he had broken through the surface, it seemed
he had no choice anymore but to die into the essential foulness of
things" (46).

Such unambiguous signposts direct our interpretation of Jamshid's adventures through the rest of the book. At Shiraz, where he
rediscovers sex with Ali's widow, he recalls how in Meshed "he had
gone over the sky night after night, until it had become for him a
vast carpet," his eyes forming the stars into familiar arrangements;
now, though, "he saw them only as wild stars" (67). Hiding out in
Tehran's New City, the squalid red-light district, he sinks deeper
into "the essential foulness of things" and of himself, discovers a
true community with other "filthy, dark beings" (111), and recognizes his gratitude for this "horrible world, peopled with the de-
generate, the sick, the used up" (98). Open to any page; a signpost
will point the interpretative way. Working with them to weave
*Black Light*'s condensed verbal texture are a series of repeated images that thread in and out of the narrative. Flames, carpets, vultures—the implications of these motifs and others don't really enlarge as the book develops, but they do accumulate power. They
help guide our understanding of the work; though operating in a
fable, finally they are less mysterious or suggestive than the images
in Kinnell's poems.

But this is in keeping with the poetics of *Black Light.* Half seriously, it seems to mistrust verse. Jamshid (who can't read) opens

the book of Hafez for an augury: "Who is it comes dancing on the grave?" (58). All his companion can offer for an exegis is, "A deep saying" (58). Who needs this?: "Poets of mystical inclination irritated Jamshid, because they gave the impression of high significance and yet kept hidden exactly what it was. . . . That, Jamshid reflected, is the way with poetry. When it is incomprehensible it strikes you as profound, and when you do understand it, it lacks common sense" (59). Jamshid, however, is himself seized by poetic impulses. About to extol Goli's beauty to a prospective customer, he felt "as if a poem were about to spring from his lips" (104) (he even manages to utter a few lines before getting his face bashed in). At its best, poetry is the handmaiden of the pimp.

So it may have been, anyway, for François Villon, legendary for dashing off verse, as Kinnell puts it, "between bouts of drinking, whoring, thieving, pimping, murdering, and general hell-raising."[8] Kinnell suggests that these escapades have often eclipsed serious consideration of the work itself, but the poetry does in any case evoke a world of elemental desire. Thus, like *Black Light* (1966), Kinnell's first translation of Villon (1965—a revised version appeared in 1977) facilitates his own descent into the unwholesome rag-and-bone shop of *Body Rags* (1968). Again, Kinnell acknowledges the connection: translation "is a way of really getting close, under the skin of a poem you admire. When you translate a poet, you invite or dare that poet to influence you. In my case I think one can see Bonnefoy in *Flower Herding* and possibly shades of Villon in *Body Rags*" (*WDS* 13). Bonnefoy's own remark about Villon, interestingly, characterizes what Kinnell will find influential: "In re-discovering and re-affirming for himself the notion of poetry which was already implicit in the works of Villon and Maynard, Baudelaire was asserting against Racine the very existence of sensible things, the particular reality as such, the stubborn entities which people our mortal horizon, as if giving himself up completely to the phenomenal world" (41).

Kinnell's comments on Villon's poems describe the premises of his own (though, apart from briefly noting that he personalized the traditional mock testament, Kinnell doesn't discuss an aspect of Villon that is crucial to his own work: as in Yeats, everywhere in Villon we sense the *presence* of a man thinking and feeling—one who can lambaste others out of a firsthand knowledge of their vices). The "mutability cantos" of *The Testament,* for example, anticipate Kinnell's chief preoccupation: "They neither assert there is peace in heaven nor moralize on the vanity of life on earth. Villon writes in a passion for reality and in deep anguish at its going. . . . He does not find a Grecian urn on which to retain some vanished scene. It has gone, and if he loved it he weeps for it" (14). Thus, "few writers have evoked these subjects [old age and death] with such harrowing reality as Villon does here or with less concern to sweeten or to compensate for them" (xvi). Even more to the point for *Body Rags* is Villon's "particularly fierce attachment to our mortal experience": like Crow, "what he holds on to is only an unspecified vitality, the vitality of decay, perhaps, or of sorrow, or simply of speech" (xvii). As in *Body Rags,* "there is nothing 'poetic' anywhere in Villon. His poetry starts from the grossest base, it is made of pain and laughter and it is indestructible" (18). To this gross base Villon retains his "fierce attachment." Last winter's snows are melted, never to return, but weren't those ladies something to look at? Even leaving the world, he is greedy for it. The last lines of *The Testament:*

> Prince graceful as a merlin
> Hear what he did as he left
> He took a long swig of dead-black wine
> As he made his way out of this world.

*Black Light* and the Villon translation can help lay bare the gross base of *Body Rags.* They can help acclimate Kinnell to the rag-and-bone shop of his psyche and the world. But they cannot guarantee the outcome of this potentially dangerous foray. One senses immediately in these poems that Kinnell has tapped some deeper power source, but, as I have suggested, such contact poses certain risks. "Once that contact has been made," Hughes warns, broaching the most dramatic, if least likely, danger, "it becomes difficult to control." Did we need Hiroshima (or Chernobyl) to tell us that elemental power sources may get out of hand? If Kinnell avoids a catastrophic meltdown, we sometimes feel that the poems' energies are allowed to seep out, unchanneled. In places there is a raw power that a poem won't know quite how to handle. And we often hunger for more tension, for the feeling that the powers have overcome some resistance. *The Book of Nightmares* will harness the energy with its pervasive lyricism and the highly wrought network of repetitions that binds together the book, even as its force threatens to explode it. *Body Rags* harnesses the power less successfully, although its best poems manage to restrain the unleashed forces with some narrative cohesion or with the craggy, tension-filled play of line against sentence. One explanation for its only partial success here is proposed by Cary Nelson. He argues that Kinnell's new "violent and immediate physicality" results partly from his "sense of recent American history" (especially the Vietnam War) but that "Kinnell is not yet equal to juxtaposing his vision with historical realities" (70).

In the act of releasing energy, then, the verse of *Body Rags* is formally broken open. But other analogies with the natural world probably convey a more accurate overall sense of these poems. They look less geometrical on the page than the early work (recall Jamshid's initial penchant for orderly geometrical shapes)—jagged like mountain ranges, not rectangular like "poems." Kinnell offers another simile: "The lines are like the river bed, so to speak, and determine the shape, depth, speed, and currents of the poem."[9] Indeed, "The Poem" is constructed primarily on connections between poetry and nature, between words and things. A hill where "a sprinkling / of soil covers up the rocks / with green" is like "the face" that "drifts on a skull scratched with glaciers," and

> The poem too
> is a palimpsest, streaked
> with erasures, smelling
> of departure and burnt stone.

The newborn and the dying speak with a "leaf / shaped tongue," and nature prefigures the elements of written language:

> On a branch
> in the morning light, at the tip
> of an icicle, the letter C
> comes into being.

Lines in wood and lines in poems describe each other: "here is a lightning-split fir the lines down its good side becoming Whitmanesque and free." And formally regular verse, too, finds a natural analogue in the rhyme of "a spike / driven crazy on a locust /

post"—"*brong ding plang ching*"—and in "a hound chasing his bitch in trochaic dimeter brachycatalectic."

Such connections bear out Charles Molesworth's view that "The Poem" illustrates Kinnell's move "beyond the suspension of irony toward the immersion in empathy" (232). He explains that "empathy in Kinnell's poetry results in an important way from the contact with the edges of experience, that boundary along which the organism and the environment become interdefinitional" (232). Thus, it involves the "surrendering" of consciousness to new forms. "Such a poetics of empathy, however, stops short of aesthetic anarchy by insisting that reality itself has forms inherent in it, or at least the mind will instinctively develop such forms for itself"— thus the poetics of "The Poem," which, with "The Porcupine" and "The Bear," Molesworth reads as a sure indicator "of a new postmodern aesthetic in contemporary American poetry" (232).

In explaining "empathy" Molesworth quotes Creeley (quoting Ginsberg—"Mind is shapely") and Levertov, but what distinguishes Kinnell's work is an awareness of how far he must come to meet the world halfway. In *Mortal Acts, Mortal Words* he writes of the "dread which throws through me / waves / of utter strangeness, which wash the entire world empty" ("The Last Hiding Places of Snow"): "empathy," paradoxically, illuminates and measures the chronic outsidership that is the origin of his poetry, reminds him of the continually renewed *need* to discover the world. He won't indulge this outsidership with irony, but everywhere Kinnell's sense of the particularity of the self makes "contact with the edges of experience" *both* terrible and glorious. When "the organism and the environment become interdefinitional," empathy can diminish the self as well as replenish it.

Consider, for example, the opening poem of *Body Rags*, "Another Night in the Ruins." Its seven fragments suggest the extreme isolation in which the poem was actually begun; Kinnell had "bought an old ruined house in Vermont": "One night I stayed up all night mainly because I was too cold to sleep, and wrote a number of disconnected fragments, some descriptive of the place, some imagined, some memories" (*WDS* 34–35). These so-called "disconnected fragments," however, won't stay apart. Mind being shapely, they begin to arrange themselves around the images of birds, of "the instant," and especially of fire—images that combine in those "lightning-flashed moments of the Atlantic" glimpsed from a plane. From his lonely outpost, the poet, like the fragments, begins to make provisional connections. He hears "nothing," but this nothing is a *presence* that unites the internal world of "bones" with the external one of "the cow": "I listen. / I hear nothing. Only / the cow, the cow / of nothingness, mooing / down the bones." The poet's brother's absence (he's dead) might ultimately outweigh his presence (in memory), but by recalling and, in the conclusion, personally asserting Derry's teaching, Kinnell achieves a kind of empathy with him. The teaching itself expresses the self's communication with the world—"the bonfire / you kindle can light the great sky"—but also the price: "though it's true, of course, to make it burn / you have to throw yourself in . . ."

By withholding his own endorsement of this maxim until the end, Kinnell maintains tension between the obvious isolation in the poem and whatever empathy is finally established (in much the same way that the title holds together death ["Ruins"] and continuation ["Another Night"]). Despite its apparent fragmentation, the poem thus retains a sense of development; the double-edged empathy appears earned because it is clearly struggled for. Indeed, although the rhetorical elevation of the long last sentence and its repeated (and elaborated) formulation of the poem's "theme" convey a strong sense of resolution, the struggle is not yet over. As Yeats so often does, Kinnell hedges his strong rhetorical closure by ending with a *question:* "How many nights must it take / one such as me to learn . . . ?" Even as he affirms the truth of his brother's lesson, he demonstrates the difficulty of learning it. The poem thus remains "alive," straining forward, intimating fulfillment but remaining unfulfilled:

How many nights must it take
one such as me to learn
that we aren't, after all, made
from that bird which flies out of its ashes,
that for a man
as he goes up in flames, his one work
is
to open himself, to *be*
the flames?

There is an undertone of frustration and complaint in these lines, as if they read, "How many *more* nights must it take?" The apparent difficulty in taking Derry's words to heart illustrates how much further *Body Rags* goes beyond Kinnell's previous work in putting the self in question. Throwing yourself on the bonfire—*being* the flames—surpasses just standing on the pulse and loving the burning earth ("Alewives Pool," *WKW*) or merely spying on a forest flower whose "invisible life . . . / Goes up in flames that are invisible" ("Flower Herding on Mount Monadnock," *FH*). If you stand on the burning earth, you must personally catch fire. In his efforts to do without the "scaffolding or occasion" to which the earlier poems still partly clung, to structure his verse wholly on the meanderings of his awareness, Kinnell here evidences his growing capacity to commit himself more directly, to "dig" deeper—to "*be* / the flames."

Still, as I have suggested, a great reluctance always accompanies these efforts. And the prosody mirrors this ambivalence. Examining an earlier version of the lines quoted above (one that, except for the lowercase line openings, looks more like a passage from *Flower Herding* than *Body Rags*)—

> that for a man
> as he goes up in flames, his one work
> is to open himself, to *be* the flames?

—Howard remarks: "It is interesting to see that in his final version of these lines, Kinnell literally opens himself, breaking apart the language until it illustrates the aperient nature of all such poetry" (316). But even as the lines open out, their extreme irregularity—the syntax-splitting line breaks, the unpredictable mix of long and short lines—creates a tension indicative of the concomitant difficulty. To open, for Kinnell, is indeed to break apart. Thus, where Whitman easily plunges right into the world, Kinnell approaches it more gingerly, with more fits and starts, like the rooster in section 6, searching for food:

> Is that a
> rooster? He
> thrashes in the snow
> for a grain. Finds

it. Rips
it into
flames. Flaps. Crows.
Flames
bursting out of his brow.

If "the lines are the river bed," they don't often allow smooth flow-ing. Rather, strewn with hidden obstructions, they reroute, tempo-rarily dam, and only finally permit climactic release, the kind of outrush that we see in the famous last line of "The Bear."

The final image of "Another Night in the Ruins" is of jumping into flames. But, as in *Crow,* life goes on. Even though "we aren't, after all, made / from that bird which flies out of its ashes," in the beginning of the volume's very next poem, "Lost Loves," the poet has survived a conflagration: "On ashes of old volcanoes / I lie dreaming." The volcano's death, and the prospect of his own, pro-vokes nostalgic dreams of other "deaths"—his lost loves. But soon, as Andrew Taylor suggests, "the poem changes from nostalgia to an affirmation of the vitality of change."[10] A tadpole "dies" as a tadpole, but—retaining its identity—is born anew as a frog:

> And yet I can rejoice
> that everything changes, that
> we go from life
> into life,
>
> and enter ourselves
> quaking
> like the tadpole, his time come, tumbling toward the slime.

"Quaking" intimates the potential violence of such self-transfigura-tion (perhaps the old volcano is only dormant) and recalls Yeats's sexual "shudder" that accompanies bloody historical succession. But at the same time the juxtaposition of that one-word line with the long concluding one accomplishes a release of tension that reinforces the rejoicing. The concluding line also testifies that, tumble and thrash about as it will, *Body Rags* at its best retains the craftsmanship (if not the manners) that Davie so admired in the very early work. Assonance is carefully controlled ("come, tum-bling") and shades into internal rhyme (like/time/slime), while the alliterated, hard-edged *t*'s (tadpole/time/tumbling toward) finally relax into the amorphous, sensual mix of sibilance and liquidity ("slime"), like the tadpole wriggling free of its old form.

"'Lost Loves' is structured on, and expresses, a transformational process," Taylor proposes, "which is basic to almost all the best of Kinnell's poetry. . . . First, through suffering of some kind the poet undergoes a death of the self, of a conscious self. He goes 'from life.' However, this does not involve death as we usually think of it. Rather, it is a withdrawal to a pre-human or pre-conscious state, an 'animal' state, consistently represented by animal imagery, in this case, the tadpole. This animal image is the second component. The third is a rebirth, a moving back 'into life,' and is accompanied by a variety of emotions, the most characteristic being rejoicing, wonder, or awe" (229). Although few poems employ this pattern as straightforwardly as "Lost Loves" or "The Bear," many make a more oblique use of it. In "How Many Nights," for example, the paradigm is slightly submerged. The emphasis falls on the third stage, the "moving back 'into life,'" as the poet, after many nights, emerges into morning; he hears the breath of sleeping animals

> and above me
> a wild crow crying '*yaw yaw yaw*'
> from a branch nothing cried from ever in my life.

Kinnell reports that some of his friends were unsure "whether I'd thought of the crow as benign or as an unwelcome presence" (*WDS* 4). But if the crow is not exactly "benign," the outrushing last line (itself venturing forward, enacting the speaker's release) unambiguously evinces the thrill of discovery itself—little matter of what. Kinnell advises that "we take seriously Thoreau's dictum, 'Be it life or death, we crave only reality'" (PPD 67). One good dictum deserves another: the crow makes it new for the poet. But, for Kinnell a discovery of the world is a discovery of the self; the poem's initial setting, "the frozen world," is finally renamed: "my life." Thus, he explicates the end of "How Many Nights" by writing a "bit of verse" called "The Mind":

> Suppose it's true
> that from the beginning, a bird has been perched
> in the silence of each branch.

> It is this to have lived—
> that when night comes, every one of them
> will have sung, or be singing.
>
> (WDS 4)

An explication of the explication: "I was thinking of those diagrams . . . that show the brain in the shape of the tree. At moments of full consciousness all the birds would be singing. Whether or not the crow's cry is beautiful mattered less to me than that this hitherto mute region comes into consciousness" (*WDS* 4).

Taylor's paradigm also structures "Night in the Forest," one of the "moment" poems in *Body Rags* that extends from those in *Flower Herding*. The opening—"A woman / sleeps next to me on the earth"—presents a version of the first stage ("the death of a self, of a conscious self"), while the "cocoon sleeping bag" in which the woman sleeps is a vestige of the second stage ("a withdrawal to a pre-human or pre-conscious state, an 'animal' state"). "A strand / of hair flows" from her bag, "touching / the ground hesitantly, as if thinking / to take root": a withdrawal involves the danger of *not* returning, of merging into the earth, rather than remaining conscious but isolated. Kinnell, however, isn't bound by these two choices. In the third stage, the "moving back 'into life,'" the focus shifts to the poet himself, who now bears within himself an echo of the world: "I can hear / a mountain brook / and somewhere blood winding / down its ancient labyrinths. . . ." The poem concludes:

> And
>
> a few feet away
> charred stick-ends surround
> a bit of ashes, where burnt-out, vanished flames
> absently
> waver, absently leap.

Drawing on the poetics of "The Poem," these lines themselves waver like flames, rise and fall capriciously, leap high and suddenly flicker out, and in this they illustrate one way that Kinnell breaks open his poetry in *Body Rags*. We have seen the effect already at the end of "Another Night in the Ruins," where in this sense the work of the verse itself also is to "*be* / the flames." The whole of "In the Anse Galet Valley" forms another striking example. "Clouds / rise . . . and sink," "A straw torch / flickers," and "fer-de-lances / writhe," but these fluctuations describe the movement of the verse as well as the events of the poem. It ends:

> The fer-de-lances
> writhe in black winding-skins,
> the grail-bearers go down, dissolving.
> What question could I have asked, the wafer-
> moon
> gnawed already at its death-edge?

"What question could I have asked?": doubt squared. Certainty twice removed, a question about a question, an interrogative cast in a conditional—trafficking in liminality, how little one knows! Going "from life / into life"—surviving—so much is jettisoned. Yeats wrote about modern poets, "we sing amid our uncertainty": [11] we may embody truth but we cannot know it, and where truth cannot be known questions and uncertainties will proliferate. And proliferate they do, from the first pages of *Body Rags* to the last— especially at the conclusion of poems, where doubts traditionally are resolved, not left hanging.

The opening and closing poems, ending with questions, frame the volume in mystery. First: "How many nights must it take . . . ?" Finally: "what, anyway, / was that sticky infusion, that rank flavor of blood, that poetry, by which I lived?" In between, "What question could I have asked . . . ?" and "How many nights / have I lain in terror . . . ?" (this single-sentence poem doesn't end with a question mark but the subject-verb inversion nevertheless indicates an interrogative). Sometimes a question occurs *near* a poem's end, but the remaining lines don't answer it directly, relating instead a sensory experience, shifting away from "knowledge" and toward "embodiment," away from what we cannot know and toward what we can. In "Getting the Mail," for example, a question arises:

> And touching
> the name stretched over the letter
> like a blindfold, I wonder,
> what did *getting warm* used to mean? . . .

Kinnell does open the letter, but the promise of a verbal answer goes unfulfilled. Instead a different sort of fulfillment follows—aural, not rational; we are thus, typically, both answered and not answered, given satisfaction and left unsatisfied:

> And tear
> open the words,
> to the far-off, serene
> groans of a cow
> a farmer is milking in the August dusk
> and the Kyrie of a chainsaw drifting down off Wheelock
> Mountain.

At the end of "Night in the Forest" the flames are simultaneously present and absent, a paradox that crystallizes in the odd coupling of the final two words—"absently leap." And in asking an unanswered question, "Last Songs" seeks a poetics—couched in a conditional—based on a mysterious "it" that can be gestured toward but not precisely defined:

> Silence. Ashes
> in the grate. Whatever it is
> that keeps us from heaven,
> sloth, wrath, greed, fear, could we only
> reinvent it on earth
> as song.

This kind of double ending—withholding but asserting, revealing our inability to know truth but also our capacity to embody it—provides many of Kinnell's poems in *Body Rags* with what Barbara Herrnstein Smith has termed "anti-closure": their conclusions avoid "the expressive qualities of strong closure"—obviously anathema to a singer amid uncertainty—"while securing, in various ways, the reader's sense of a poem's integrity."[12] The withholding precludes strong closure, while the assertion secures the sense of an ending; even as a question conveys ignorance, it can also express discovery—discovery of what precisely to ask. The end of "Another Night in the Ruins," for example, discloses even as it inquires: the lesson is defined and affirmed, even if it remains unlearned. In "The Bear" the poet is left "wondering," but at the same time we feel something climactic has been revealed (the concluding question is thus sometimes quoted out of context—as an epigraph to a student literary magazine or a newspaper interview—as if it conveyed some great Truth about Poetry). One reason is that this conclusion sifts through the hallucinatory confusions of the poem to arrive at the center of things: "What was that thing? What was this all about anyway? What am *I* about?" Moreover, that central thing *is* named, even as it is wondered about: it is a "sticky infusion," a "rank flavor of blood" and finally (out with it now) "poetry" itself. The poem's true subject, hidden throughout, making its claims only implicitly, is finally, dramatically unveiled. *Voilà!*

The drama is sharpened by the culminating, *spent* effect of the last line. The lineation of the preceding few works up a tension—

> the rest of my days I spend
> wandering: wondering
> what, anyway,
> was . . .

—that is released in the rhapsodic gush of the overflowing final line, the longest in the poem: the poet, near the finish, gives out all of his remaining breath in a last-second sprint for the wire. The closural effect of such an ending—even though it is cast as an unanswered question—is striking. Thus, "anti-closure."

Kinnell's master, here again, is Yeats.[13] As I have suggested, closing questions express his sense that although we cannot know truth we can embody it. But, stylistically as well as thematically justified, frequent questions also help Yeats achieve a poetry that uses a "speech so natural and dramatic that the hearer would feel the presence of a man thinking and feeling," that dramatizes the "actual thoughts of a man at a passionate moment in life": most poetic utterances, even in Yeats, are cast in the indicative mode, so that when a question does occur, by virtue of its relative oddity it calls attention to itself *as* a question and, thus, to the questioning voice that utters it. Questions thus personalize tone. Insofar as Kinnell (unlike Hughes) shares Yeats's interest in dramatizing the presence of the speaker, they become a stylistic trademark of *Body Rags*.

If a poem in the volume doesn't conclude with a question, chances are it will end by addressing the act of ending itself (here Kinnell is on more traditional ground, for Smith shows that the use of "closural allusions" has historically been an important way of securing poetic closure). Sometimes this is a matter of leave-taking: when "we go from life / into life," farewells are always in order. Thus, the final gesture of "The Fly"—"And yet we say our last goodbye / to the fly last"—or the ending (and title) of "The Correspondence School Instructor Says Goodbye to His Poetry Students":

> Goodbye,
> you who are, for me, the postmarks again
> of shattered towns—Xenia, Burnt Cabins, Hornell—
> their loneliness
> given away in poems, only their solitude kept.

Sometimes, although a final image describes cessation, Kinnell dispenses with goodbyes altogether, as in the last lines of "The Burn": "The mouth of the river. / On these beaches / the sea throws itself down, in flames." And sometimes, when "into life" eclipses "from life," "goodbye" transmutes into "hello." In addition to the tadpoles "tumbling toward the slime" and the sunrise finale of *Black Light,* there is the ending of "The Fossils":

> Outside
> in dark fields
> I pressed the coiled
> ribs of a fingerprint to a stone,
> first light in the flesh.
>
> Over the least fossil
> day breaks in gold, frankincense, and myrrh.

## II

Part 2 of *Body Rags* consists entirely of the long poem "The Last River," a work which looks back to "Avenue C," not merely in its length, but in its Whitmanesque concern with the American experience. However, in keeping with the general direction of Kinnell's writing, "The Last River" is a more personal work than "Avenue C": while in the earlier poem the poet remains relatively anonymous, here everything is filtered through his consciousness, and the whole is openly structured by his memory, associations, dreams, and fantasies. The exploration of America is simultaneously a revelation of the self.

The poem is set in a Southern jail into which Kinnell has been thrown, presumably for his civil rights activism. His cellmates, however, aren't other activists, but "real" criminals—copbeaters, carthieves, pimps. Kinnell identifies them solely by these epithets— the copbeater did this, the pimp said that—as if to emphasize the sordid milieu. But he doesn't set himself against the depravity; rather, in the course of the poem he discovers what he calls "the world-braille of my complicity." One thinks again of the risk in digging: "If we are willing to face the worst in ourselves, we also have to accept the risk . . . that probing into one's wretchedness one may just dig up more wretchedness."

Only a small part of the poem actually describes prison experiences. The jail cell becomes a brain cell, as external events flow into internal ones. The present (the jail) is intercut first with recollections of Kinnell's trip south and then with boyhood memories, and his meditative responses to these scenes punctuate his account. Recalling the air-transfiguring smile of an "ancient ex-convict / who teaches voter-registration," for example, Kinnell wonders: "What is it that makes the human face, / bit of secret, / lighted flesh, open up the earth?" After a Whitmanesque catalogue of American rivers he has heard, he puts another question (echoing "First Song"):

> Was there some last
> fling at grace in those eddies, some swirl
> back toward sweet scraping, out there
> where an Illinois cornstalk
> drifts, turning the hours,
> and the grinned skull of a boy?

The tone of these meditations is essentially ominous, but as Mills notes, it "is alleviated by sudden flashes of grace, instances of dignity and love, usually revealed through images of lightning, fire, or sunlight" (112). (These flashes are the poem's strongest example of the motivic strategy Kinnell will refine and extend in *The Book of Nightmares*; "The Last River" also rings changes on images of the human face, birds, and of the river itself.)

These flashes don't break the underlying gloom, however, and eventually the poem settles into an extended dream journey into Hell, the poet led along by a boy named Henry David. They encounter the tortured damned, and predictably the ones we see suffering most gruesomely are Establishment types, public evil-doers—Northern and Southern politicians, "a man / with stars on his shoulders," his Secretaries of Profit and Sanctimony. But also numbered among the damned here are those who were more banally evil, who, Henry David explains, " 'weren't for or against anything,' " who " 'looked out / for themselves.' " Indeed, even life's victims have landed in this hell, victims of lynch mobs, of "sexual dread," of, we gather, the anonymous political killings of totalitarian regimes, " 'unknown persons' / killed for 'unknown reasons' / at the hands of 'persons unknown' . . ." What most unnerves Kinnell, however, is his glimpse of a man "signing restrictive covenants with his fingernails / on a blackboard" (a teacher?), who was "well-meaning" and "believed / in equality and supported the good causes," and who must remind the poet of himself: "Hearing us talk, the man half turns . . . / 'Come on,' I say sweating, for I know him." As the journey probes the underside of American society, it unveils the poet's own "complicity."

This revelation, indeed, is the target toward which much of "The Last River" points. By the penultimate section, not only have the earlier periodic flashes not cleansed the desolate landscape with light, but the darkness has eclipsed everything: "My brain rids itself of light, / at last it goes out completely." There *is* illumination, however—internal, not external: "slowly / slowly / a tiny cell far within it / lights up." What is illuminated by this internal light is an image of "My old hero," Thoreau again, trying to wash his knives of "buffalo blood . . . Indian blood . . ." Thoreau (though, like Kinnell, jailed for civil disobedience) is implicated here in America's crimes, but the entire scene occurs in Kinnell's own brain cell, revealing the contents of his own mind: he too is guilty.

Eventually, even the internal light gives out and the darkness is complete. Then "In the darkness / a letter for the blind / arrives," a message, presumably from Thoreau. Kinnell anticipates that it will expose his guilt:

> Did I come all this way only for this, only
> to feel out the world-braille of my complicity,
> only to choke down these last poison wafers?

But his complicity is by this point well established; instead of level-ing accusations, the letter bears a gift. Thoreau sends Kinnell "mortality," having learned, we gather, that this is all he finally has to give, that it is the truest, if most painful gift:

> *For Galway alone.*
> *I send you my mortality.*
> *Which leans out from itself, to spit on itself.*
> *Which you would not touch.*
> *All you have known.*

This passage is the poem's climax, not least because of its con-trolled quietness, its air of intimacy. The rest of the poem consists of Kinnell's more typical, unbalanced, sawed-off lines and long, sweeping sentences often chopped to pieces by the lineation. As be-fits a poem of exploration, there is a sense of floundering. However, at the climax, set off by italics, symmetry reigns: visually and met-rically, the lines lengthen out and then, at the same pace, recede back to their point of origin. Reinforcing this symmetry, the first and last lines rhyme in both of their two feet (For Gál / All you . . . -way alone / have known). Instead of the enjambed, over-spilling sentences, here each line begins with a capital and ends with a period (even though this creates mostly fragments): each line is "alone," like Galway. In addition to establishing the tone of re-straint, the lineation adumbrates the semantic content of the pas-sage. As they lengthen, the lines "lean out" from themselves—en-acting some escape?—but then shorten to where they start (the rhyme underscores this), just as Kinnell, wanting to lean out from and spit on mortality, must return to it, for it is all he can really know (what spits on mortality here is mortality itself: there is no escape).

The closeness of the writing, the level of abstraction (after pages of narrative), and the air of final pronouncement (*"All you have known"*) contribute to the lines' climactic charge. But although the passage defines the very parameters of human knowledge, it is less a bardic culmination than a quiet, intimate one. The form, after all, is conducive to intimacy—a personal letter, one fellow to one other; things are literally on a first-name basis.

Thoreau assumes the pivotal role in "The Last River" because he, like Kinnell, seems torn between purity and corporality. But while Kinnell ultimately aspires to the fullest acceptance of his bodily life, the historical Thoreau often opts for transcendence. Especially in "Higher Laws," how he loathes—or wants to loathe— things physical! "The true harvest of my daily life," he writes, "is somewhat as intangible and indescribable as the tints of morning or evening. It is a little star-dust caught, a segment of the rainbow which I clutched." [14] In extreme contrast to Kinnell, he extols chastity and continence. In this mood, divinity interests him more than humanity: "Man flows at once to God when the channel of purity is open. By turns our purity inspires and our impurity casts us down. He is blessed who is assured that the animal is dying out in him day by day, and divine being established. Perhaps there is none but has cause for shame on account of the inferior and brutish nature to which he is allied. I fear that we are such gods or demigods only as fauns and satyrs, the divine allied to beasts, the creatures of appetite, and that, to some extent, our very life is our disgrace" (220). "Our very life is our disgrace"; if he is frank about his inclination for purity, how quickly the Transcendentalist, for all his evident vitality, begins to sound like a Calvinist.

Although he heavily revised *Walden* (filtering out the more troubling aspects of the presented self), Thoreau does at least profess frankness as a virtue. Again, the dictum to which Kinnell appeals: "Be it life or death, we crave only reality." Thus, though he abhors his animality, he doesn't disown it; indeed, a few pages before concluding "life is our disgrace," Thoreau reveals a true "reverence" for his vital "lower" instincts, for that half of his life, Kinnell might say, that belongs to the wild darkness:

> As I came home through the woods with my string of fish, trailing my pole, it being now quite dark, I caught a glimpse of a woodchuck stealing across my path, and I felt a strange thrill of savage delight, and was strongly tempted to seize and devour him raw; not that I was hungry then, except for that wildness which he represented. . . . I found in myself, and still find, an instinct toward a higher, or, as it is named, spiritual life, as do most men, and another toward a primitive rank and savage one, and I reverence them both. I love the wild not less than the good. The wildness and adventure that are in fishing still recommend it to me. I like sometimes to take rank hold on life and spend my day more as the animals do. (210)

In any case, it is Thoreau the craver of purity, Thoreau the continent vegetarian, who can write, "Nature is hard to overcome, but she must be overcome"—it is this Thoreau who, "wiping / a pile of knifeblades clean / in the rags of his body," suffers for his old ways in "The Last River":

> "Seeking love . . . love
> without human blood in it,
> that leaps above
> men and women, flesh and erections,
> which I thought I had found
> in a Massachusetts gravel bank one spring . . .
> seeking love . . .
> failing to know I only loved
> my purity . . . *mein herz! mein* fucking *herz!*"

And it is this Thoreau who, having had a change of heart, sends Kinnell the final message: *"For Galway alone. / I send you my mortality."*

The last section of the poem shifts from the personal to the political, although their close connection has by now been well established. An enigmatic "man of no color" (neither a white man nor a black), made of purified non-human parts—beryl, lightning, polished brass, lamps of wild fire—starts to deliver a high-sounding speech. But like Thoreau, he is overtaken by the mortal flesh, and from the Prophet of Better Times to Come he dissolves into Charon, the ferrier to Hell:

> Here his voice falters, he drops
> to his knees, he is
> falling to pieces,
> no nose left,
> no hair,
> no teeth,
> limbs dangling from prayer-knots and rags,
>
> waiting by the grief-tree
> of the last river.

## III

*The Book of Nightmares* is Kinnell's most accomplished work, but to some readers he is perhaps better known for the final two poems of *Body Rags*, "The Porcupine" and "The Bear." Despite their increased violence and virtual absence of conventional autobiography, Mills (writing before *Nightmares*) finds these poems "the most personal Kinnell has written" (115). For Nelson, they are "the first full fruition" of Kinnell's "new sophistication with harsh realism" (71). Even Davie inadvertently testifies to the new power of "The Bear," having evidently been so shook up by the poem that he fears it will lead unsuspecting readers into bestiality, and he warns Kinnell against becoming another Charles Manson.

Davie here lines up with the Thoreau who, craving purity, quotes John Donne: "How happy's he who hath due place assigned / To his beasts and disaforested his mind!" (220). But what exactly *is* that "due place"? As I've shown, Thoreau also sometimes hungered for wildness, sometimes spent his days "more as the animals do." Indeed, from the Romantics on, a number of important poems—and Kinnell's are two of the most interesting contemporary examples—center on the poet's relationship to the animal world: in tones from nostalgic to vatic, poets since then have found themselves in animals (to their delight or dismay), or ruefully mused on their distance from them, or wanted to live with them or be them or be like them. In deciding on that "due place," much depends on what significance one locates in beasts or, rather, on which of many true meanings one takes up (Kinnell and Davie might disagree with each other on bears, Thoreau with himself on woodchucks). Defending his jaguar poems from charges that they celebrate violence, Hughes writes:

> A jaguar after all can be received in several different aspects . . . he is a beautiful, powerful nature spirit, he is a homicidal maniac, he is a supercharged piece of cosmic machinery, he is a symbol of man's baser nature shoved down into the id and growing cannibal murderous with deprivation, he is an ancient symbol of Dionysus since he is a leopard raised to the ninth power, he is a precise historical symbol to the bloody-minded Aztecs and so on. Or he is simply a demon . . . a lump of ectoplasm. A lump of astral energy.

The symbol opens all these things . . . it is the reader's own nature that selects. (199)

But if there are even more than thirteen ways of looking at a jaguar or a porcupine or a bear, most of them have in common at least the sense that, as Helen Vendler puts it, "animal life is pure presence, with its own grandeur. It assures the poet of the inexhaustibility of being."[15]

Poetic responses to this "pure presence" cover the spectrum. At one end (sometimes called "romantic") reside works of an un-adulterated yearning for it. These human speakers concentrate on the seductive purity of animal life, and they either seem to achieve it somehow or at least retain the hope of doing so. The young snake slithers away, but it stays on Roethke's mind:

> I felt my slow blood warm.
> I longed to be that thing,
> That pure, sensuous form.
>
> And I may be, some time.
> ("Snake")

Whitman could "turn and live with animals, they are so placid and self-contain'd," and, indeed, he finally outdoes them even on their own vitalistic terms:

> I but use you a minute, then I resign you, stallion,
> Why do I need your paces when I myself out-gallop them?
> Even as I stand or sit passing faster than you.
>
> (SM 32)

Shelley has a more difficult time trying to scorn the ground and join the skylark, but he never does renounce the desire to do so. Although he remains grounded and realizes that, unlike those of the bird, the "sweetest songs" of humans "are those that tell of sad-dest thought," his gaze stays skyward; his appeal to heaven never does break off, even as he acknowledges that if he *could* sing like the lark it would be "harmonious madness" ("To a Skylark"). "Harmonious madness": too complete a merger is dangerous to sanity and to life. Plath dissolves into the "Ariel"—"God's lioness, / How one we grow"—but knows the price: she becomes

> The dew that flies
> Suicidal, at one with the drive
> Into the red
>
> Eye, the cauldron of morning.

Encounters with horses needn't be as confident as Whitman's or as self-consuming as Plath's; James Wright's contact with the slenderer of two Indian ponies is more tenuous but is contact nonetheless:

> She is black and white,
> Her mane falls wild on her forehead,
> And the light breeze moves me to caress her long ear
> That is delicate as the skin over a girl's wrist.
> Suddenly I realize
> That if I stepped out of my body I would break
> Into blossom.
>
> ("A Blessing")

Wright's exchange is more compatible with life than Plath's. Where his leaving the body (in the conditional) is a blossoming, hers (in the declarative present) is a dissolution:

> White
> Godiva, I unpeel—
> Dead hands, dead stringencies.
>
> And now I
> Foam to wheat, a glitter of seas.

Varied as these poems are in other respects, the attraction of animal purity and at least the hope of sharing it align them with one another. At the other end of the spectrum reside poems (which, again, may have little else in common) that define a gulf between humans and the "pure presence" of the animal world. In "In Monument Valley," James Merrill recollects riding a sorrel mare

> Who moved as if not displeased by the weight upon her.
> Meadows received us, heady with unseen lilac.
> Brief, polyphonic lives abounded everywhere.
> With one accord we circled the small lake.

But this is only a pleasant memory. After he shifts into the present tense (from innocence to experience?), we see him sitting "in the cool Hertz car," insulated. A "stunted, cinder-eyed" horse comes to the window, to whom he offers an apple core (yes, experience):

> But she is past hunger, she lets it roll in the sand,
> And I, I raise the window and drive on.
> About the ancient bond between her kind and mine
> Little more to speak of can be done.

We are even further removed from the ancient bonds in John Ashbery's "Ode to Bill." As soon as the horse appears in the poem, its very status as a being is thrown into question as the poet focuses not on the creature itself but on the nature of his perception of it:

> One horse stands out irregularly against
> The land over there. And am I receiving
> This vision? Is it mine, or do I already owe it
> For other visions, unnoticed and unrecorded
> On the great, relaxed curve of time.

When he does return to the horse, it is only—regretfully perhaps, but inevitably—to dismiss it:

> He moves away slowly,
> Looks up and pumps the sky, a lingering
> Question. Him too we can sacrifice
> To the end progress, for we must, we must be moving on.

Between these broadly defined poles lie works that combine elements of each or are more overtly ambivalent about the "due place" of their beasts. The snake enraptures D. H. Lawrence, as it did Roethke, but it also appalls him, and he tosses a log at it. Where Roethke believes he may yet achieve "that pure, sensuous form," Lawrence, a landlocked Ancient Mariner, rues his separation from it (although we sense the ancient bond is not inevitably severed); he concludes, not with a sense of expectancy, but with a sense of transgression:

> And so, I missed my chance with one of the lords
> Of life.
> And I have something to expiate;
> A pettiness.
>
> ("Snake")

When a moose stops Elizabeth Bishop's bus, everyone feels a "sweet / sensation of joy" (the romantics often used "joy" in this enlarged sense). But she risks less than Lawrence, for she imagines the creature as virtually domesticated: "it sniffs at / the bus's hot hood" like a dog, it is "high as a church," "homely as a house" and "safe as houses"—" 'Perfectly harmless. . . .' " ("The Moose"). Although she has intimations of the ancient bond, like Merrill she remains ensconced in a motor vehicle, in which she must, she must be moving on.

Analyzing Keats's "Ode to a Nightingale," Robert Pinsky clarifies one of the issues inherent in this spectrum I have sketched. He argues that Keats, at the wellspring of the conflict-ridden line that defines one "Romantic" tradition, yearns to be "with" the unselfconscious, untroubled bird but also, finally, realizes that such union is the "easeful death" of the conscious self and so withdraws, remaining alive and conscious, but isolated:

> The nostalgia for unconsciousness, the nostalgic wish to live only in each unreflecting moment, is strong, but nevertheless it is firmly identified as a nostalgia for death. Anything else is a sorry delusion. . . . The complexity of conflicting truth and desire here is a caution against facile reference to "imaginative one-ness with nature" and similar phrases of the "Romanticism" which sometimes appears in writing about poetry. For Keats, the situation is inherently, and not temporarily, a quandary: to be a "sod" or to be "forlorn." (55)

The terms of the quandary, of course, derive from and are defined by Keats's poem. To be entirely "with" the nightingale is to become like a lump of earth: "Still wouldst thou sing, and I have ears in vain— / To thy high requiem become a sod." And "Forlorn" is the "very word" which tolls the poet back from the bird to his unmerged, isolated "sole self."

It is "the very word" that shocks Keats away from the nonhuman, fairy lands. That language itself functions here as the agent of alienating self-consciousness is crucial for Pinsky's argument: "Language is absolutely abstract, a web of concepts and patterns; and if one believes experience to consist of unique, ungeneralizable moments, then the gap between language and experience is absolute" (59). His larger point is that modern and contemporary poets—going in fear of abstraction, grasping for the particularity of experience—have inherited the problem of this "gap," and his analysis of the various strategies they employ to "make the gap seem less than absolute" (59) is wide-ranging and incisive. The implication of his discussion for the spectrum I have proposed is clear: poems that cluster around the first pole, those that envision the gap as *actually* less than absolute, are "naive" or limited by a "'pre-Keats' insistence that the poet is somehow 'already with thee' or . . . has received an apprehensible, loving response from the unconscious world" (75).

Although Pinsky doesn't discuss Kinnell at this point, I want to defend "The Porcupine" and "The Bear," poems that concern the poet's merger with the animals, from the judgment implicit in Pinsky's analysis, that of "pre-Keats" naïveté. Indeed, two defenses pertain, the first applying to the whole group of poems which join Kinnell's at the traditionally "Romantic" end of the spectrum, the second based on qualities of his work which distinguish him from Whitman, Roethke, and many of the rest.

The first issue concerns the definition of "Romantic." For Pinsky, the term implies an unresolvable conflict "between conscious and unconscious forces within the mind: between the idea of experience as unreflective, a flow of absolutely particular moments, and the reality of language as reflective, an arrangement of perfectly abstract categories" (47)—the unbridgeable "gap." The "reality of language" as "perfectly abstract" marks his starting point. The basic conditions of the dilemma are set out in the first paragraph of his book: modern poets try "to grasp the fluid, absolutely particular life of the physical world by using the static, general medium of language" (3).

As my use of the term above to describe Roethke and the others suggests, there is another way to understand "Romantic." Pinsky stresses the inevitable separation of articulate subject and mute object, and thus he focuses on Keats. But one traditional interpretation of the romantics holds that, starting with this separation, they envisioned the imagination—and its manifestation in poetic language—as capable of bridging the gulf. The essential assumption of Wordsworth and Coleridge is that the abstracting mind and the world of particulars can interpenetrate, that poetry itself can effect a reconciliation—what Coleridge calls a "unity in multeity." Indeed, in his view, the separation itself (multeity) is the very condition that allows for a connection (unity): "The artist must first eloign himself from nature in order to return to her with full effect."[16] Nature itself possesses a "language," and if it remains "unspoken," it is nevertheless apprehensible to the artist, who "merely absents himself for a season from her [nature], that his own spirit, which has the same ground with nature, may learn her unspoken language in its main radicals." The artist "must master the essence, the *natura naturans,* which presupposes a bond between nature in the higher sense and the soul of man," or, as W. J. Bate glosses this passage, "What must be mastered are the living forms that work organically through nature according to principles which are the same as those that characterize human reason itself" (396n). In this way poets can "make the external internal, the internal external . . . make nature thought and thought nature," a notion of a bridgeable gap which informs Coleridge's poetry as well as his criticism. In "Frost at Midnight," for example, he predicts that his son, wandering "like a breeze / By lakes and sandy shores," beneath "the clouds / Which image"—like the mind—"in their dark bulk both lakes and shores," shall

> see and hear
> The lovely shapes and sounds intelligible
> Of that eternal language, which thy God
> Utters, who from eternity doth teach
> Himself in all, and all things in himself.

Charles Altieri distinguishes Coleridge, heading the "symbolist" tradition committed to the "creative, form-giving imagination," from early Wordsworth, who represents "an essentially *immanentist* vision of the role of poetry" in which "poetic creation is conceived more as the discovery and disclosure of numinous relationships within nature than as the creation of containing and structuring forms" (17). But since, for Coleridge, the mind as it creates these "containing and structuring forms" operates by the same organic principles as nature, the difference between these two poets (although not between the symbolist and immanentist traditions themselves) is a matter of emphasis. (Indeed, reversing Altieri, one could cite passages where Coleridge seems to stress perception—as in the quotation from "Frost at Midnight" above—and

Wordsworth recognizes that the eye and ear "half-create" as well
as "perceive.") For both, mind and world are unified by means of
the poem.

For Keats, it is a different matter. Perhaps because of a more precarious sense of self, for him nature both seduces and threatens. In
joining the world, the negatively capable self is eclipsed rather than
completed. As "The Fall of Hyperion" suggests, Keats didn't altogether *trust* poetry or, rather, didn't trust that he *was* really a poet,
a "physician to all men," and not one of the escapist "dreamer
tribe." For Coleridge, a feeling of unity with the world, of ex-
panded consciousness, is often accompanied by a blissful silence;
for Keats, silence is chilling and deadly: "Thou, silent form, dost
tease us out of thought / As doth eternity: Cold Pastoral!" ("Ode
on a Grecian Urn"). Language, thus, is for him a defense, the agent
of self-preservation through self-consiousness, rather than the
means of reconciliation.

For all that Kinnell shares Keats's pervasive sense that Delight
and Melancholy can be worshipped only jointly, "The Porcupine"
and "The Bear" operate from premises about poetry closer to
those of Coleridge and Wordsworth. These poems enlarge upon
the relatively impersonal catalogue of connections in "The Poem,"
but in all three works art doesn't alienate Kinnell from the physical
world; rather, in the Coleridgean tradition, it is the process by
which he discovers it.

In perhaps a truly "naive" sense, this is possible because he often
imagines poetry less as words, which are inevitably self-conscious,
than as an utterance analogous to song. From "First Song" to
"Last Songs," poetry's power to wake our hearts to the darkness is
figured as a musical one. But even if one dismisses the musical
analogy as facile, more remains than words: "Poetry consists of
inner experience, things of the world, and language" (*WDS* 75).
Third place. Or else, poetry is a "sticky infusion," a "rank flavor
of blood" ("The Bear"), rather than slick nouns and wholesome
verbs.

Readers of a less mystical bent might protest that poems are
plainly composed of words, period. But even if, like Humbert
Humbert, we have only words to play with, must that doom us to
Keats's dilemma? If, as Pinsky claims, words are "absolutely abstract," it certainly must. But Kinnell ('in a manner very different

than the imagists') sees words as physical entities too: "Since words form in the poet's throat muscles, they can be said to come out of his very flesh. And since the reader's throat muscles also have to form the words, the words enter the reader's very flesh. Poetry goes not merely from mind to mind, but from the whole body to the whole body" (WIW 55). Not mere azoic lumps, words have a "secret life" which "the music of the voice releases" (WIW 55). Rather than floating down from an abstract realm on high, words for Kinnell bubble up from lower, more corporal regions: he agrees with Sartre that "language itself comes from the deepest place, from sex" (WDS 112). Echoing Bonnefoy's distinction between French and English poetry, Kinnell asserts that poetry can call forth the physical world and (like sex) join us to it, making us, for once, less forlorn: "In this country, we have another, equally rich tradition, of trying to evoke physical things, of giving them actual presence in a poem. Our language has more physical verbs and more physical adjectives than most others, and is more capable of bringing into reality—bringing into presence—those creatures and things that the world is made up of—through words bringing them to reality."[17]

In bringing physical things into reality, Kinnell goes on, we become "one with them, so that they enter into us as Rilke says." Indeed, Rilke himself goes even further. In the *Duino Elegies,* he envisions poetry as the medium through which the visible world enters into consciousness and is fulfilled. For Rilke, "The poets are the vehicles of consciousness," as Stephen Spender interprets the ninth elegy, and "Rilke conceives of it as their task to bring what is symbolized by things into consciousness; that is, to make them achieve invisibility."[18] The *Elegies* imply "a world in which every other significance in order to attain its meaning within a higher wholeness has to enter into the imagination which is poetry" (60).

In apotheosizing the transforming powers of the mind, Rilke here represents the radical element in the Coleridgean "symbolist" tradition. He won't waste consciousness, the story goes, on his daughter's wedding (one thinks of Coleridge's Wedding Guest turning from the Bridegroom's door) for fear of missing whatever world-redeeming poem might come to him otherwise. Because the readiness is all, the world is, paradoxically, nothing. This extremist symbolism is rooted in Coleridge's view that "body is but striving to become mind,—that it is mind in its essence!" If Kinnell leans more toward an "immanentist" position, his basic premises are nevertheless those shared by both Wordsworth and Coleridge. For him, "The mind is only a denser place in the flesh" (PPD 69), but his reversal of Coleridge points toward the same unity of self and world.

My objective here isn't to stage a critical debate about poetic language and referentiality. I want only to remind us that there is a viable Romantic tradition that derives from Coleridge as well as one that derives from Keats and that if Kinnell, like Roethke, Wright, and others, doesn't feel forced to choose between being a "sod" and being "Forlorn," it isn't necessarily because of a damning poetic naïveté. Pinsky does expose some instances of "facile reference to 'imaginative oneness with nature,'" but their failings don't compromise the entire Coleridgean tradition. A presumed "'one-ness'" with nature needn't be "facile," as Coleridge's writing itself demonstrates. For Kinnell especially, as I've repeatedly suggested, participation in the natural life comes hard. Indeed, even as his presumption of kinship aligns him with Whitman and the others, his ingrained sense of the difficulty of this kinship distinguishes him from many of them. Writing of "the effort to make the gap seem less than absolute," Pinsky argues that "the difference between the dross and the vulgarization on the one hand, and genuine work on the other, is a sense of cost, misgiving, difficulty" (59). By this criterion—suspending the question as to whether or not the gap is finally absolute—Kinnell's work numbers among the most "genuine" of the postmoderns.

Kinnell's recognition of the costs differs markedly, however, from Coleridge's sense of misgiving. In "The Eolian Harp," participation in nature is easy and blissful, but as the poet begins to interpret his experience—

> Or what if all of animated nature
> Be but organic Harps diversely fram'd,
> That tremble into thought, as o'er them sweeps
> Plastic and vast, one intellectual breeze,
> At once the Soul of each, and God of all?

—he is cut short by his dour "pensive Sara":

> But thy more serious eye a mild reproof
> Darts, O beloved Woman! nor such thoughts
> Dim and unhallow'd dost thou not reject,
> And biddest me walk humbly with my God.
> Meek Daughter in the family of Christ!
> Well hast thou said and holily disprais'd
> These shapings of the unregenerate mind.

Coleridge backs off. The rub isn't a difficulty in achieving the vision or a harrowing sense of becoming a "sod" but rather a sense of religious transgression, of an "unregenerate" lapse into pantheism. As regards "cost, misgiving, difficulty," Kinnell looks back more to Keats than to Coleridge. The difficulty isn't an awareness of *transgression*, but one of *danger*. Indeed, in "The Poetics of the Physical World," he demonstrates a pointed awareness of the dangers that Pinsky insists accompany a desire for "'one-ness with nature'" (although what is *inevitable* for Pinsky remains *potential* for Kinnell): "In the great poems affirming life we may be even more clearly in the presence of the hunger to die. Freud says: 'The most universal endeavor of all living substance [is] to return to the quiescence of the inorganic world'" (123).

Insofar as the "pure presence" of the animal world can involve unconsciousness (rather than extended consciousness), Kinnell doesn't glorify the impulse to be "with" the animals, doesn't assume the "'pre-Keats,'" unconflicted attitude of which Pinsky accuses Roethke (75). When Kinnell quotes Roethke's "Snake" in his essay, he adds that "the desire to be some other thing is in itself suicidal, involving as it must a willingness to cease to be a man, to be extinct" (123). Thus the songbird is cousin to the scavenger, Keats's nightingale to Jeffers's "Vulture," the poem with which Kinnell illustrates the suicidal element. As it does for Keats, the prospect of being "with" the bird tempts Jeffers. The vulture inspects the poet lying "death-still" on a hillside, and Jeffers, not yet actually dead and thus relatively inedible, is sorry to disappoint him:

> To be eaten
> by that beak and become part of him, to share those
> wings and those eyes—

What a sublime end of one's body, what an enskyment;
    What a life after death.

Jeffers concludes with these lines, but he has declared his strongest
allegiances earlier on:

                    I said, "My dear bird, we are
        wasting time here.
    These old bones will still work; they are not for you."

Language, here again, sides with life and isolation; Jeffers's rejection of the vulture is an act of *speech*, or at least an act of mind
evinced by speech, directly calling attention to itself as such by "I
said" and by the quotation marks. If Jeffers lets himself fall half in
love with enskyment, it is because his very words have already
tolled him back to the ground.

If Kinnell's essay reveals one theoretical kind of "cost, misgiving,
difficulty," "The Porcupine" and "The Bear" demonstrate a more
immediate one. Although they share Coleridge's view that poetic
language can reunite subject and object, these poems cannot be
dismissed as nostalgic or soft. For the mergers they concern are
hardly escapist. Although he ends up thinking twice about it, at
first Keats wants to "fade away" with the nightingale, to get drunk
and quite forget "the weariness, the fever, and the fret" of a world
which the immortal bird, "not born for death," has never known.
What is absolutely central about Kinnell's animals is that they *were*
born for death. Their bloody lot is so much sorrier than the nightingale's or the snake's or the vulture's that no one would choose it
for escape. Where Whitman "could turn and live with animals" because "they are so placid and self-contain'd," Kinnell *becomes*
them—and placid they aren't. Whitman's animals "do not sweat";
the porcupine pays out gut. If "In character / he resembles us in
seven ways," those resemblances don't soothe but draw us, rather,
into his weary, feverish, fretful life.

The nightingale alters Keats's consciousness, not by enriching it,
but by diminishing it. Where the bird flies, the poet feels "sunk";
where the bird sings "*full*-throated" (my italics), the poet *empties*
opiates. Oblivion, easeful death—that's the whole point. Kinnell's
poems, in contrast, don't want to get rid of consciousness, to merge
with ursine physicality at the expense of painful awareness. Rather,

they want to join consciousness to its animal underpinnings, to complete, not reduce, it. Kinnell tentatively explains: "The bear seems to be like the dark, non-mental side of a person. And the hunter, who is stalking the bear, is like the mental side. In the central moment of the poem, the hunter opens up the bear, crawls inside, and perhaps he then becomes whole."[19] This may involve a *symbolic* death, but it is not an easeful one. It results in the very opposite of suicide—more life, not less: "The death of the self I seek, in poetry and out of poetry, is not a drying up or withering. It is a death, yes, but a death out of which one might hope to be reborn more giving, more alive, more open, more related to the natural life. I have never felt the appeal of that death of self certain kinds of Buddhism describe—that death which purges us of desire, which removes us from our loves. For myself, I would like a death that would give me more loves, not fewer. And greater desire, not less" (PPD 74).

Pinsky admires how Keats comes to his senses at the last, how he doesn't naively ignore the cost of mindless merger. If no sudden tolling back to the self occurs at the end of Kinnell's animal poems, it is not because they are naive; rather, never having gotten drunk, the poet has no need to sober up. Clearly the nightingale represents a different prospect (self-obliteration) than the porcupine and bear (self-discovery). And while the bird contrasts with the self, the porcupine resembles it in seven ways. But in addition to embodying a different meaning, the bird also has a different dramatic status as an image, one more typical of how snakes or vultures or horses usually function in animal poems. Keats's ode unfolds in a fixed dramatic context in which the bird is one realistic element: the poet is sitting, perhaps, by a window; he hears the nightingale singing; he meditates on it; it flies away. The poem could be spoken as a soliloquy in a conventional stage drama. But there is no specific porcupine, no fixed scene; it is a more fluid image, seen in a changing and tenuous dramatic context. A certain bear is singled out, but it operates in a dream world; we would need Strindberg to stage this. The real setting of these poems is the poet's consciousness (one might say that the important action of Keats's ode "takes place in the poet's mind," but that is a different matter), so porcupine and bear are not integrated, separate beings out there in the world that the poet can long to be with or admire and move on. They operate both in the world and in the poet's mind. Evoking them in poetry becomes a dig into the unexplored self: "For me those animals had no specific symbolic correspondences as I wrote the poems about them. I thought of them as animals. But of course I wasn't trying simply to draw zoologically accurate portraits of them. They were animals in whom I felt I could seek my own identity, discover my own bearness and porcupinehood."[20]

Even as "our own inner life finds expression through them," the "creatures that surround us . . . enter us, so that they are transformed within us" (*WDS* 52). Since this is a two-way street, the porcupine seeks us out, even as we reach toward him. Like an "ultra- / Rilkean angel," he is "Unimpressed—bored— / by the whirl of the stars" (by the heavenly), but "astonished" by ordinary things, salted by human use, by "hand / crafted objects / steeped in the juice of fingertips," by "clothespins that have / grabbed our body-rags by underarm and crotch."

For his part, the poet isn't so much astonished at the porcupine as he is ineluctably drawn into him. Early in the poem they merely *resemble* each other in seven quirky ways; they alchemize by moonlight, shit on the run, etc. But, as the mood swings from jaunty to feverish, and as Kinnell broaches his own experience directly (initially he refers to humanity in general, then to "A farmer," and finally to "I"), resemblance becomes identity: he rolls around in bed,

> the fatty sheath of the man
> melting off,
> the self-stabbing coil
> of bristles reversing, blossoming outward—
> a red-eyed, hard-toothed, arrow-struck urchin
> tossing up mattress feathers,
> pricking the
> woman beside me until she cries.

Earlier, Kinnell describes a porcupine's death in terms that accentuate its vulnerable, desperate, brutal existence but also its heroic tenacity, its Villonesque, vital lust for the salt-strewn mortal realm it leaves:

> A farmer shot a porcupine three times
> as it dozed on a tree limb. On

> the way down it tore open its belly
> on a broken
> branch, hooked its gut,
> and went on falling. On the ground
> it sprang to its feet, and
> paying out gut heaved
> and spartled through a hundred feet of goldenrod
> before
> the abrupt emptiness.

Later, his own innards strewn over the goldenrod, glorifying the landscape, it is his own tenacity that is on display. Indeed, if the poem is self-exploration, what is discovered is the passion for earthly existence, despite its barbarousness—the Crow-like will to live.

After paying out his guts, the porcupine-poet is still dragging himself around. The death scene isn't the final one, for it enacts a death "out of which one might hope to be reborn more giving, more alive." Clearly a rebirth is imminent. Spewing his mental innards, Kinnell was "seeking home." At the moment of death he writes, "I have come to myself empty." This paradoxical conflation of selfhood and emptiness then dominates the first half of the final section:

> And tonight I think I prowl broken
> skulled or vacant as a
> sucked egg in the wintry meadow, softly chuckling, blank
> template of myself, dragging
> a starved belly through the lichflowered acres.

"Shattered and essential," as Nelson interprets it, the poet "is resolved into the 'blank/template' of himself, the hollow but potent original mold that shaped him. The template is an image of renewal through regression, reminiscent of Roethke's figures for a primary and anonymous selfhood" (73).

If Kinnell's regressions are less easeful than Roethke's, if what is left behind is relinquished with more difficulty and a sharper sense of loss, his sights nevertheless remain set on renewal, that "hope to be reborn more giving, more alive." Thus "The Porcupine" concludes with images "hollow but potent": the poet prowls

where
burdock looses the arks of its seed
and thistle holds up its lost blooms
and rosebushes in the wind scrape their dead limbs
for the forced-fire
of roses.

Out of the burdock's loss—more life. For the thistle and rosebush, death anticipates flowers. Loss and blooming balance.

At the beginning of the poem, the porcupine has had plenty to eat, but his fullness seems sterile, unnourishing—deadweight rather than lifegiving plenitude: he is "fatted," "swollen," "ballooned," and "puffed up on bast and phloem." This initial image is answered by the final ones of the poet as "sucked egg" and "blank / template," the mix of deprivation and expectancy. Pivoting on the poet-porcupine merger, enacting a renewal through regression, "The Porcupine" arcs from sterile fullness to pregnant emptiness as Kinnell comes to himself.

When he comes to himself in "The Bear," the renewal through regression takes a more straightforwardly narrative form. The poet-hunter whittles a wolf rib, hides it in blubber for the bear to ingest, and follows the trail of blood. Literally following in the bear's footsteps, resting when he does, crawling across the same stretches of bauchy ice, the hunter is guided (in some sense, *taught*) by his prey. And he is also sustained by it, gnashing down "a turd sopped in blood" for nourishment. Eventually he finds the carcass, eats raw flesh and drinks blood, tears the body open, crawls inside, sleeps, and in dream, becomes the bear, shamanistically reliving its ordeal of being hunted and dying. Waking reality cannot remain unchanged; indeed, he is not sure he *does* awake. Part hunter now, part prey, part man, part bear, he has undergone a metamorphosis—an initiation perhaps, but certainly a renewal. Winter has given way to spring. His thoughts turn to "the dam-bear" (*his* mate now?) and her just-born cubs. He heads off, "one / hairy-soled trudge stuck out before me" (part bear) and spends the rest of his days "wandering: wondering" (part man) about what happened.

"In the central moment of the poem," as Kinnell sees it, "the hunter opens up the bear, crawls inside, and perhaps then he becomes whole." Heavy with parataxis and anaphora, as if the poet were too weary to subordinate or vary line openings, the writing of this central moment mirrors the hunter's sheer exhaustion:

> I hack
> a ravine in his thigh, and eat and drink,
> and tear him down his whole length
> and open him and climb in
> and close him up after me, against the wind,
> and sleep.

If this essential union of the "dark, non-mental side of a person" with "the mental side" isn't easeful, neither is it merely primitive (nor, as Davie has it, literally bestial). Soul isn't bruised to pleasure body. Rather, flesh and spirit liberate each other. "Like Norman O. Brown," Nelson observes, Kinnell "believes language can redeem the body by elevating it to consciousness. Language and consciousness can come into their own full power only by occupying the territory of the physical world. The mind's descent into the body, like the hunter's dream while he sleeps in the bear's carcass, is a submission to flesh that brings enlightenment" (80). Though more ecstatic in mood and more attuned to the enlivening possibilities of "the mind's descent into the body," the passage Nelson quotes from *The Book of Nightmares* to illustrate this point reformulates the central image of "The Bear":

> And the brain kept blossoming
> all through the body, until the bones themselves could think,
> and the genitals sent out wave after wave of holy desire
> until even the dead brain cells
> surged and fell in god-like, androgynous fantasies—
> and I understood
> the unicorn's phallus could have risen, after all,
> directly out of thought itself.

(59)

The possibility of this mutual redemption is the Romantic ground of Kinnell's poetry. In "The Bear," poetry *is* redemption, although it is a terrible one. Kinnell returns to the key Romantic image for the organic basis of art, the Eolian harp, but what was ecstatic for Coleridge is agonizing for the hunter:

> and now the breeze
> blows over me, blows off
> the hideous belches of ill-digested bear blood
> and rotted stomach
> and the ordinary, wretched odor of bear,
>
> blows across
> my sore, lolled tongue a song
> or screech, until I think I must rise up
> and dance. And I lie still.

"Poetry" may at first surprise in the poem's final line—made synonymous with "that sticky infusion" and "that rank flavor of blood"—but many readers will share William Heyen's impression that "on subsequent readings it seemed to me, mysteriously, what the whole poem was about."[21] Kinnell's rhetorically climactic placement of "poetry"—the dramatic withholding, the flourish as the true subject is finally unveiled—makes strong and strange claims for his art, the power by which he lives. With "The Porcupine" and "The Bear"—watershed poems of his career—Kinnell begins to substantiate those claims. Having worked his poetic way into their wretched, vital world, he can proceed in his next book to explore this new territory with less desperation, less turd-gnashing frenzy, more love. He can bring to this hard-won, hard-bitten poetic terrain the "'Tenderness toward Existence'" which lighted his earlier work and which, *The Book of Nightmares* reveals, has always been "the dream / of all poems" (29), his secret subject all along.

## CHAPTER 4

# The Web of Words and the Outrage of History: *The Book of Nightmares*

I

"The supreme awareness that we can have," Stanley Kunitz writes, "is that all existence is a continuous tissue, a gigantic web of interconnected filaments, so delicately woven that if touched at any point the whole web trembles."[1] Much of Kinnell's work before *The Book of Nightmares* poses such a conception of "all existence," but not until this book-length poem does the web become the text itself. ("Text"—and "tissue"—derive from the Indo-European root *teks*, "to weave.") This "supreme awareness," however, has always been grounded in his tragic sense of the integrity and perishability of particular flesh. It is, after all, a book of nightmares. Kinnell weaves his verbal web with an intricacy approaching that of *Pale Fire*, but does it tremble with the ecstasy of participation or the terror of paranoia? Artistry may be "plexed," in Nabokov's terms, but is the world? "O Lord!" Coleridge cries, "What thousands of Threads in how large a Web may not a metaphysical spider spin out of the Dirt of his own Guts / but alas! it is a net for his own super-ingenious Spidership alone!"[2] If this is one nightmare, finally it haunts Kinnell less than Coleridge or Nabokov. Sharing Whitman's vision of a physical unity of being, his most persistent nightmare is this: a web is a weapon of prey. At the center of *The Book of Nightmares,* in section 5, Kinnell watches a fly "tangled in mouth-glue" await the spider (35). The poet, for all his "super-ingenious Spidership," must also identify with the fly, whose wings "flutter out the music blooming with failure / of one who gets ready to die" (35).

The fly "ceases to struggle." Reading the passage, we catch hold of a strand, follow it back to the beginning of "The Hen Flower"—

> if only
> we could let go
> like her, throw ourselves
> on the mercy of darkness, like the hen
>
> (11)

—and then forward a few pages:

> Listen, Kinnell,
> dumped alive
> and dying into the old sway bed,
> a layer of crushed feathers all that there is
> between you
> and the long shaft of darkness shaped as you,
> let go.
>
> (14–15)

And forward again: "Little Maud, / . . . I would let nothing of you go, ever" (49). And again: "I can see in your eyes / . . . a tiny kite / . . . and the angel / of all mortal things lets go the string" (52). And yet again: "a lamp / at one window, the smarled ashes letting / a single flame go free" (57). The fly "ceases to struggle"—we could have followed the strand forward to begin with, almost to the end:

> Stop.
> Stop here.
> Living brings you to death, there is no other road.
>
> (73)

Then, roadblocked, back to the "love-sick crab lice" who

> struggle to unstick themselves and sprint from the doomed
>     position—
>
> and stop,
> heads buried
> for one last taste of the love-flesh.
>
> (36)

And again back, to the first sentence now:

I stop,
gather wet wood,
cut dry shavings, and for her,
whose face
I held in my hands
a few hours, whom I gave back
only to keep holding the space where she was,

I light
a small fire in the rain.

(3)

Face holding points us forward to . . . but we are getting ahead of ourselves. Having touched, we are getting tangled in the trembling web.

*The Book of Nightmares* is remarkable among contemporary poems for this cohesiveness of its verbal texture, this sense that it is composed of a "continuous tissue." The temptation is to dive right in, to start flipping forward and back, as I've begun to do, connecting up passages at an accelerating, dizzying pace. But first things first. Before we dive in, it may help us keep our bearings to consider *Nightmares* against two of the central reference points for many twentieth-century poetic sequences, the *Duino Elegies* and *Four Quartets*. Elegiac, musical, Kinnell's work harks back to both of these poems. The debt to Rilke, from whom Kinnell takes his epigraph, is certainly the more obvious, but all three sequences, as Stephen Spender puts it, linking the *Elegies* and *Quartets*, "have affinities on the level of the deepest seriousness" (58); Kinnell might say of himself or Eliot what he says of Rilke, that he "writes only what is for him a matter of life and death. There's nothing trivial, no bright chatter, no clever commentary. He writes at the limit of his powers" (*WDS* 43). Kinnell looks back to Eliot and Rilke also in that his "seriousness," like theirs, recognizes a threat to the self. The web of existence in *Nightmares* connects but also traps. "Human kind / cannot bear very much reality," Eliot realizes at the outset of "Burnt Norton," echoing the first lines of the *Elegies:*

Who, if I cried, would hear me among the angelic
orders? And even if one of them suddenly

pressed me against his heart, I should fade in the strength of his
stronger existence. For Beauty's nothing
but beginning of Terror we're still just able to bear,
and why we adore it so is because it serenely
disdains to destroy us. Each single angel is terrible.[3]

Rilke's angels aren't angels of God. Representing the absolute
potential of human consciousness, having "no existence independent of . . . [the poet's] power to imagine forces so incomparably
greater than his" (Spender 49), they differ from us not in kind but
in degree. They betoken not another world but a flowering (in consciousness) of this one. "For Rilke the 'final facts' are the visible
reality which has to be transformed into the invisible [by the
poet]," in Spender's view (58), while "with Eliot the 'final facts' are
the supernatural, objectively true, incredibly believed in claims of
Christianity" (69). If Kinnell is more tolerant of—more *interested*
in—the unheroic, unpoetic ordinary people who cannot transform
reality, more attuned to the vagaries and failures of consciousness,
his "final facts" are nevertheless Rilke's—"visible reality." Indeed,
the facts of the physical world are perhaps even more "final" in
*Nightmares,* since for Kinnell they have a significance of their own,
independent of what consciousness can make of them. This emphasis on the objective aligns him, oddly, with Eliot (although
where what is objective for Eliot is tradition or God, for Kinnell it
is the natural world). But Rilke remains the dominant ghost, the
*Elegies* explicitly the father of *Nightmares:*

> I began it as a single ten-part sequence. I had been rather immersed
> in the *Duino Elegies.* In the Ninth Elegy, Rilke says, in effect, "Don't
> try to tell the angels about the glory of your feelings, or how splen-
> did your soul is; they know all about that. Tell them something
> they'd be more interested in, something that you know better than
> they, tell them about the things of the world." So it came to me to
> write a poem called "The Things." Like the *Elegies* it would be a
> poem without a plot, yet with a close relationship among the parts,
> and development from beginning to end. I did write a draft of that
> entire poem one spring, while I was living in Seattle. I didn't like it
> and I threw it away, almost all of it. One of the surviving passages
> became "The Hen Flower." Then I started again. The poem has

moved far from its original intention to be about things and now probably does try to tell the angels about the glory of my feelings! (*WDS* 35–36)

If *Nightmares* departs from Rilke's advice to tell of things, it retains the *Elegies*'s sense of development over a ten-sectioned, interconnected whole. More important, it keeps a Rilkean focus on the unity of life and death. In "The First Elegy," Rilke writes:

> Yes, but all of the living
> make the mistake of drawing too sharp distinctions.
> Angels (they say) are often unable to tell
> whether they move among living or dead. The eternal
> torrent whirls all the ages through either realm
> for ever, and sounds above their voices in both.

J. B. Leishman elucidates this passage with a quotation from Rilke's letter to his Polish translator: In the *Elegies*,

Affirmation of life *and* affirmation of death reveal themselves as one. To concede the one without the other is, as is here experienced and celebrated, a restriction that finally excludes all infinity. Death is our reverted, our unilluminated, side of life: we must try to achieve the greatest possible consciousness of our existence, which is at home in both of these unlimited provinces, which is inexhaustibly nourished out of both. . . . The true form of life extends through both regions, the blood of the mightiest circulation pulses through both: there is neither a here nor a beyond, but only the great unity.[4]

Kinnell is as unwilling as ever to deny the particularity of our moments "here," but his distinctions between here and beyond have grown less sharp: "In the greatest moments of our lives, we grasp that there's an element beyond our reach, from which we came, and into which we will dissolve, which is the mother and father of all the life of the planet" (*WDS* 97–98).

*Nightmares* is an effort to grasp this "element," and thus "from one point of view the book is nothing but an effort to face death and live with death" (*WDS* 45). Indeed, the book seems shot through with an elegiac wisdom, as if Kinnell were continually keeping the unilluminated side of life in mind, even when his subject is birth. Like Rilke, he envisions childhood as a time when the "element" was easily grasped. Kinnell dedicates *Nightmares* to

Maud and Fergus, his daughter and son—whose births frame the volume—because children

> have glimpses of death . . . through their memory of the non-existence they so recently came from. They seem to understand death surprisingly clearly. But now time passes slowly for them. It hardly exists. They live with death almost as the animals do. This natural trust in life's rhythms, infantile as it is, provides the model for the trust they may struggle to learn later on. *The Book of Nightmares* is my own effort to find the trust again. I invoke Maud and Fergus not merely to instruct them, but also to get help from them. (*WDS* 45–46)

Kinnell thus imagines that the alchemical engraving on the front cover of *Nightmares* shows two young angels (his children) drawing forth the breath (the poem) from a dying man (the poet) below (although this is not the actual alchemical meaning, which I will discuss later). And in the text, baby Maud cries in this world, but she expresses "a sadness / stranger than ours, all of it / flowing from the other world" (7). The dedication thus feeds into the epigraph, appearing on the same page, from the Spender and Leishman translation of "The Fourth Elegy":

> But this, though: death,
> the whole of death,—even before life's begun,
> to hold it all so gently, and be good:
> this is beyond description!

Earlier in that elegy Rilke himself anticipates Kinnell's view of the intimacy between children and the element beyond our reach:

> O hours of childhood,
> hours when behind the figures there was more
> than the mere past, and when what lay before us
> was not the future! We were growing, and sometimes
> impatient to grow up, half for the sake
> of those who'd nothing left but their grown-upness.
> Yet, when alone, we entertained ourselves
> with everlastingness: there we would stand,
> within the gap left between world and toy,
> upon a spot which, from the first beginning,
> had been established for a pure event.

Like death and life, death and love imply each other for Rilke and Kinnell. In "The Poetics of the Physical World," published in the same year as *Nightmares*, Kinnell quotes a Rilke letter elucidating this connection: our "deepest raptures" are "independent of duration and passage; indeed, they stand vertically upon the courses of life, just as death, too, stands vertically upon them. . . . Only from the side of death (when death is not accepted as an extinction, but imagined as an altogether surpassing intensity), only from the side of death, I believe, is it possible to do justice to love" (124). Leishman interprets this passage: "Love, like death, he regarded as an extension of human life into the infinite, as a snatching-up of it into the great cycle, as a plunging of it into the eternal stream. Its passion and hunger cannot and should not (so he always felt) be satisfied by the object that awakens it; it is for something infinite, it extends beyond this visible 'side of life' into the reverted, invisible side we call death, it can find its fulfillment only in 'the Whole'" (123). At the end of "The Fifth Elegy" Rilke thus asks us to "suppose there's a place we know nothing about, and there, / on some indescribable carpet, lovers showed all that here / they're for ever unable to manage," to

> suppose they could manage it there,
> before the spectators ringed round, the countless unmurmuring
>    dead:
> would not the dead then fling their last, their for ever reserved,
> ever-concealed, unknown to us, ever-valid
> coins of happiness down before the at last
> truthfully smiling pair on the quietened
> carpet?

This passage typifies the fulfillment and relief with which Rilke imagines the Whole; death "is not accepted as an extinction, but imagined as an altogether surpassing intensity." Thus, when considering the "early-departed," the "youthfully-dead," in "The First Elegy," the poet "must remove the appearance / of suffered injustice, that hinders / a little, at times, their purely proceeding spirit." "True," he concedes, "it is strange to inhabit the earth no longer," to "be no longer all that one used to be." But "one's gently weaned from terrestrial things as one mildly / outgrows the breasts of a mother." All in all, to die young is rather a fine thing. Kinnell, despite his profound debt to Rilke, is less cheerful about the prospect of being weaned from terrestrial things. If he now sees death and life as elements of a greater whole, his deep love of "particular flesh" precludes a Rilkean dismissal of grief. If he is less defiant now, his position remains essentially unchanged from his earlier response to the premature departure of his brother from earthly life—a *refusal* to "remove the appearance / of suffered injustice":

> But an incarnation is in particular flesh
> And the dust that is swirled into a shape
> And crumbles and is swirled again had but one shape
> That was this man. When he is dead the grass
> Heals what he suffered, but he remains dead,
> And the few who loved him know this until they die.
> ("Freedom, New Hampshire")

"One of Rilke's *Sonnets to Orpheus*," Kinnell recounts, "tells us to 'keep ahead of all parting.' I guess I'm not doing that very well, and there is a sense in which I don't even want to" (*WDS* 91). Death *is* accepted as "extinction" in *Nightmares*, even as it lends an "altogether surpassing intensity" to terrestrial life. The conclusion of "The Poetics of the Physical World" helps explain the paradox: "That we last only for a time, that everyone and everything around us lasts only for a time, that we know this, radiates a thrilling tragic light on all our loves, all our relationships."

"From the side of death," then, both Kinnell and Rilke "do justice to love." But, consistent with their contrasting perspectives on "extinction," the kind of relief Rilke feels at doing so is mixed in Kinnell with pain. In "The Call Across the Valley of Not-Knowing," where, characteristically, love is more explicitly sexual than in Rilke, "it must be the wound, the wound itself, / which lets us know and love" (58). Time-bound, sexual union—representing not a degradation of love (as it sometimes does for Rilke), but its flowering—is

> that purest,
> most tragic concumbence, strangers
> clasped into one, a moment, of their moment on earth.
> (58)

Put succinctly at the end of "Little Sleep's-Head Sprouting Hair in the Moonlight," *the wages / of dying is love.*
Kinnell's tragic sense of love reflects his understanding of its physical origin. Life itself, in *Nightmares,* cannot be teased away from its perishable, material base. The interdependence of love and death in the poem is thus adumbrated by the relationship between sex and death. As Elizabeth Sewell explains this connection, "Sex and death are delivered to us by our bodily nature and heritage. They are part of our condition as living organisms. . . . Biologists tell us that they entered the world together in the history of living creatures, at the point of the differentiation of the individual and development of sexual reproduction."[5] Rilke preserves the distinction between what Leishman calls "that sublime love which is an end in itself, the love of the great feminine lovers such as Gaspara Stampa" and "the blind animal passion which is always the foundation, and often the whole content, of masculine love" (96):

> One thing to sing the beloved, another, alas!
> that hidden guilty river-god of the blood.
> ("The Third Elegy")

For Kinnell, the two songs are one. As melodramatic as Zola, Rilke in "The Third Elegy" is repulsed by our animal origins. The sleeping babe may appear to be protected by his mother, but his outward calm belies his atavistic inner life:

> who could avert,
> divert, the floods of origin flowing within him?
> . . . . . . . . . . . . . . . . . . . . . .
> He, so new, so timorous, how he got tangled
> in ever-encroaching roots of inner event,
> twisted to primitive patterns, to throttling growths, to bestial
> preying forms! How he gave himself up to it! Loved.

Like Kinnell, the babe continues "into his own roots and out into violent beginning / where his tiny birth was already outlived," an image which anticipates Kinnell's description of a dying derelict:

> Violet bruises come out
> all over his flesh, as invisible

fists start beating him a last time; the whine
of omphalos blood starts up again, the puffed
bellybutton explodes, the carnal
nightmare soars back to the beginning.

(37)

Where Rilke bemoans the "hidden guilty river-god of the blood,"
Kinnell acknowledges the sacred character of the babe's journey
back "into his own roots and out into the violent beginning." He
himself undertakes that journey. Indeed, Rilke's description of the
babe's descent could stand as the sacred text on which *Nightmares*
is an extended meditation: the boy

> Descended,
> lovingly, into the older blood, the ravines
> where Frightfulness lurked, still gorged with his fathers. And
>      every
> terror knew him, and winked, and quite understood.
> Yes, Horror smiled at him.

Although Kinnell's temperament is less rarefied, he joins Rilke in
apotheosizing the ephemeral. In "The Ninth Elegy" Rilke asks
why, when our lives are so fragile, "why / *have* to be human, and,
shunning Destiny, / long for Destiny?" His answer suffuses every
line of *Nightmares:* "Not out of curiosity," but

> because being here amounts to so much, because all
> this Here and Now, so fleeting, seems to require us and
>      strangely
> concerns us. Us the most fleeting of all. Just once,
> everything, only for once. Once and no more. And we, too,
> once. And never again.

In this spirit, Kinnell tells baby Maud that if, with a lover one day,
she commits "the error / of thinking, / *one day all this will only be
memory*," she must "learn to reach deeper / into the sorrows / to
come":

> Kiss
> the mouth
> which tells you, *here,*

> *here is the world.* This mouth. This laughter. These temple
> bones.
>
> The still undanced cadence of vanishing.
>
> (52)

The sacred ("temple") and the material ("bones") meet in the human face, our only place of worship.

The sorrow Rilke professes about the fleeting "Here and Now"
remains muted. Grief is implicit in "Once and no more. And we
too / once. And never again," but "even the moaning of grief" can
"escape / to a bliss beyond the fiddle." The "things that live on departure" aren't lost but "look for / rescue from something in us."
The Earth can have "an invisible re-arising in us" and its "holiest
inspiration's / Death, that friendly Death." "The Ninth Elegy" concludes not in surrender to departure but in timelessness:

> Look, I am living. On what? Neither childhood nor future
> are growing less. . . . . Supernumerous existence
> wells up in my heart.

When Rilke does focus on sorrow, in the final elegy, the allegorical
treatment keeps the sadness at a remove. One of the "youthfully-
dead" leaves the "City of Pain," the false life from which death—
and reality—have been banished, and he follows a girl, one of the
Lament family, once a powerful clan but now outcasts. Wearing
"Pearls of Pain and the fine-spun / Veils of Patience," she "leads him
through the spacious landscape / of Lamentation," pointing out
"the fields of flowering Sadness" and "the pasturing herds of Grief."

That the "Here and Now" is "so fleeting" is a personal matter
for Kinnell, not a theoretical or allegorical one. What takes its
leave of earth isn't some imagined "early-departed," but Kinnell's
father, or his daughter, or himself. Where the particular contexts
of Rilke's life are filtered out—the voice is purified, disembodied—
*Nightmares,* as Kinnell puts it, "does stay fairly close to the experiences of my life" (*WDS* 22). Acknowledging this distance from
Rilke, he knows his nighttime songs to Maud aren't "the songs / of
light said to wave / through the bright hair of angels, / but a blacker /
rasping flowering" (7). Death has for him a specificity, a physical
presence, a valence it mostly lacks in the *Elegies.* The conclusions

of both poems exemplify what Yeats called "tragic gaiety," but where Rilke's final words refer obliquely to what death in general offers—

> And we, who have always thought
> of happiness climbing, would feel
> the emotion that almost startles
> when happiness falls

—Kinnell's last lines, anticipating a very specific prospective departure, present his own fleabag corpse:

> On the body,
> on the blued flesh, when it is
> laid out, see if you can find
> the one flea which is laughing.

If Kinnell proudly announces the *Elegies* as the thematic father of his long poem, he is quieter about what may be its structural mother. He does not speak much about T. S. Eliot, but *Four Quartets* nevertheless lurks, unobtrusive but persistent, behind *The Book of Nightmares*. Robert Langbaum suggests some specific echoes,[6] but the pivotal connection is the manner in which the works formulate images of themselves. At its end, Kinnell figures his book as a "Bach concert" (74), the union of counterpointing voices, a "concert of one / divided among himself" (75). In his final section, Eliot's poetic ideal verbally manifests itself in a sentence "where every word is at home, / Taking its place to support the others, / . . . The complete consort dancing together."[7] Kinnell's "concert" and Eliot's dancing "consort" suggest the quasi-musical ambitions of the sequences: both are heavily motivic, introducing, repeating, and modifying verbal elements in the manner of a musical composition developing a theme. And these two key words also point toward the double preoccupation of each poem: the particularity of things in the historical, temporal world (the individual instruments, the isolated words) and their simultaneous identity in a visionary, eternal one (the verbal web woven from the repetition of those words).

The nature of the poetic sequence—a whole comprised of separate parts—reflects this double subject, but, more importantly, the doubleness is embodied in the verbal texture of the *Quartets* and the *Nightmares*. In both works, the interconnecting verbal filaments (recovering the etymological link) make the text a tissue. The weave is the relation *among* words in the *Quartets*, the threads spun between, for instance, the "rose-garden" or the "first gate" in "Burnt Norton" and "the moment of the rose" and the "unknown, remembered gate" in "Little Gidding." Isolated words or phrases, moving "Only in time," "will not stay in place," for "The detail of the pattern is movement" (19), but arranged in an interdependent whole, they rise above the flux. Through time, thus, time is conquered:

> Words, after speech, reach
> Into the silence. Only by the form, the pattern,
> Can words or music reach
> The stillness, as a Chinese jar still
> Moves perpetually in its stillness.
>
> (19)

But even as the tapestry of the *Quartets*—"the form, the pattern"—reconciles flux and permanence, the balance tips toward eternity:

> Or say that the end precedes the beginning,
> And the end and the beginning were always there
> Before the beginning and after the end.
> And all is always now.
>
> (19)

Arranged in pattern, words may "reach / The stillness," but in general for Eliot they are inadequate: they "strain, / Crack and sometimes break"; they "Decay with imprecision" and "Will not stay still" (19). Worse, they must be degraded by speech, by "Shrieking voices / Scolding, mocking, or merely chattering" which "Always assail them" (19). His underlying concern, moreover, is anyway less with words than with the Word, which "Is most attacked by voices of temptation" (19). For Eliot, "the word of poetry has a very small 'w,'" Spender tells us, "compared with the infinitely large 'W' of the Word made flesh" (59): "The seriousness of poetry lies in the poet's realization that it is not serious: this realization opens a door onto what is serious—the Word beyond the word. 'The poetry does not matter'—but the realization that it does not do so occurs when the language of poetry coincides with that of religion. And this releases a spring which opens a door onto the language of truth that does matter" (59–60).

Through "the form, the pattern," *Nightmares* "Moves perpetually in its stillness," like Eliot's Chinese jar. It is structured on a linear, spiritual journey, but even as the journey unfolds in time, because of the threads of repetition which stitch together the text, the book seems to happen all at once. Just as Eliot, his eye on the "one end, which is always present" (13), conflates beginnings and endings, Kinnell, gazing at that "mysterious element beyond our reach," superimposes death on birth and birth on death. As she enters the world, Maud "dies / a moment, turns blue as a coal" (6). In her first moment her father tells her, "It is all over, / little one, the flipping / and overleaping, the watery / somersaulting alone in the oneness / under the hill" (5).

> We shall not cease from exploration
> And the end of all our exploring
> Will be to arrive where we started

concludes Eliot (59), while in *Nightmares,* when a Southern sheriff dies, he

> floats out
> on a sea he almost begins to remember,
> floats out into a darkness he has known already.
> (60)

In the final section (its number, "10," made of "one / and zero"), Kinnell writes,

> It is right
> at the last, that one
> and zero
> walk off together,
> walk off the end of these pages together,
> one creature
> walking away side by side with the emptiness.
> (73)

Time ("one": number, division, linearity) and eternity ("zero": su-
pernumerous existence, wholeness, circularity) stroll arm in arm.
But where in Eliot the balance tips toward the "one end which is
always present," in Kinnell time finally just outweighs (but does
not deny) eternity. One and zero are walking "off the end of these
pages," themselves traveling the temporal road; positioned in relation to what comes before, they are "at the last." Complaining that
words and music move "only in time," Eliot pronounces blankly,
"that which is only living / Can only die" (19). Kinnell reformulates this stripped-down pronouncement, retaining the grimly insistent tone, the bald confrontation of mortality: "Living brings
you to death, there is no other road" (73). But where Eliot miti-
gates death even as he confronts it (leaving room for that which
isn't "only living," which moves, presumably, *outside* of time), Kinnell discards the extraterrestrial possibility; "only living" becomes
merely "Living."

The Christian imagery of *Nightmares* and the allusions to the
Gospels suggest the religious stakes of the poem, its concern with
final things, but Christianity itself is subverted. Sacredness resides
not in the "Word" but in the "word" and, thus, the poetry *does*
matter. Where Eliot bemoans that both Word and word are as-
sailed and attacked by the human voice, Kinnell follows Whitman,
who "knew that for the voice which loves it every word is virginal,"
that "the original music of the human voice . . . rescues words and
makes them fresh" (WIW 55). Since "poetry is wasted breath," it
"needs the imperfect music of the human voice" (PPW 125). The
"Shrieking voices" Eliot decries evince and affirm for Kinnell our
perishable lives; his description of Villon is also a self-portrait:
"What he holds on to is only an unspecified vitality, the vitality of
decay, perhaps, or of sorrow, or simply of speech" (xvii).

Although the interplay between time and eternity structures
both poems—Kinnell's "concert" is surely indebted to Eliot's "consort" here—the "final facts" in *Four Quartets,* as Spender suggests, are Christian, otherworldly, eternal. Eliot may emphasize the
intersection of this world and the other, but his interest often appears as a concession, as the only move left. Since we are temporarily stuck on earth, an intersection provides the only access to eternity, but best of all, I sense Eliot thinking, would be an unmediated
apprehension of the other world. Thus "sense and notion" are

obstructions (50), earthly life a "waste sad time" (20), unless it is
visited by the sacred presence in an Incarnational moment. The
"final facts" of *Nightmares* are the dying things and creatures of
the temporal world. Sacredness resides here—not Incarnation but
Immanence. Kinnell's question is rhetorical, the affirmative answer
shining out of every crevice of the poem: "Is it true / the earth is all
there is, and the earth does not last?" (73). "Love is most nearly
itself," for Eliot, "When here and now cease to matter" (31). In
*Nightmares*, love flourishes *only* in the here and now; Kinnell,
again, wants his daughter not to absent herself from the present,
but rather to

> Kiss
>
> the mouth
> which tells you, *here,*
> *here is the world.* This mouth. This laughter. These temple
> bones.
>
> (52)

*Four Quartets* climaxes in those moments when time is conquered through time, "the intersection of the timeless moment"
(51), for example, at Little Gidding, one of those places which are
"the world's end" (50). If you came there, "you would have to put
off / sense and notion" (50). This vacancy echoes Eliot's earlier
prescriptions:

> Shall I say it again? In order to arrive there,
> To arrive where you are, to get from where you are not,
>     You must go by a way wherein there is no ecstasy.
> In order to arrive at what you do not know
>     You must go by a way which is the way of ignorance.
>
> (29)

Inscribing his own circuitous journey, Kinnell too goes "by a way
wherein there is no ecstasy." But because his arrival is an immersion in time, not a conquering, *Nightmares* climaxes in the very
taking on of sense and notion:

> And the brain kept blossoming
> all through the body, until the bones themselves could think,
> and the genitals sent out wave after wave of holy desire
> until even the dead brain cells

surged and fell in god-like, androgynous fantasies—
and I understood
the unicorn's phallus could have risen, after all,
directly out of thought itself.

(59)

For Eliot, "the enchainment of past and future / Woven in the weakness of the changing body" protects us from the Absolute but thereby thwarts our spiritual possibilities, "Protects mankind from heaven and damnation / Which flesh cannot endure" (16). For Kinnell, the weave of time affords our only entrance to these conditions, the changing body underlies any conception we may entertain of heaven: "But isn't the very concept of paradise also only a metaphor? Our idea of that place of bliss must be a dream we extrapolated from our rapturous moments on earth, moments perhaps of our infancy, perhaps beyond that, of our foetal existence" (PPW 121).

II

Where Eliot embraces Christianity, Kinnell is drawn to what Jung calls "an undercurrent to the Christianity that [historically] ruled on the surface"—to alchemy.[8] Alchemy is to Christianity, Jung proposes, "as the dream is to consciousness, and just as the dream compensates the conflicts of the conscious mind, so alchemy endeavors to fill the gaps left open by the Christian tension of opposites" (23). Where the religion, that is, separates spirit and matter, the medieval science insists on their shared identity. For alchemy was more than a greedy and wrongheaded attempt to get rich. As H. Stanley Redgrove explains, it "was both a philosophy and an experimental science" dedicated to "the attempt to demonstrate experimentally on the material plane the validity of a certain philosophical view of the Cosmos" (2). Kinnell's only prose statement on the subject, although idiosyncratic, indicates a similar unity of material and non-material: "Alchemy, the search for the philosopher's stone, was, on the surface, an attempt to master nature, to change base metals into gold; secretly, however, it was a symbolic science, and its occult aim was to propitiate the sexual, creative forces in nature, and to transfigure the inner life" (PPD 61).

For this and other reasons alchemy lies at the heart of *Night-mares*, is (one might say, applying its premise of underlying unity) thematic father and structural mother in one. Kinnell acknowledges this parentage in a variety of ways, most explicitly in the illustrations that introduce and pictorially comment on each section. These are all from "old books," Kinnell explains (*WDS* 56), some of them alchemical texts, and with the verbal alchemical and astrological images, they lend the volume a talismanic aura. (Alchemy and astrology are closed linked, partly because both interpret physical phenomena in psychological terms: "such projections repeat themselves," Jung explains, "whenever man tries to explore an empty darkness and involuntarily fills it with living form" [245].) *Nightmares* makes its first eerie impression with the alchemical woodcut depicted on the front cover, an illustration whose appearance there itself seemed uncannily fated: "When I saw a reproduction of the woodcut that's used on the cover I knew I wanted it, though I hadn't yet figured out who those two little angels were who were drawing the words from the mouth of the man about to be devoured. I wrote the Library of Congress and asked if there was a copy in the United States of the original book in which the woodcut appeared. I was living in Iowa City at the time. They wrote back and said there was only one copy in the country, at the Medical Library in Iowa City. So I walked down the street and had it photographed" (*WDS* 57). Kinnell's fanciful interpretation suggests the cover's purely representational aptness, but its symbolic alchemical meaning pertains as well: it depicts the *nigredo*, the first stage in the alchemical process of producing the philosophers' stone; the "little angels" arc, in fact, the *spiritus* (spirit) and *anima* (soul) which are being exhaled by Mercurius. Mercurius, however, as Jung tells us, is a figure of arrival as well as departure: "Mercurius stands at the beginning and end of the work. . . . He is metallic yet liquid, matter yet spirit, cold yet fiery, poison and yet healing draught—a symbol uniting all opposites" (293, 295). Just as a metal needs to be "killed" (stripped of its identity, its form) before it is "resurrected" into gold (the desired material change, as always, expresses a desired spiritual one), the protagonist of *Night-mares* must "die," in section 5, before his eventual regeneration.

The alchemists were solitaries, endlessly repeating in their laboratories their strange procedures, reworking the same material over and over, driven to get it right. Kinnell too, obsessively solitary, repeatedly gathers up in his alembic the same handful of images and casts them out, restlessly recombining the same elements over and over. "The book's flesh, its words, would be spiritualized," Cary Nelson writes, "by the endless alchemy of its formal reverberations" (93). The analogy extends beyond the workshop to the philosophy of both postmodern poet and medieval scientist, particularly the refusal to discount the spiritual and intellectual consequence of the material world.

In this, the alchemists followed Aristotle, whose biological interests led him to reckon seriously with impermanence. "Plato had looked with suspicion upon susceptibility to change," Arthur Hopkins explains, tracing alchemy back to Greek philosophy, while "Aristotle emphatically denied that this introduced unreality" (20). Indeed, Aristotle's basic understanding of matter provides the theoretical ground for alchemical thought, which in turn underlies Kinnell's conception of identity in *Nightmares*. Matter is unified; it consists of the same four elements (earth, air, fire, water—elements as well of the vocabulary that constitutes the verbal matrix of *Nightmares*) in varying proportion. Aristotle saw the material world constituted by this prime matter, or substratum, but actual existence combined this unifying matter with a *differentiating* "form"—not shape only, as E. J. Holmyard explains, but "all that conferred upon a body its specific properties" (19). As one entity changes into another by an alchemical process, so the alchemical theory went, "It is only the form that alters; the prime matter of which the elements are made never changes." Theoretically, if one altered the mix of elements, matter, which in *itself* remains constant, could assume a new "form." Lead could be transmuted into gold.

Here we see precisely the doubleness of Kinnell's vision. Self and other are identical, composed of the same unifying matter: "every atom belonging to me as good belongs to you" (SM 1), Whitman declaims, and Kinnell assents, the question posed in section 4—

Can it ever be true—
all bodies, one body, one light
made of everyone's darkness together?

—implicity answered in section 8, "*yes . . . yes . . . ?*" This affirmation, however, ends with a question mark. He *asks*, "might not we hear" this word "yes," and the question isn't entirely rhetorical. Kinnell, like Whitman and the alchemists, *does* strongly hold to a visionary materialism, but his vision is often qualified. "*Yes,*" but "*yes . . . ?*" Lovers can achieve "that purest / most tragic concumbence, strangers / clasped into one," but that togetherness lasts only "a moment, of their moment on earth" (58). We accomplish the "wholeness" Aristophanes proposed, but even as Kinnell appeals to this authority he compromises him: "Aristophanes ran off / at the mouth—made it all up, nightmared it all up" (57); he is a "drunk Greek," who "extrapolated from his high / or flagellated out of an empty heart," the "wholeness" of which he speaks (58).

Aristotelian "matter," in any case, never supersedes "form" for Kinnell. "That everything proceeds from the One is a fundamental tenet of alchemy," Jung explains (450), but this monistic tenet paradoxically implies a dualistic conclusion: existence derives from the *means* by which "everything proceeds" as well as from syncretizing matter. "At some level all things *are* each other," Kinnell knows, "but before that point they are separate entities" (*WDS* 52). Thus, although "all bodies" are eventually "one body," *Nightmares* is shot through with an abiding attachment to what vanishes, to the world's particular bodies—to "This mouth. This laughter. These temple bones" (52). Aging may have mellowed the fierceness of this attachment, "matter" may have gained ground, but *Nightmares* works the same conflict Kinnell articulated most brashly in the early poem, "Freedom, New Hampshire." "It is true / That only flesh [read "form"] dies, and spirit [read "matter"] flowers without stop." But "an incarnation is in particular flesh": if existence rests in matter, identity resides in form. "The dust that is swirled into a shape / And crumbles and is swirled again"—that is, the undifferentiated matter—"had but one shape," its form, "That was this man."

Wholeness and division, then, keep turning into one another in *Nightmares*, as they do in alchemical thought. "One of the central axioms of alchemy," according to Jung, is the saying of Maria Prophetissa: "'One becomes two, two becomes three, and out of the third comes the one as the fourth'" (23). Since they derive from the "One," metals can be resolved back into their origin, into gold. Or, as Kinnell remarks in connection with *Nightmares*, "in the greatest moments of our lives, we do grasp that there's an element beyond our reach, from which we came, and into which we will dissolve" (*WDS* 97). We see Maud emerging from this element, "glowing / with the astral violet / of the underlife" (6), and the old tramp dissolving back into it, "violet bruises" coming out over his flesh as "the carnal / nightmare soars back to the beginning" (37).

But this synonymy of birth and death parallels a more encompassing equivalence, between the human and the cosmic. Kinnell calls the "element beyond our reach" the "mother and father of all life of the planet" (*WDS* 97–98). Hovering behind this analogy is one of the most frequently cited of mystical alchemical equations, reputed to be inscribed on an emerald tablet in the tomb of (the probably mythical) Hermes Trismegistus: "'What is below is like that which is above, and what is above is like that which is below, to accomplish the miracles of one thing'" (Read 16). "In one of its aspects," M. M. Pattison Muir tells us, this saying meant "processes happen within the earth like those which occur on the earth; mineral and metals live, as animals and plants live; all pass through corruption toward perfection" (29). This connection parallels the familiar alchemical association between the heavenly bodies and the earthly metals: gold represents the sun, silver the moon, iron Mars, and so on. But more directly to the point for Kinnell is Muir's second gloss: "In another aspect the saying meant 'the human being is the world in miniature; as is the microcosm, so is the macrocosm; to know oneself is to know all the world'" (29–30).

At the end of "The Path Among the Stones" Kinnell directly incorporates this key alchemical aphorism:

> As above: the last scattered stars
> kneel down in the star-form of the Aquarian age:
> a splash
> on the top of the head,
> on the grass of this earth even the stars love, splashes of the
>     sacred waters . . .

So below: in the graveyard
the lamps start lighting up, one for each of us,
in all the windows
of stone.

This pronouncement synopsizes the whole of the ninth section, in which Kinnell descends into the earth and crawls back up to discover a cosmic harmony, just as section 9 itself recapitulates the descent and eventual affirmation of *Nightmares* as a whole. The mystical utterance, thus, structurally demonstrates its own meaning; microcosm mirrors macrocosm, which in turn becomes mirroring microcosm. Indeed, by quoting the ancient emerald tablets Kinnell at once affirms his terrible kinship with the dying physical world and his connection to his spiritual predecessors, those solitaries who spent lifetimes concocting spiritual gold. This bond, however, doesn't lead Kinnell into the laboratory. He literalizes Hermes' precept, not essentially in metallurgic terms, but in anthropomorphic ones (although the distinction, for the alchemists, was more apparent than real); at the birth of Kinnell's son, the newborn infant (below) is like "the newborn planet" (above), the father (below) like "empty space" (above). Throughout *Nightmares,* above and below (like form and matter) are similarly yoked together. When newborn Maud cried in her crib here below, the Archer, above, "lay / sucking the icy biestings of the cosmos, / in his crib of stars" (7). Maud is born "clotted with celestial [above] cheesiness [below], glowing / with the astral violet [above] / of the underlife [below]" (67). The Crone counsels Kinnell that he lives *"under the Sign / of the Bear, who flounders through chaos / in his "starry* [above] *blubber* [below]" (22–23).

As this floundering suggests, Kinnell's access to the original One is achieved only in time (indeed, only in the process of writing poems). Kinnell formulates this "One" in the "element beyond our reach," in the "underlife" (an inversion of Emerson's "Oversoul"), in the "strangers / clasped into one" (58), in the binding network of the poem's language; but, as for the alchemists and Whitman, everywhere unity is predicated on our existence as physical beings, on a visionary materialism that surpasses mere catabolism: we contain "in ourselves our own animal and plant and stone life, our own deep connection with all other beings"[9]—"all bodies" are "one body." Woven from the volatile threads of physical beings, Unity grows complicate—single but multiple. One keeps turning into two and three. The alchemists, gazes fixed resolutely on the unity of creation, need to ply their metals repeatedly, endlessly starting from scratch. The alchemical climax of *Nightmares*, "As above . . . So below," is ever-present but also arrived at. Like Eliot's Chinese jar, *Nightmares* "Moves perpetually in its stillness"—a single object (in space) and a divided one (in time), a "concert of one / divided among himself." It is an intricate and simple thing.

### III

But one thing at a time. First, motion. "I write long poems," Kinnell has explained, because "it is possible for them to begin and then wander around, search around for some way out, and to come to a climax and resolution. . . . Long poems are made out of time."[10] "As above, so below" might translate to Eliot's epigraph from Heraclitus, "the way up and the way down are one and the same." With this in mind, I want to follow closely the temporal development of *Nightmares*, the "search around for some way out," the journey Kinnell undertakes, down and up, from his haunted, lone room, through the "whorled / archway of the fingerprint of all things" (68), to his final "walk off the end of these pages" (73).

Section 1 begins by locating Kinnell on a journey, "On the path," but "Under the Maud Moon" actually precedes the journey proper. Functioning as prologue, it establishes the verbal and thematic territory the rest of the book will traverse. As in the poems of *Body Rags*, at the start things here have flamed out:

> On the path,
> by this wet site
> of old fires—
> black ashes, black stones . . .

Immediately, we sense Kinnell's spiritual hunger, as he stops at a campsite

> where tramps
> must have squatted down,
> gnawing on stream water,
> unhouseling themselves on cursed bread,
> failing to get warm at a twigfire—

Like the tramps, he is "unhouseled," "cursed bread" having replaced the eucharist wafer, but this likeness affords as yet no communion. Next, he strikes the note of not-having again, now with a more personal focus: in lines which derive from "The Fourth Elegy"—

> the space within your faces changed,
> even while I loved it, into cosmic space
> where you no longer were . . .

—he thinks of her

> whose face
> I held in my hands
> a few hours, whom I gave back
> only to keep holding the space where she was.
>
> (3)

"She" may anticipate Kinnell's other half, the "lost other we keep seeking across time," the woman he met in an airplane where he "held her face a few hours / in my hands" (58); but more immediately, "she" is Maud, whose birth and infancy are the main events of section 1. As he takes up these subjects, his restlessness and solitude recede. At the fire, the daughter or lover exists only in memory, but when Maud does appear—"A round- / cheeked girl-child comes awake"—Kinnell retains the present tense; they are together, and his floundering is put on hold.

Writing about Maud affords Kinnell the tone which will characterize the rest of *Nightmares*. Some critics have called the work "confessional," and if the epithet minimizes the visionary streak, it is nonetheless true that, more than ever, Kinnell speaks directly from his own experience. Yet, as befits the occasion of birth—personal and transcendent, common and miraculous—his voice becomes bardic and intimate at once, a contemporary reformulation of Wordsworth's. Indeed, just as Wordsworth believes "Our birth is but a sleep and a forgetting" ("Intimations of Immortality"), Kinnell imagines Maud's just-born "limbs shaking / as the memories rush out of them." Wordsworth asserts, "The Soul that rises with us, our life's Star, / Hath had elsewhere its setting," while Kinnell intones over Maud (speaking of intra-uterine life, her most recent "elsewhere"), "It is all over little one" and supposes that "as they cut / her tie to the darkness / she dies / a moment." Maud, "the mist still clinging about her face," enters the world, in effect, "trailing clouds of glory."

It is in addressing his daughter at the end of "Maud Moon" that Kinnell draws closest to Wordsworth.[11] As Wordsworth, near the end of "Tintern Abbey," anticipates his eventual death and offers his sister the poem, "these exhortations," in his stead—"in after years" (the future), he tells her,

> If solitude, or fear, or pain, or grief,
> Should be thy portion, with what healing thoughts
> Of tender joy wilt thou remember me,
> And these my exhortations! Nor perchance,
> If I should be where I no more can hear
> Thy voice, nor catch from thy wild eyes these gleams
> Of past existence, wilt thou then forget
> That on the banks of this delightful stream
> We stood together;

—so Kinnell, imagining she'll one day be "orphaned," "exhorts" his daughter (also, like Dorothy, a "*sister*"):

> And in the days
> when you find yourself orphaned,
> emptied
> of all wind-singing, of light,
> the pieces of cursed bread on your tongue,
>
> may there come back to you
> a voice,
> spectral, calling you
> *sister!*
> from everything that dies.

And then
you shall open
this book, even if it is the book of nightmares.

Maud's birth parallels the poem's emergence. If she is its audience, she is also its muse. "I *invoke* Maud and Fergus," Kinnell tells us (my italics), "not merely to instruct them, but also to get help from them." As we have seen, Kinnell fancies that the woodcut on the front cover depicts "two little angels" (his children) "drawing the words" (the poem) from a "man about to be devoured" (the poet). Infant Maud thus "puts / her hand / into her father's mouth, to take hold of / his song." Maud is a muse not primarily in and of herself, however, but because of her close connection (as an infant) with the "element beyond our reach, from which we came, and into which we will dissolve." Her sadness is "stranger than ours," and she glows "with the astral violet / of the underlife," with the Rilkean, unilluminated side of life, which is the true origin of *Nightmares:* when the "Maud moon / glimmered in those first nights," Kinnell "crept down / to riverbanks," to

> where the earth oozes up
> in cold streaks, touching the world
> with the underglimmer
> of the beginning,
> and there learned my only song.

Maud is muse, then, in that her birth dramatizes for Kinnell his thinking about Rilke, about the "extended whole" of life and death invoked in the epigraph. "Those little lumps of clinging flesh, and one's terrible, inexplicable closeness to them," he says, "make one feel very strongly the fragility of a person. In the company of babies, one is very close to the kingdom of death" (*WDS* 44). And, as we have seen, the birth itself is figured repeatedly as a death, the rising life's star elsewhere setting. Here at the start Maud "turns blue," just as, at the end, the poet's corpse is "blued flesh." But this "extended whole" isn't static in *Nightmares.* Caught in mysterious rhythm, lives emerge from and dissolve back into the underlife, just as on the level of language specific words and images emerge from the verbal matrix, dissolve back, and re-emerge. The blueness of Maud's flesh, for example, re-emerges in the "blue, vanished water" (29), the "Violet bruises" on the tramp's dying flesh (37), the "blue spittle / of snakes" (68), the "eerie blue light" that "blooms / on all the ridges of the world" (68), and the "blued flesh" of the poet's corpse (75). Form and matter marry and divorce, only to marry again. Maud separates out from the underlife and will, soon enough, merge again, just as her father holds her for a while and then gives her back. When it rains,

> The raindrops trying
> to put the fire out
> fall into it and are
> changed: the oath broken,
> the oath sworn between earth and water, flesh and spirit,
>     broken,
> to be sworn again,
> over and over, in the clouds, and to be broken again,
> over and over, on earth.

Kinnell invokes his children because "they live with death almost as animals do," with a "natural trust in life's rhythms" which "provides the model for the trust they may struggle to learn later on"; *Nightmares,* he tells us, "is my own effort to find the trust again" (*WDS* 45—46). The back and forth of the oath sworn and broken, of emergence and dissolution: "life's rhythms" are there at the start. As the introduction, "Under the Maud Moon" invokes what the rest of the volume will struggle toward. Calling up the underlife, it sets pulsing the sustaining, daunting rhythm, the bass line whose vibrations underlie both Kinnell's flounderings and his terrible findings.

Having foreglimpsed what he will ultimately affirm, in "The Hen Flower" Kinnell plunges into his own orphaned days of cursed bread. Here commences the way down. This second section, he remarks, "states one of the problems the poem is to explore and attempt to deal with. The second, third, fourth, fifth, and sixth parts all do more or less the same thing. The rest of the poem tries at least to understand, if not solve, the problems."[12] If "The Hen Flower" does "more or less" what the following sections do, still, it must precede them. The first section completed, a remnant of the discarded "The Things," it "expresses the dread that is the poem's starting point. It addresses the protagonist before he begins the

journey of the poem, instructing him to let go, to surrender to existence" (*WDS* 47).

Where his response to Maud's birth provoked "Maud Moon,"
Kinnell's appalled attraction to the hen stirs up the verse here. He
imagined his unborn daughter as a foetus, happily "flipping / and
overleaping" in the womb, warmly "drifting there furled in the
dark"; now that dread predominates, a chill has come over his vision of the unborn, and the poet himself is implicated in their non-
being:

> I have glimpsed
> by corpse-light, in the opened cadaver
> of hen, the mass of tiny,
> unborn eggs, each getting
> tinier and yellower as it reaches back toward
> the icy pulp
> of what is, I have felt the zero
> freeze itself around the finger dipped slowly in.

The closeness of birth and death, so sustaining in "Maud Moon,"
has thus taken on a ghastliness. Even as "the ax- / scented breeze
flourishes / about her," even as the hen woozes off into the darkness,

> the next egg, bobbling
> its globe of golden earth,
> skids forth, ridding her even
> of the life to come.

The egg "skids forth," that is, as Maud "skids out" (6), but the
emotional valence has altered drastically.

"The Hen Flower" directly "addresses the protagonist" only at
its end. Perhaps in retreat from the "dread" that his vision of the
hens has evoked, Kinnell drifts into a childhood memory about
them:

> I remember long ago I sowed
> my own first milk
> tooth under hen feathers, I planted under hen feathers
> the hook
> of the wishbone,
> which had broken itself so lovingly toward me.

Just as "first milk" briefly recalls the celestial, nourishing "icy biestings" of the Archer's infancy (7) only to jolt us back to earth with "tooth," Kinnell abruptly snaps back from his optimistic boyhood expectations to the sprawling, troubled present:

> For the future.
>
> It has come to this.

Then, amidst "this," the address:

> Listen, Kinnell,
> dumped alive
> and dying into the old sway bed,
> a layer of crushed feathers all that there is
> between you
> and the long shaft of darkness shaped as you,
> let go.
>
> Even this haunted room
> all its materials photographed with tragedy,
> even the tiny crucifix drifting face down at the center of the
>     earth,
> even these feathers freed from their wings forever
> are afraid.

Letting go, abandoning oneself to "life's rhythms," is dreadful, especially if it means offering up one's neck to the hatchet like the hen, relinquishing one's hold on earthly life. And layered on such dread is the poetic risk of this kind of self-probing poem, the fear I discussed earlier that nothing will turn up but violence or wretchedness. Describing the instruction he gives himself here, Kinnell places "let go" in apposition to "say all."[13] His instructions are poetic as well as spiritual. But we sense in the tortured lurching of the verse the sheer difficulty of such saying all. "I suspect it isn't a matter of theory," Kinnell remarks about poetry, "but a personal, psychological, question: whether one can get past the censors in one's mind and say what really matters without shame or exhibitionism" (*WDS* 105).

The more overtly autobiographical turn of *Nightmares* may index Kinnell's progress in saying what really matters. Thomas Gardner connects "The Hen Flower" to the animal poems in *Body*

*Rags* (429), and while it is true that the innards of all three creatures spill out in a violent merging of self and world, where "The
Bear" presents an imagined poet-hunter as protagonist and "The
Porcupine" only belatedly centers on the poem's "I" (by then envel-
oped in hallucination), "The Hen Flower," self-addressed, consists
of material more plainly personal. The earlier poems, structured by
the meanderings of the poet's consciousness, *are* deeply personal,
as I have argued, but in the later one, as throughout *Nightmares*,
Kinnell creates a more fully dramatized sense of the particular personality ultimately probed beneath and transcended. This sense derives partly from an autobiographical content which keeps in check
the fantastical strain of the book; for all its abandon, *Nightmares*
never reaches the level of hallucination where the poet can merge
with porcupine or bear. These totem animals extend Kinnell's
imagination, but the hen, in addition, taps his early memories:

> My family had a henhouse out behind our house until the Pawtucket
> city fathers zoned it away. I was very young then, perhaps six or
> seven, and I remember the chickens mostly through a few images.
> One is of my sisters plucking them. I don't suppose they ever stuffed
> a pillow with these feathers of a hen we were at that moment digest-
> ing—but it seemed a possibility. And I can see my father hatcheting
> the hens' heads off on the old grey log he'd set on end for the pur-
> pose, and then letting the headless creatures run about. I don't think
> any of the times I've killed hens myself are more vivid than these
> memories. (*WDS* 107)[14]

In "The Shoes of Wandering," according to Kinnell, "the actual
journey begins."[15] In the Salvation Army Store he finds an old pair
of dead man's shoes, perfectly fitting "eldershoes," in which to
begin his letting go. (That these shoes cling "down to the least
knuckle" suggests his readiness, as it recalls the hen's surrender
when stroked "down the throat knuckles" [11]). Kinnell has the-
orized that poems search for the "absolutely new"—that every
poem is a journey—and in poems like "Where the Track Vanishes"
(*WKW*) he writes explicitly of probing into the unmarked. But
even in that early work, he discovers that "where the track vanishes
the first land begins": discovering the absolutely new is a rediscovery of origin, the absolutely old. Shod, he thus walks out "in *dead*
shoes, in the *new* light" (my italics). And although *"the first step,"*

as the Crone told him, *"shall be to lose the way,"* he is guided by history, the eldershoes which say *"turn* or *stay* or *take / forty-three giant steps / backwards."* These backward steps are "the way" even as they return him to his beginnings (Kinnell is forty-three years old as he writes these lines); the way back and the way forward, now, are one and the same. The regression to pure being imaged in Maud's intra-uterine thrashing and the eggs in the hen's opened cadaver is now manifest in terms of the poet's own life.

The journey, thus, isn't spatial, but mental. After assuming the eldershoes Kinnell returns to the Xvarna Hotel, the physical setting of the rest of "The Shoes" (and of "Dear Stranger," "In the Hotel," and probably, we realize in retrospect, "The Hen Flower"—all the sections on the way down; on the way up, in "Little Sleep's-Head" and "The Call," domestic settings replace this transient one). Leaving "unlocked the door jimmied over and over," the poet follows Whitman's exhortation to "Unscrew the locks from the doors!" but he remains isolated, "self-hugged on the bedclothes," stewing in his own juices, "love-acid, night-sweat, gnash-dust / of tooth." He "lapse[s] back into darkness," into nightmares haunted by "the elderfoot / of these shoes, the drunk who died in this room." We see these probings beneath consciousness approach the origin: "the road / trembles as it starts across / swampland streaked with shined water," a scene which recalls the "underglimmer / of the beginning" in "Maud Moon," "marshes / where the earth oozes up / in cold streaks." But again, what is passed intertwines with what's to come as "memory reaches out / and lays bloody hands on the future." Summarizing his journey, Kinnell acknowledges both its self-generation and his longing for an even purer spontaneity, for "the mantle / of the great wanderers," absolutely ancient figures, presumably, who create the absolutely new. "On this road," he begins, virtually repeating the volume's initial line,

> on which I do not know how to ask for bread,
> on which I do not know how to ask for water,
> this path
> inventing itself
> through jungles of burnt flesh, ground of ground
> bones, crossing itself
> at the odor of blood, and stumbling on,

I long for the mantle
of the great wanderers, who lighted
their steps by the lamp
of pure hunger and pure thirst,

and whichever way they lurched was the way.

The verse lurches around like those great wanderers, driven by primitive and urgent need. Syntactic and grammatical units are hacked up by unpredictable line breaks; lines jag out like broken bones. Yet, as throughout *Nightmares,* the writing is careful. When Kinnell doesn't know how to ask for something, his preschool vocabulary and grammatical repetitiveness express the sense of verbal limitation. Since the long *o*'s, long *i*'s, and a variety of short vowels predominate in the passage, the two long *a*'s in the last line introduce a new sound just as the line itself points toward a new place. We hear newness as the wanderers lurch into it.

"Dear Stranger Extant in Memory by the Blue Juniata" further elaborates on the poet's isolation. From the hotel, Kinnell hears "the chime / of the Old Tower, tinny sacring-bell drifting out / over the city," but no Eucharist is consecrated, no sacrament now at hand. Instead, the "chime" of the sacring-bell becomes "chyme" [digested food] / of our loves," that

the peristalsis of the will to love forever
drives down, grain
after grain, into the last,
coldest room, which is memory.

Kinnell reformulates the spiritual "chime" into the material "chyme" not to proffer an alternate, physical communion—not yet, anyway—but rather to reveal, given our "will to love forever," how little accomplished we are at letting go. Despite this will, however, we are characters in "the book of solitude" kept in the brain by nerves which are cut only by maggots; we are unconditionally released from solitude, that is, only in death.

Much of the rest of "Dear Stranger" concerns Virginia, the stranger of the title. In an interview, Kinnell helps us sort things out here:

The Juniata is a river that flows through southern Pennsylvania. It's Virginia who lives near it . . . Virginia is an actual person I've had a long correspondence with. She is a mystic, a seer. She is one of those born without the protective filtering device that allows the rest of us to see this humanized, familiar world as if it were all there is. She sees past the world and lives in the cosmos. In an old issue of *Poetry*—or perhaps it was *Time*—there's a review of Malcolm Cowley's book of poems, *The Blue Juniata*. The review says the region Cowley writes about belongs to the past, no longer exists. So I allude to the fact that Virginia found it amusing to have her own sense of non-existence thus confirmed. ("You see," I told Mama, "we just *think* we're here.") In this case, the "I" is Virginia. (*WDS* 108)

Despite Virginia's struggle with her "sense of non-existence" and his own floundering, Kinnell initiates a tentative affirmation. Not a mystic, he can only "see this humanized, familiar world as if it were all there is":

> And if there is one more love
> to be known, one more poem
> to be opened into life,
> you will find it here
> or nowhere.

Virginia's ghastly letters, partly forced on her by her demon lover, are balanced by what comes unbid to Kinnell:

> a poem writes itself out: its title—the dream
> of all poems and the text
> of all loves—"Tenderness toward Existence."

The descent is temporarily arrested here in "Dear Stranger" as terror and tenderness are held in equipoise.

Not that Kinnell has rid himself of his nightmares. Love has entered the poem as Tenderness (an abstraction, a "text") but also (more vividly) as a demon. He still thrashes about in his saggy hotel mattress, listening for maggots, thinking of those who have nightmared there before. But, lying there, he also thinks back to flinging the dead hen into the night, a memory which now is mysteriously steadying, almost comforting:

> I lie without sleeping, remembering
> the ripped body

of hen, the warmth of hen flesh
frightening my hands,
all her desires,
all her deathsmells,
blooming again in the starlight. And then the wait—

not long, I grant, but all my life—
for the small, soft
thud of the return among the stones.

Indeed, the memory triggers a tentative vision of, or a wish for, the yet unrealized material communion pointedly absent earlier:

Can it ever be true—
all bodies, one body, one light
made of everyone's darkness together?

Just as Kinnell had earlier "lapse[d] back / into darkness," Virginia now closes her second letter, "Forgive my blindness. Yours, in the darkness, Virginia." But now that the possibility of "one light / made of everyone's darkness together" has been introduced, their solitudes seem less absolute. As the section ends, Kinnell acknowledges that each isn't entirely lost to the other, that at least they share "these letters":

Dear stranger
extant in memory by the blue Juniata,
these letters
across space I guess
will be all we will know of one another.

Kinnell here draws the reader into the constellation of solitudes. The "stranger" is Virginia, but also the unknown reader; "these letters" are the correspondences, but also the poem. When he writes (succinctly translating the visual image of the section's introductory illustration, a single, plucked eye atop a lone tower in a desolate valley) "So little of what one is threads itself through the eye / of empty space," he broaches the limitations of his work. Kinnell remarks, "I think it's the opposite of what Plato thought. I think that if people know each other only mind to mind they hardly know each other at all" (*WDS* 109). Yet, "empty space,"

merely a void here, by the end of *Nightmares* itself becomes pro-
creative, bending over the "newborn planet" it has fathered. The
final lines of "Dear Stranger," each an isolated sentence, composed
mostly of discrete monosyllables, nevertheless point beyond the
alienated self to the provisional, material communion implicit in
the opening "chyme / of our loves":

> Never mind.
> The self is the least of it.
> Let our scars fall in love.

If the self is the least of it, gone through only to be reached beyond, it is nevertheless the death of the self which generates "In the
Hotel of Lost Light," the section Langbaum calls the "book's
nadir, its inferno" (31). Here, the journey bottoms out. At the start
Kinnell has poured himself into a death mold:

> In the left-
> hand sag the drunk smelling of autopsies
> died in, my body slumped out
> into the shape of his, I watch, as he
> must have watched, a fly
> tangled in mouth-glue, whining his wings.

The poet is the spider, spinning his web of words, but also the fly,
whose imminent demise announces his own. It, like Kinnell, is
"concentrated wholly on / *time, time.*" Just as the poet's first step
on his descent was "to lose the way," the fly is "losing his way
worse / down the downward-winding stairs." Kinnell has tried to
"let go," to "surrender to existence"; the fly "ceases to struggle"
and, as it does, is linked directly to the artist:

> his wings
> flutter out the music blooming with failure
> of one who gets ready to die, as Roland's horn, winding down
> from the Pyrenees, saved its dark, full flourishes
> for last.

"In the Hotel" then turns from the fly's death to that of the old
man, the past resident of Kinnell's hotel room, the previous owner
of his perfectly fitting eldershoes. As Virginia takes dictation from
her demon lover, Kinnell receives his words from the dead drunk:

after-amanuensis of his after-life,
I write out
for him in this languished alphabet
of worms, these last words
of himself, post for him
his final postcards to posterity.

As the perfect fit of the mattress sag and eldershoes suggests, this drunk is a version of Kinnell himself, "Flesh / of his excavated flesh." The first line of the drunk's "last words / of himself" recapitulates the poet's own experience in sections 1 and 2: "I sat out by twigfires flaring in grease strewn from the pimpled limbs of hen." (Nelson accurately connects the epitaph to Ginsburg's "Howl," and, indeed, the lines incorporate their own acknowledgment: " 'I heard my own cries already howled inside bottles the waves washed up on beaches.' ") The drunk's reference to the "sweet excremental / odor of opened cadaver" also identifies him with the poet, who earlier glimpsed "the opened cadaver / of hen"; and his advice on what to tell the deskman about this mess,

> Friend, *To Live*
> has a poor cousin,
> who calls tonight, who pronounces the family name
> *To Leave,*

evinces a familiarity with Rilke's tenth *Elegy,* where the family name is Lament, equal to the poet's own.

As Kinnell describes the drunk's death, then, he illustrates the death of part of himself, the self that is the least of it perhaps. But it is "a death out of which one might hope to be reborn more giving, more alive, more related to the natural life" (PPD 74). Thus the language of the old man's leaving the world reformulates Maud's coming into it. Kinnell had described her somersaulting "under / the old lonely bellybutton," "the stream / of omphalos blood humming" all about her, her "stunned flesh" glowing "with the astral violet / of the underlife"; here he scoops up these same images and redeals:

> Violet bruises come out
> all over his flesh, as invisible
> fists start beating him a last time; the whine

> of omphalos blood starts up again, the puffed
> bellybutton explodes, the carnal
> nightmare soars back to the beginning.

The "nightmare soars back to the beginning": once again Kinnell takes *"forty-three giant steps / backwards,"* although here the regression is more explicitly morbid than renewing. *Nightmares* nevertheless pivots on this passage; "if the poem begins with Maud's birth and ends with Fergus's," Nelson writes, "it also offers the old man's death as an image of its center" (86), its *own* omphalos.

Here in the middle of the way, resurrection impends. The drunk's bones, "tossed / into the aceldama back of the potting shop," shall "re-arise / in the pear tree, in spring, to shine down / on two clasping what they dream is one another." Kinnell here foresees the scene of sexual communion with his wife in section 8, although, still mired in the Hotel of Lost Light, he qualifies even that anticipation with the solipsistic suggestion that they only clasp "what they dream is one another." Resurrection, in any case, remains merely imminent, as yet unrealized. The section rounds off, not pointing forward to rebirth, but returning us to the fly's—and the poet's— dilemma: "The foregoing scribed down," Kinnell writes,

> in the absolute spell
> of departure, and by the light
> from the joined hemispheres of the spider's eyes.

Kinnell previously in the poem has alluded to his age (forty-three steps backward) and to "a brother / shipped back burned / from the burning of Asians" (21), but as "In the Hotel" concludes, he extends these temporal references and locates *Nightmares* explicitly in history. The section was "scribed down / in March, of the year Seventy / in my sixteen-thousandth night of war and madness." "In the Hotel" represents the "poem's nadir, its inferno," but only on the personal level. "The Dead Shall Be Raised Incorruptible" broadens the work's concerns to Kinnell's historical moment, to the inferno of Western history as it is typified by the war and madness wrecking Vietnam in the year Seventy. In this sense, sections 5 and 6, taken together, constitute a double nadir, encompassing both the personal and the political.

Just as the old man's death in "In the Hotel," soaring him back to the beginning, anticipated new life, so too "The Dead," as the title (taken from 1 Corinthians) foretells, "Shall Be Raised Incorruptible." Not that these re-arisings are announced with hosannas. By now we understand that Kinnell's resurrections are profoundly secular—worldly, material, endlessly corruptible. Indeed, given the enlarged scale it introduces, it is questionable whether or not "The Dead" *can* merge the way down with the way up. Nelson, for example, thinks the center of *Nightmares* is "an historical weight the poem cannot transcend" (86). Death, in any case, predominates at the section's start. Picking up from "In the Hotel," the first image is a dead body—one, we gather below, still flaming on a battlefield: *"Lieutenant! / This corpse will not stop burning!"* The corpse is presented as so much waste, placed in apposition with "carrion, / caput mortuum [alchemical residue], / orts [fragments of food], / pelf [ill-gotten gain], / fenks [refuse of melted whale blubber], / sordes [filth], / gurry [fish offal] dumped from hospital trashcans."

"The Dead" locates thanatos first in the individual psychology that makes war possible—in Burnsie, an openly deranged permutation of Dickey's firebomber, whose name links him to his burnt victims—and then in "Christian man" in general (a term for "technological man," Kinnell says in *WDS* 98), who speaks the section's central passage, a Villonesque mock-testament where Kinnell broaches the unredeemable demise of human civilization. By its end, the section offers a world devoid even of the technocrat war makers, an earth inhabited only by human remains:

> Membranes,
> effigies pressed into grass,
> mummy windings,
> desquamations,
> sags incinerated mattresses gave back to the world,
> memories left in mirrors on whorehouse ceilings,
> angel's wings
> flagged down into the snows of yesteryear.

Yet, even these do not give up. "It is the membranes, effigies, etc.," Kinnell glosses the passage, "the memories of itself left on the earth by the human race, which is imagined to have destroyed itself, who pray for earthly experience to continue no matter how painful or empty it has become" (*WDS* 109). Echoing Christ's prayer (Matthew 26:42) (and more distantly, what Villon—whose ghost already haunts the section in its mock-testament and the "snows of yesteryear"—says to conclude *The Testament:* "He took a long swig of dead-black wine / As he made his way out of this world"), the membranes and the rest pray,

> do not let this last hour pass,
> do not remove this last, poison cup from our lips.

Countering this holocaust, however, "The Dead" also envisions a provisional resurrection. Once again, even in the aceldama, what is death from one angle is birth from another. At the start, "Orts, / pelf, / fenks" indicate leavings, waste, decay, but the very appearance of these forgotten words represents a linguistic *revival*, a re-emergence from the underlife of the language. About this list of strange words, Kinnell has remarked, "I love it when I run across an archaic word that seems to me terribly expressive, I entertain the possibility of its resurrection."[16] The corpse—of the hotel drunk, a soldier, human civilization—at the center of "The Dead" is also, ironically but ineluctably, a breeding ground from which "a mosquito / sips a last meal" and "the fly, / the last nightmare, hatches itself." Amidst the wreckage, "A few bones / lie about in the smoke of bones," but this image points back at the section's introductory illustration, a kneeling figure above a scattering of bones, taken from Jan Lascinus Therapus's *The New Pearl of Great Price*, where the image represents an allotment of bones before a resurrection. The final lines repeat *"Lieutenant! / This corpse will not stop burning!"* but where at the start *"corpse"* and *"burning"* dominated, by the end, when the fire *still* hasn't consumed itself, the emphasis has shifted to *"will not stop."*

I have suggested that "The Dead," extending to the historical level what "In the Hotel" accomplishes on the personal level, "envisions" a re-arising. But *can* poetic vision gather into itself the nightmare of history? Nelson's thesis is that it cannot. "In the sixth poem, near the center of *The Book of Nightmares*," he writes, Kinnell "opens the book to precisely those historical circumstances it cannot undo" (94): "The language's interconnectedness absorbs all temporal process, seeking to replace history with its own inclusive space. Yet it cannot transform the national history it acknowledges" (95). Its "mythic, archetypal form," thus, "can never wholly surmount its singular American content" (96). Nelson suggests that Kinnell self-consciously exploits this failure: "Following an historical imperative," in "The Dead" Kinnell "deliberately subverts the self-referential perfection of the book's formal development" (94). Burnsie's monologue "is essentially untouched by the verbal matrix of the surrounding poem [section 6], and that is exactly the point," Nelson argues (94), and indeed the point pertains as well to the relationship between "The Dead" and the rest of *Nightmares;* the tapestry of verbal interconnections wears thin in "The Dead" and the book falters, noticeably out of sync with itself.

Nelson implies that the relative weakness of "The Dead" is a poetic inevitability—vision undone by unredeemable history. But, granted that poetry cannot "replace" or "surmount" history, can it not at least *acknowledge* history—even a history characterized by genocide and ethnocide—without thereby coming unraveled? We do not, after all, ask of poetry that it somehow put right the grotesque spectacle of history, although Nelson's verbs imply just such an expectation; vision or poetry or inclusive form cannot, he repeats, "alleviate," "transform," "surmount," "compensate for," "transcend," "replace," "absolve," "undo," "overcome," or "absorb" history. Of course. We might, however, look to poetry to help us *understand* history, to help us *comprehend* what appears, and must partly remain, incomprehensible. It can tell us something about how human beings could have done these terrible things. Anyone who has heard, for example, repentant Vietnam combat veterans try to account for (not "absolve" or "undo") their own participation in burning a country—how they found themselves in circumstances where this was expected, what it felt like, why they sometimes enjoyed it, how they came to rebel, what inner conflict such rebellion ignited—can recognize in these frequently moving testimonies the raw material of one kind of poetry. When a poet "opens the book to precisely those historical circumstances it cannot undo," this need not precipitate the undoing of his vision. On the contrary, insofar as "vision" implies a seeing into, a more inclusive account of the world, an opening to history can keep vision viable. Carolyn Forché's *The Country Between Us* offers a sober, powerful vision successful precisely *because* she opens the book to the as yet unsurmountable circumstances in El Salvador.

Forché's work, however, is essentially reportorial. Her poems disturb and challenge because they *present*. "What you have heard is true" ("The Colonel") runs her theme, and it is a necessary theme. We need shaking up. But if she doesn't "undo" the historical reality she acknowledges, neither does she illuminate how it comes about. And on this score, Kinnell too falls short. "The Dead," where Kinnell explicitly opens the book to history, is a weak (if ambitious) link in the chain of *Nightmares*. He has complained in an interview about war poems which "separate humanity into two camps: we, the 'good people,' poets and lovers; and *they*, Rusk and Johnson, Nixon, and so on, who are killers and therefore a different species."[17] "The great poems about the war," he concludes, "have been those whose outrage never allows the poet to forget that he and Lyndon Johnson are also brothers." *Hypocrite lecteur,—mon semblable,—mon frère!* Discussing James Dickey's "The Firebombing," Kinnell quotes Whitman—"Latent in a great user of words, must be all passions, crimes, trades" (PPD 60)—and although he feels that by resorting to a persona Dickey doesn't truly "explore this region of himself," he does admire Dickey "for exposing the firebomber within himself." In "The Dead," however, Kinnell temporarily abandons his project of transcending the self by digging into it, partly because, as he suggests discussing the poem, of his anger: "I don't think I solved the problem particularly well there—to try to remain identified but at the same time to express outrage."[18] To the extent that in "The Dead" outrage eclipses identification, Kinnell forgets that he and LBJ are brothers, and to that extent Christian man (Kinnell's evasive persona here) appears as a "different species," his last will defused by its irony.

We cannot blame Kinnell for not equaling Villon, who manages to achieve tenderness in his testament without sacrificing wickedness. But we can wish that he had exposed and explored the Christian man in himself or that Burnsie's orgy of killing was personally testified to by the poet himself, not merely quoted (Burnsie's language, quite literally, does not originate in the poem's verbal matrix; Kinnell "copied down that speech nearly verbatim" from a Korean war veteran [*WDS* 110]). The dream idiom of *Nightmares* provides the opportunity to undertake just this kind of exploration, to extend the actual experience without forsaking the personal focus; "The Dead" might have sounded less familiar, less like the anti-technological jeremiads which are "correct" but unmoving. Broadening the implications of the private death in "In the Hotel," "The Dead" admits into the poem the public death contained in American history, but while it cannot, and does not set out to, absorb or transform that history, it might have illuminated, have testified to, the psychological capacity that has made such public death possible.

With "Little Sleep's-Head Sprouting Hair in the Moonlight," the worst of the journey is over. Kinnell, having suffered the nightmares of the previous sections, himself now "ceases to struggle" and lets himself go into kinship, at once glorious and terrible, with the perishable world. Although by absenting himself from the historical nightmare in "The Dead" he skirts an important issue, this does not mitigate the implications of his sacramental vision, and it certainly does not eclipse its beauty or lessen its power. Kinnell and Christian man are brothers, but they are also enemies, and if the poet retains the awareness of his sacred, interdependent relationship with other human beings and the Earth itself, the very absence of which awareness is precisely what allows Christian man to kill his brothers and sisters and destroy his planet—well, we should not fault Kinnell for that. The more (and the more persuasively) this kinship is proclaimed, the better. Christian man exterminates "a whole continent of red men for living in unnatural community / and at the same time having relations with the land"; but when Kinnell, in the face of this extermination, makes up a loving papoose name for Maud, "Little sleep's-head sprouting hair in the moonlight," he doesn't *deny* American history, but rather *affirms* his connectedness to its victims and their values.[19]

As "Little Sleep's-Head" begins, the malign spell of corpses and spiders breaks: "You scream, waking from a nightmare." No longer thrashing about on a dead man's mattress in the Hotel of Lost Light, his own nightmares now suffered through, Kinnell has come home, and he goes to his daughter. His voice, too, has been domesticated, the frequently tortured, floundering, febrile tone giving way to one more consistently elegiac, heavy with tenderness toward existence. Waking from his own nightmare, joining his child, the poet hasn't, of course, put death out of his mind. Indeed, even as his "broken arms heal themselves around" Maud, Kinnell's first thought is that their moments together on earth will soon pass.

Even so, togetherness pervades the section. Maud has told the sun *"don't go down"* and the flower *"don't grow old, / don't die";* poeticizing her diction, Kinnell echoes his daughter's wish:

> I would blow the flame out of your silver cup,
> I would suck the rot from your fingernail,
> I would brush your sprouting hair of the dying light,
> I would scrape the rust off your ivory bones,
> I would help death escape through the little ribs of your body,
> I would alchemize the ashes of your cradle back into wood.

Temporarily abandoning his resolve to "let go," he "would let nothing of you go, ever." And yet, like Maud herself, Kinnell well knows the two of them live "forever / in the pre-trembling of a house that falls," and he tells her, again emphasizing their likeness, "I, like you, only sooner / than you, will go down / the path of vanished alphabets." Extending the likeness, he foresees that "in the year Two Thousand and Nine" (when she is his age, that is) she "will walk out / among the black stones / of the field, in the rain"—

> and the raindrops
> hitting you on the fontanel
> over and over, and you standing there
> unable to let them in.

She will repeat, that is, the opening scene of her father's book (the field, the stones, the rain, the phrase "over and over," the unhouseled estrangement). That is the future. For now, Kinnell reintegrates her into the familial network and stitches together present and past as he sees in his daughter's eye "the hand that waved once / in my father's eyes, a tiny kite / wobbling far up in the twilight of his last look."

Putting her back into her crib at the section's end, Kinnell does finally let Maud go. The nightmares now passed, in her dreams "the hours begin to sing." The conclusion stresses their togetherness and leads to Kinnell's reformulation of St. Paul, a summarizing dictum which resolves the section's intertwined emotions:

Little sleep's-head sprouting hair in the moonlight,
when I come back
we will go out together,
we will walk out together among
the ten thousand things,
each scratched too late with such knowledge, *the wages
of dying is love.*[20]

En route to this resolution Kinnell has given Maud some revealing advice. As I pointed out earlier, he here apotheosizes the present. Again, this isn't a rejection of history or time but rather a re-
affirmation of tenderness toward existence, the absence of which is
one definition of the horror with which history confronts us. "If
one day it happens / you find yourself with someone you love," he
tells her, "and if you commit then, as we did, the error / of thinking, / *one day all this will only be memory,*" he goes on, then
"learn to reach deeper / into the sorrows / to come":

Kiss

the mouth
which tells you, *here,*
*here is the world.* This mouth. This laughter. These temple
    bones.

The still undanced cadence of vanishing.

The final sentence of this passage, Kinnell's response to the knowledge that the wages of dying is love, is itself undanced, incomplete,
fragmentary. Yet "still" suggests the doubleness of time in *Nightmares*. It means, on the one hand, "as yet": the cadence of vanishing, it implies, will soon enough be danced. But it also means "always": the cadence will never be danced out, the present lived
intensely partakes of eternity, time is conquered through time. The
oath between flesh and spirit is broken over and over, and over and
over it is sworn again.

"Little Sleep's-Head" is the most limpid, most lyrical of the
*Nightmares*. It has a tonal purity and simplicity commensurate
with its theme, a father's love for his young child. But what about a
husband's love for his wife? This is not so simple. "The Call Across
the Valley of Not-Knowing" addresses sexual love, and here the

language thickens, takes on body, its texture more crosshatched. Fulfillment is possible but intermittent; the call across the valley may be answered, but we must renew it again and again.

The section opens with another domestic scene, the poet lying by his sleeping and pregnant wife (Fergus makes his first, fetal appearance here). The scene suggests completion, but at the same time the two are "mismatched halfnesses" and his wife is "far away, in some other, / newly opened room of the world." Kinnell thinks of Aristophanes' nightmare:

> that each of us
> is a torn half
> whose lost other we keep seeking across time
> until we die, or give up—
> or actually find her.

Kinnell *had* found his lost other in an airplane once, heading to Waterloo, Iowa, but, because of "all which goes by the name 'necessity,'" left her. And, indeed, this separated condition is what allows us our earthly experience of love, momentary and tragic as it is:

> And yet I think
> it must be the wound, the wound itself,
> which lets us know and love,
> which forces us to reach out to our misfit
> and by a kind
> of poetry of the soul, accomplish,
> for a moment, the wholeness the drunk Greek
> extrapolated from his high
> or flagellated out of an empty heart,
>
> that purest,
> most tragic concumbence, strangers
> clasped into one, a moment, of their moment on earth.

Kinnell thus offers two verbally interlinked but contrasting climaxes, the first with his "mismatched halfness" (his wife), the second with his true "lost other" (the "woman of Waterloo"). In both, the poet and the woman "lay out together," concumbent under a tree or on the grass, and accomplish some sort of wholeness. But the second scene results in a diminution of sensual experience, a withdrawal from earthly life; had he lain out with the Waterloo woman, he thinks,

> I might have closed my eyes, and moved
> from then on like the born blind,
> their faces
> gone into heaven already.

Kinnell's concumbence with his "misfit," on the other hand, results in the *extension* of the senses; it is an opening to the world, not a withdrawal. Love here doesn't transcend earthly life but is rather the agent of our belonging (thus the scene echoes sections 5 and 6 of "Song of Myself"). As it unifies, for at least the moment, self and world, brain and body, male and female, the scene is the visionary climax of *Nightmares*, the (only temporarily realized) goal of the poem's journey:

> we two
> lay out together
> under the tree, on earth, beside our empty clothes,
> our bodies opened to the sky,
>
> .  .  .  .  .  .  .  .  .  .  .  .  .  .  .  .  .  .  .  .  .  .
>
> And the brain kept blossoming
> all through the body, until the bones themselves could think,
> and the genitals sent out wave after wave of holy desire
> until even the dead brain cells
> surged and fell in god-like, androgynous fantasies—
> and I understood
> the unicorn's phallus could have risen, after all,
> directly out of thought itself.

Between the two concumbences, Kinnell includes a scene which extends the sacramental union beyond the condition of sexual love. What he remembered most about being fingerprinted by a sheriff in a Southern jail "was the care, the almost loving, / animal gentleness of his hand on my hand." Sympathy here joins enemies as well as lovers. In yet one more passage conflating regression to the beginning of life with the moment of leaving it, the sheriff too is incorporated (or lets himself go) into the unifying element beyond our reach:

> And when he himself floats out
> on a sea he almost begins to remember,
> floats out into a darkness he has known already;
> when the moan of wind
> and the gasp of lungs call to each other among the waves
> and the wish to float
> comes to matter not at all as he sinks under,
>
> is it so impossible to think
> he will dream back to all the hands black and white
> he took in his hands
> as the creation
> touches him a last time all over his body?

*Nightmares* might have ended with "The Call," the journey more or less complete, but the conclusion would have been perhaps too upbeat—gaiety insufficiently tempered with tragedy. In sections 9 and 10 Kinnell, no longer located domestically, spirals back to the landscapes of the earlier sections—in the first words of section 9, he is back "On the path"—but his wandering now is informed by what he has learned. The sense of belonging he has discovered is now tested against the undomesticated condition of an ancient battlefield. With its thick layering of verbal echoes from the previous sections, the landscape of "The Path Among the Stones" seems to encapsulate the history of the whole poem. Indeed, in the image of the "wafer-stone / which skipped ten times across / the water," leaving "zeroes . . . that met / and passed into each other," the landscape figures the very structure of the volume, its ten sections merging into one another like ripples on the water.

Amidst this landscape, the poet recapitulates the journey, down and up, already inscribed in the first eight sections. First,

> A way opens
> at my feet. I go down
> the night-lighted mule-steps into the earth.

This descent into the abandoned coal mine ("goaf"—another linguistic resurrection) is, given the poem's conflation of man and planet, a dig into the self: the "pre-sacrificial trills / of canaries" link the mine shaft to the poet's body, in which "the canaries of the blood are singing" (59); going down the goaf is a confrontation with "everything I ever craved and lost." These craved and lost things refer us to the Waterloo woman, or the "more perfect state" she represents in the poem, an "other dimension of happiness."[21] Plumbing the self, he unearths this lech for transcendence. "The narrator," Kinnell explains, "has gone down into the earth and found an old man trying to perform some kind of alchemical transformation, or transcendence." The old man (trying to transcend time, surmount history, live forever) salts down his witches' brew "with sand / stolen from the upper bells of hourglasses"—with grains, that is, which will never reach the lower bells, moments that will never pass. Kinnell, however, leaves his perfect "lost other"; the old man's alchemy amounts to

> Nothing.
> Always nothing. Ordinary blood
> boiling away in the glare of the brow lamp.

The poet has reached "a decision to remain in and happily accept the imperfect condition." Not the heaven of perfect lost others, but the earth of mismatched halfnesses. Just as his concumbence with his misfit had occasioned his climactic reunion with the dying world, now, accepting "the imperfect condition," he ascends to ground level, aware of the "sympathetic and permanent linking of my life and the life of all things on earth":

> And yet, no,
> perhaps not nothing. Perhaps
> not ever nothing. In clothes
> woven out of the blue spittle
> of snakes, I crawl up: I find myself alive
> in t ie whorled
> archway of the fingerprint of all things,
> skeleton groaning,
> blood-strings wailing the wail of all things.

About his interpretation of this passage Kinnell observes, "it's curious how sometimes very little of what one intends actually gets into the explicit content, that content which is available to readers." And yet, the "sympathetic linking" seems unambiguous. The "whorled / archway of the fingerprint of all things" points back to the "whorls and tented archways" of Kinnell's own fingerprint

(59); world and poet *both* leave fingerprints. A fingerprint itself is a collective of *discrete* markings, signifying *identity*. Moreover, the imagery of the passage suggests that the poet's ascent here is a literal re*birth*. The blueness of his clothes connects the scene to previous ones of birth, and their fabrication from the "spittle of snakes" suggests his kinship with even lowly forms of life and his primitive but vital state of being. Like an emerging infant, he "crawl[s] up" and finds himself alive "in the whorled / archway" (in a threshold, an entrance) or, as the pun (effected by the line break) implies, "in the world." The death in section 5, recapitulated in the fruitlessness of the old man's alchemical scheming to avert death, is now seen literally as "a death out of which one might hope to be reborn more giving, more alive, more related to the natural life" (PPD 74). His own sounds, his "skeleton groaning" (he is linked as well here to the birth-giver), now echo the sounds of the cosmos as his newly reborn body becomes an Eolian harp, "blood-strings wailing the wail of all things."

This identity of the human and the cosmic is figured, at the conclusion of "The Path," in Kinnell's elaboration of Hermes Trismegistus's precept:

> As above: the last scattered stars
> kneel down in the star-form of the Aquarian age:
> a splash
> on the top of the head,
> on the grass of this earth even the stars love, splashes of the
> sacred waters . . .
>
> So below: in the graveyard
> the lamps start lighting up, one for each of us,
> in all the windows
> of stone.

I have discussed earlier the centrality of this equation in *Nightmares*, but notice here how the passage verbally demonstrates itself. As the stars, *above*, kneel *down*, so in the graveyard, *below*, the lamps light *up*; "the top of the head" and "the grass of this earth" are syntactically and linearly equivalent. Indeed, the interplay between above and below has operated throughout the volume, most extensively perhaps in the battlefield landscape of this very section. Just as in Kinnell's formula a raindrop splashes down to "this earth even the stars love" (one thinks of Rilke's Angel, astonished by terrestrial things), so each stone in the field sends up a "ghost-bloom" which seeks "to be one / with the unearthly fires kindling and dying" (the stars) but which we see inevitably "falling back, knowing / the sadness of the wish / to alight" (66). Within the section's first few lines "the path winding / upward, toward the high valley" is balanced by the downward plunging "waterfalls" there; vipers may have "urges to fly," but they "drape the black stones." The landscapes in this section, Nelson observes, "call up the elemental underlife of the earth and draw us near to the movements of the constellations" (83), positioning above and below on the same verbal field. And since Hermes' equation refers to the identity, not just of heaven and earth, but of self and world (or, as Emerson puts it, "Within and Above are synonyms"), the landscapes, as Nelson again interprets, "are composed in a verbal territory neither exclusively internal nor external," and he aptly quotes Kinnell's view here that "when you do get deep enough within yourself, deeper than the level of 'personality,' you are suddenly outside yourself, everywhere." (PPD 65–66)

At the end of "The Book of Ephraim," James Merrill sees "the stars have wound in filigree / The ancient, ageless woman of the world." This woman wound in the sky is one avatar of Rosamund Smith, the earth mother, the earth itself; like Kinnell's sequence, Merrill's draws together above and below. "Ephraim," like *Nightmares*, poetically embodies this interdependence as each individual part is structurally linked to the whole, as one character turns into another and all turn into the ageless Mrs. Smith, she with the commonest of names, who after all "is not particular" ("Z"). Merrill and Kinnell even arrive at equivalent images of Immanence, of heaven's dependence on, and presence in, the earth. In "The Path," as we have seen, the stars splash down water to the earth they love, while in "Q" Ephraim (from heaven) tells JM: "AT LAST DEVOTION WITH THE COMBINED FORCES OF FALLING & WEARING WATER PREPARES A HIGHER MORE FINISHED WORLD OF HEAVEN THESE DEVOTIONAL POWERS ARE AS A FALL OF WATERS PUSHED FROM BEHIND OVER THE CLIFF OF EVEN MY EXPERIENCE." "I HAVE

BUILT THIS HIGH LOOKOUT BUT FIND," Ephraim adds, "I AM
WISEST WHEN I LOOK STRAIGHT DOWN AT THE PRECIOUS GROUND I
KNEW."
Merrill finishes his poem with a vision of Mrs. Smith wound in
the stars, and we might also expect Kinnell's like-minded vision,
"As above . . . So below," to conclude his. But "Ephraim" first ap-
peared as one of Merrill's *Divine Comedies*. There *are* gaps in its
unifying verbal texture—black holes into which time is elided,
"CYSTS IN THE TISSUE OF ETERNITY" ("P")—but the outlook is essentially comic. Time passes, but by the end "nothing's gone," or at
least "nothing we recall." "Nothing's lost," Merrill writes earlier in
*Divine Comedies*, "Or else: all is translation / And every bit of us is
lost in it"; but "in that loss a self-effacing tree, / . . . turns the waste /
To shade and fiber, milk and memory" ("Lost in Translation"). In
*Nightmares*, a work of less sanguine temperament, waste remains
waste—carrion, orts, sordes, gurry—but is also turned to the
physical breeding ground of more life. If every bit of us is lost in
the translation of our life into another's, this provokes grief as well
as inspiring trust. Mrs. Smith "is not particular"; but identity resides "in particular flesh" for Kinnell, and the specific incarnations
of those we love *are* lost, translation or no: "in the graveyard / the
lamps start lighting up, one for each of us." *Nightmares* concludes,
thus, not with the relatively comic formula at the end of "The
Path," but with the prospect of the poet's own particular demise.
   "Lastness" spirals back to the opening landscape of the book.
The same "small fire," which we understand now is the poem itself, "goes on flaring in the rain." In "Maud Moon" Kinnell lit this
fire "for her, / whose face / I held in my hands / a few hours," but

> No matter, now, whom it was built for,
> it keeps its flames,
> it warms
> everyone who might wander into its radiance,
> a tree, a lost animal, the stones,
>
> because in the dying world it was set burning.

The same black bear sits alone, "nodding from side / to side," but
when a no-longer-estranged poet rewrites the scene—having con-

firmed his own relationship to the land, having discovered he lives
*"under the Sign / of the Bear"* (22–23)—he is now a participant.
Indeed, man and bear can no longer quite be told apart: the bear

>        sniffs the sweat
> in the breeze, he understands
> a creature, a death-creature
> watches from the fringe of the trees,
> finally he understands
> I am no longer here, he himself
> from the fringe of the trees watches
> a black bear
> get up, eat a few flowers, trudge away,
> all his fur glistening
> in the rain.

He is a participant, too, in the birth scene (Fergus's), which balances the opening one. The poet had been observer at his daughter's birth, but having let go, he is now front and center, "empty
space" incarnate, directly implicated in the natural life:

> When he came wholly forth
> I took him up in my hands and bent
> over and smelled
> the black, glistening fur
> of his head, as empty space
> must have bent
> over the newborn planet
> and smelled the grasslands and the ferns.

One feels occasionally perhaps Kinnell is *too* front and center.
We cannot take exception to Kinnell's intentions, Richard Howard
observes, "without simultaneously opposing motherhood (though
Kinnell, in his exaltation of fatherhood, might be said to do just
that)" (317). The absence of reference to the mother in the birth
scenes is striking. In "Ephraim," Merrill acknowledges "the absence from these pages / Of my own mother" but explains "of
course she's here / Throughout, the breath drawn after every line, /
Essential to its making as to mine" ("X"); Kinnell seems less aware
of troubling absences in his work.

Kinnell's bending over Fergus rivals his lying under a tree with his wife as the most self-extensive moment of *Nightmares*. But, like that earlier epiphany, it is presented as a memory. When "Lastness" returns to the present tense, it is to consider the death for which these moments of love are wages. The infant Archer sucked "the icy biestings of the cosmos" in "Maud Moon," but now there is a "hole torn open in the body of the Archer." As the poet approaches an "echoing / cliffside," he senses "the line / where the voice calling from stone / no longer answers, / turns into stone, and nothing comes back"—senses, that is, the point of no return. He stands "between answer / and nothing" (echoing Eliot's "The Hollow Men"), between life and death. No longer unhoused, he knows communion, but this sacrament is figured in

> the bones
> which ripple together in the communion
> of the step,
> and which open out
> in front into toes, the whole foot trying
> to dissolve into the future.

Communion consists, that is, in the very process of journeying, in motion itself, in following the road to the point "between answer / and nothing," to the brink of dissolution. The journey, in other words, has come to its end:

> Stop.
> Stop here.
> Living brings you to death, there is no other road.

Or rather, it has reached the point where life passes into the Rilkean extended whole, where life itself finds its "lost other," a point beyond which it can no longer be written about. The text must "Stop here," but it gestures beyond itself into the unsayable:

> It is right
> at the last, that one
> and zero
> walk off together,
> walk off the end of these pages together,
> one creature
> walking away side by side with the emptiness.

It is at this juncture, then, that dissolution is figured not as a going beyond but as a return. Throughout *Nightmares,* the extinction of identity has been simultaneous with regression to an undifferentiated, fertile blank, the "blank template" of "The Porcupine," all matter and no form; here these instances are generalized:

> the dead lie,
> empty, filled, at the beginning,
>
> and the first
> voice comes craving again out of their mouths.

*Nightmares* ends, or almost does, with three representations of itself, two of them concerts. The poem, like the contrapuntal music at "That Bach concert," keeps in play disparate and simultaneous strains, suspending conflicting desires in a single solution. The violin sounding "the wail, / the sexual wail / of the back-alleys and blood strings we have lived" is like the poet, his "blood strings wailing the wail of all things" (68). More explicitly, Kinnell calls the poem a "concert of one / divided among himself." "Each creature or thing you write about," he explains, "brings out some aspect of yourself . . . and all together make up the 'concert'";[22] the self, like the poem and the poem's world, is single *and* multiple. As he relinquishes alchemical transcendence in "The Path" and, *ascending* to ground level, comes home, so he lets himself *fall* to earth here at the end:

> this earthward gesture
> of the sky-diver, the worms
> on his back still spinning forth
> and already gnawing away
> the silks of his loves, who could have saved him,
> this free floating of one
> opening his arms into the attitude
> of flight, as he obeys the necessity and falls . . .

In the course of the book Kinnell emerges from the underlife, sends up a "ghost-bloom / into the starlight," floats out "over the trees, seeking to be one / with the unearthly fires," only "to alight / back among the glitter of bruised ground" (66); inscribing the same curve, his sentences typically rear up, extend themselves in subtle syntactic flights, fly off into new associations, but eventually, fulfilling their periodicity, arc back to their point of departure. But because the syntactic action here coincides with the semantic sense, the summarizing sentence about the sky diver never does return to itself; the point at which the falling body thuds down is the point beyond which language may gesture but cannot reach.

In "Dear Stranger" Kinnell recalls flinging up the body of a hen,

> And then the wait—
>
> not long, I grant, but all my life—
> for the small, soft
> thud of her return among the stones.

Life brief as free fall, life *as* free fall—Kinnell now plays the metaphor over his own body. Inevitably, the last image in *Nightmares* is the poet's corpse:

> Sancho Fergus! Don't cry!
>
> Or else, cry.
>
> On the body,
> on the blued flesh, when it is
> laid out, see if you can find
> the one flea which is laughing.

Holding together weeping and laughter, tragically gay, the conclusion summarizes Kinnell's ambivalence about death, "the extinction, which we fear, and the flowing away into the universe, which we desire" (*WDS* 23). After the incantatory sweeps of language that characterize the volume, in this final subsection (almost the book's shortest) the voice attenuates, the passion bleeds out, the lines refuse to lengthen. And yet the passage remains resolutely focused on the physical world. This is the moment after the end, but it points us back to life; "Lastness," Kinnell remarks, was written "imagining the heightened feeling she would have for the world when she left it" (*WDS* 23). "She" is Emily Dickinson, whose buzzing fly prefigures Kinnell's laughing flea. His reading of her poem is likewise a commentary on the end of the road of his own: "Of course, it is repulsive that a fly come to you if you are dying and if it may be a corpse fly, its thorax the hysterical green color of slime. And yet in the illumination of the dying moment, everything the poet knew is transfigured. The fly appears, physical, voracious, a last vital sign. The most ordinary thing, the most despised, may be the one chosen to bear the strange brightening, this last moment of increased life" (PPW 120).

## IV

Thus concludes the motion, the journey of *Nightmares*. But, as I have suggested, like *Four Quartets,* Kinnell's poem "Moves perpetually in its stillness." "Long poems are made out of time," as he has observed, but this is only half the story: "The strength of the long poem is its capacity to show an experience in its stages. Therefore time is an essential part of it. And yet because a long poem can bring a series of experiences to a climax, and transfigure them, it also, in its own way, can transcend time" (*WDS* 53). *Nightmares* unfolds in time along the narrative line I have traced, but because of the highly wrought system of verbal interconnectedness, it seems to happen all at once. The resultant interplay—between eternity and time, unity and multeity, communal spirit and particular flesh—is the true subject of the book. And it also forms the basis of its prosody—the unity of the long, overarching sentences playing against the particularity of the unpredictable, distinct lines; one keeps turning into many, the many keep resolving back into the one, and the poem is thereby drawn in opposing directions simultaneously. Kinnell might have gone back to Whitman for his epigraph:

> Let me glide noiselessly forth;
> With the key of softness unlock the locks—with a whisper,
> Set ope the doors O soul.
>
> Tenderly—be not impatient,
> (Strong is your hold O mortal flesh,
> Strong is your hold O love.)
>
>             ("The Last Invocation")

Or more simply: "Always a knit of identity, always distinction" (SM 3). Kinnell speaks of wanting "to bring from the central core of the poem a sort of light onto—well I could say onto any subject whatever. . . . . This light would bind each unconnected thing into the wholeness of the poem" (*WDS* 25–26).

This binding light is neither particle nor wave, but language. *Nightmares* coheres by its words; each part repeats and presses on every other, as if a single poetic impulse were being incessantly re-written, as if the same verbal dice—the same collection of words and images, rhythms and motifs—were cast and gathered up and cast again, over and over (just as "the oath sworn between earth and water, flesh and spirit" is alternately sworn and broken). The "unity" of any poem resides in its language, of course, but what distinguishes *Nightmares* is the closeness and obsessiveness of its verbal weave, the centripetal force of the sheer number and concentration of verbal interlinkings. As in a dream, each single element seems aware of and co-present with all the others; everything being foreknown and almost forgiven in advance, no explanations are necessary.

Cary Nelson performs a telling analysis of the way *Nightmares* is stitched together primarily by its words. He surveys the "verbal ground" (78) of the poem and partially itemizes the "covert verbal matrix" (79) (what I have called the "verbal dice" and Kinnell the binding "light") out of which it is composed: "His recurrent terms—death, emptiness, flowers, darkness, and light—are interwoven with images of blood, bone, and stone. This verbal tapestry is linked to a number of motifs introduced in the poem's separate narratives, such as the hen's death, the old man's shoes, and the births of his children. The result is a matrix of repetition and variation, in which the narratives of the ten individual sections begin to lose their identity through their relationship to the poem's larger form" (77). To illustrate one feature of this matrix, Nelson delineates "the pervasive binarism of Kinnell's language" (77): "the 'long rustle / of being and perishing' (7)," the "'unearthly fires kindling and dying' (66)," the poet himself "'dumped alive / and dying' (14) into his bed"—Nelson could have traced such typical couplings down to the final lines, "Don't cry! / Or else, cry." "Renewal and extinction are linked as always by the temporal process that extends from one to the other. In moments of change, ends and origins come together," Nelson argues (77), and thus "Kinnell's binarism is unstable and reversable" and—this is the key—he "wants to make the opposite terms of polarities coalesce" (77–78). Nelson details, for example, how the vocabulary that Kinnell introduces in "Maud Moon" suggests associations which subsequent appearances "both reinforce and invert" (78). The first appearances of the verb "to suck" in relation to Maud's birth, for instance, are affirmative, but, Nelson notes, soon the range of connotation widens: "soon we read of 'the sucked / carcass' of a hen," and later the poet "wills his twentieth-century brain to the fly, 'that he may suck on it and die' (43)." As in the repeated permutations of other words and images, "eventually any use of the word implies all its meanings; none are exclusively positive or negative." "Kinnell would demonstrate," that is, "that language coheres beneath a surface of differences" (79).

For writers like Merwin and Beckett, Nelson accurately claims, a "covert verbal matrix sets conclusive limits to everything we can say. Language for them is a tool whose use and function are predetermined" (79), and thus "they see language as either ironic or suffocating" (80). "Kinnell reacts differently to the same data," however; "for him, as for Whitman and Duncan, the celebration of the warp and weft of words is intrinsically liberating" (80). A matrix, after all, both substantiates and contains; it is "that which gives origin or form to a thing," the dictionary tells us, as well as that "which serves to enclose it." If Kinnell celebrates "the warp and weft of words," if language for him is renewing, he also knows that renewal cannot be teased away from extinction, even on this verbal level. "His Whitmanesque democritization of language does . . . infuse a strain of melancholy into his poetry," as Nelson observes, though I think his sadness traces as much to the constraints set by the life-giving matrix as to America's "dubious public achievements" (80), to which Nelson connects it.

Insofar as language is liberating for Kinnell, he departs "from the modernist revulsion with language as the foremost evidence that human thought degenerates into materiality" (80). As I suggested earlier, he inverts Eliot's preference for the Word over the word: the poetry *does* matter. "Kinnell's poetic," Nelson goes on, "travels the same hierarchy as the modernists in reverse. Like Norman O. Brown, he believes language can redeem the body by elevating it to consciousness. Language and consciousness can come into their own full power only by occupying the territory of the physical world" (80). At the book's climax, the poet understands "the unicorn's phallus could have risen, after all, / directly out of thought itself."

At the beginning of this chapter I followed up a few of the poem's verbal threads, and in passing I have pointed to many other strands in the verbal fabric. But the extreme closeness of the knit in *Nightmares* is difficult to illustrate. Almost every passage links up to several others, and upon each re-reading one discovers new connections. Because this pattern of recurrence draws together disparate and often contradictory single instances, it renders these instances analogous to "the bones / which ripple together in the communion / of the step" (73). This self-referential image itself completes one of the more obvious verbal filaments in the poem: Kinnell continually returns to images related to shoes and feet (not only because he tramps a journey but also because the lowly foot is the point of contact with the earth). From the pattern of "The Shoes of Wandering," the image intertwines into the other sections. Anticipating the end of the journey, Kinnell writes, "'I painted my footsoles purple for the day when the beautiful color would show'" (36) (i.e., when he is flat on his back). When he temporarily leaves the road for home, we see "a shoe of dreaming iron nailed to the wall" (57), and when he thinks of "the roadlessness" (50), Maud's arms become "like the shoes left behind" (51). Such simple designs, however, suggest more complex embroideries. In "The Shoes" Kinnell asks:

> Is it the foot,
> which rubs the cobblestones
> and snakestones all its days, this lowliest
> of tongues, whose lick-tracks tell
> our history of errors to the dust behind,
> which is the last trace in us
> of wings?

Later, he quietly recombines many of these verbal elements:

> A way opens
> at my feet. I go down
> the night-lighted mule-steps into the earth,
> the footprints behind me

filling already with pre-sacrificial trills
of canaries, go down
into the unbreathable goaf
of everything I ever craved and lost.[23]

(67)

The rewriting overtly changes the subject, but under the surface the language stitches the passages together. "Is it the foot" echoes in "at my feet"; "lick-tracks" reaches toward "footprints"; the "history of errors" calls across to "everything I ever craved and lost"; even "wings" anticipates "canaries." This semantic stitching, moreover, is adumbrated by a syllabic one; each of the first five lines in one passage contains an identical number of syllables as its counterpart in the other (4, 6, 10, 6, 12), and the sixth lines differ only by one (7/6).

More than a rewriting of the first, the second passage in turn puts out feelers in several other directions. The trilling canaries, for example, look back to "the canaries of the blood" (59): the later group of birds trills below the surface of the earth and the self, while the earlier sings in the "underlife"; the later are associated with footprints, the earlier with "the whorls / and tented archways" of a fingerprint. Even as they look back, however, the "pre-sacrificial trills / of canaries" simultaneously send us forward to "the legends of blood sacrifice" (68). To take another example, the "unbreathable goaf" (old coal mine) recalls the early scene where "as they cut / her tie to the darkness" Maud "turns blue as a coal" (6), not only because of the comparison to anthracite, but also because the baby turns blue for the very reason that, the cord cut, the world *is* momentarily "unbreathable."

The forkings proliferate rapidly, but let us make our way back to shoes and feet. The momentarily coal-blue Maud sucks in her first breath only "When / they hold her up by the feet" (6). This life-starting example is later reversed by the destruction implied in the "hoof-shattered / meadows" (65). And even the vipers in these meadows get into the act as, undercutting their "urges to fly," they hiss out their pun, *"pheet! pheet!"* Although the instances of shoes and feet express a range of meanings, eventually they all come to imply one another. It is in this sense that the poem happens all at once, that it both depends upon and transfigures time. Again, even as the single instances retain their identity, they compose a whole, just as the individual bones function jointly in the step:

> Here, between answer
> and nothing, I stand, in the old shoes
> flowed over by rainbows of hen-oil,
> each shoe holding the bones
> which ripple together in the communion
> of the step.
>
> (73)

This culminating instance, however, isn't the final one. As if to extend the meditation on his foot beyond himself, after this passage Kinnell briefly returns us to the landscape: "A clatter of elk hooves." As each instance implies every other and, thus, the network of which it is a part, so the human inevitably implies its own contextualization in the natural world.

Indeed, the interdependent system of the natural world vies with the fragmenting condition of human history for the primary context in which *Nightmares* will locate itself. Or, rather, the poem locates itself in *both* space (nature) and time (history). Discussing *Nightmares*, Howard claims that Kinnell "does not give much heed to the past, for is there not the future?" and observes, "he is forever opening up, and so what is left behind, untended, tends to assume a charred and neglected aspect" (317). But with the advent of parenthood, history presses on Kinnell in a way it hadn't before. Just as a dream rehearses events from the dreamer's infancy as well as the present, *Nightmares* consistently has one eye on the past—personal, poetic, and public. This backward-glancing tendency is evident right from the outset where Kinnell, by an old fire, thinks of tramps who have squatted down before him. His journey, indeed, can only begin when he dons his "eldershoes," shoes of a dead stranger, which themselves face him back to his origin (*"take / forty-three giant steps / backwards"*) even as they lead him on. As I have suggested, much of the poem's material, even when hallucinatory, is highly personal; everywhere "memory reaches out / and lays bloody hands on the future" (21).

Paralleling the incorporation of his personal history is Kinnell's inclusion of his poetic one. Not only does he "rescue" old words— "orts," "pelf," and so on—but his forays into originality often overtly depend on a verbal given. Marjorie Perloff complains about Kinnell's use of "cumbersome coinages like 'halfnesses,' 'night-mared,' or 'biopsied,'"[24] but if the strategy is less successful in some instances than others, it nonetheless reveals Kinnell's careful attention to his linguistic inheritance, since a coinage calls as much attention to the "old" verbal elements as to the "new" way of com-bining them, to recounting as to invention. Of course, poets can work only with the existing language, but Kinnell's interest in re-vivifying lost words and in coinages suggests a more pointed his-torical awareness than he has displayed before. So too does what Alan Helms calls Kinnell's "revised borrowings" (*"the wages / of dying is love,"* etc.), which function as coinages raised to the sen-tence level.[25] Indeed, in the way the volume keeps rewriting the same material, it consists largely of revised borrowings from itself.

Kinnell's most obvious acknowledgment of the poetic past, how-ever, is his incorporation of various literary ancestors. He has never been an overly allusive writer, but in *Nightmares* we do hear clear echoes of Rilke, Eliot, Villon, and others. The conclusion of "Maud Moon," to take one example, seems rooted in the end of "Tintern Abbey," as I have suggested. Or, to take another instance, the sex-ual union of brain and body that Kinnell experiences lying with his wife "on the grass of the knowledge / of graves" (59) harks back to the erotic scene between Whitman and his soul as he loafs on the grass in "Song of Myself," section 5. More directly, just as he res-cues lost words and coins new ones, Kinnell tries to effect an even larger scale "coinage," to revivify, or reinterpret from a modern perspective, the mock-testament genre of Villon's *The Testament,* which, according to Kinnell, itself turns the convention of the me-dieval comic genre to new, more serious ends (xv).

This modern perspective assumes an awareness of the troubling record of "technological man." Howard's claim that Kinnell leaves the past untended is most pointedly belied by the poem's concern with the Vietnam War and the historical reality it typifies:

> In the Twentieth Century of my trespass on earth,
> having exterminated one billion heathens,
> heretics, Jews, Moslems, witches, mystical seekers,
> black men, Asians, and Christian brothers,
> every one of them for his own good,

> a whole continent of red men for living in unnatural community
> and at the same time having relations with the land,
> one billion species of animals for being sub-human,
> and ready to take on the bloodthirsty creatures from the other
>     planets,
> I, Christian man, groan out this testament of my last will.
>
> (42)

But what is the relationship between the cohesion figured by the language of *Nightmares* and the violence of the history it acknowledges? This is, finally, Nelson's central concern. He argues that "in the verbal connectiveness of *The Book of Nightmares* we are to see . . . a collective life that compensates for a unity the nation has never achieved" (81) or, rather, that *wants* to compensate but cannot: "The verbal apotheosis of *The Book of Nightmares* is also its failure" (96). His reading of the poem is shaped by a provocative thesis that the political reality of the Vietnam War undermines, or at least severely compromises, the possibilities of writing about it; the most successful attempts are the most precarious, are those "whose forms cling tenaciously to their own dissolution" (30). But as the verbs I listed earlier demonstrate, Nelson's assumption remains that *compensation* is the issue: Kinnell means the collective life of his language to "absolve" (etc.) history, or at least Kinnell plays off of its inability to do so.

The implication of Nelson's argument is that the commonality figured in Kinnell's plexed artistry is falsified by the historical reality it broaches, that it remains merely an impotent verbal construct. "The dream [that "language can overcome history"], however often thwarted, persists," Nelson writes (80), but this begs the question. If Kinnell means to "overcome history," his vision *must* remain a dogged but endlessly thwarted dream. But if his intention is rather merely to evince in language the interdependence of all parts of the planet, then his "dream" is no dream at all, but a persuasive and timely testimony to a *reality* that Christian man has tragically repressed. The ripples of similitude set off by the splash of "As above, so below" do not stop at the margins of the page; just as the microcosm of "The Path Among the Stones" mirrors the macrocosm of the entire poem, the entire poem, in its verbal cohesiveness, suggests the world beyond the text.

If, in a political sense, it is all too true that, as Nelson claims, this is "a unity the nation has never achieved," in another sense this unity isn't a matter of achievement at all. It is the condition, recognized or not, of our existence on earth. Kinnell never slights identity, but what distinguishes the self need not entrap it. Emerson's Oversoul is inverted in Kinnell's "underlife" (as over, so under), but both terms imply an a priori commonality—one that, in Kinnell anyway (as in Whitman, if not Emerson), derives from our existence as physical beings:

> The "nature poem" as opposed to, say, the poem of society or the urban poem, doesn't have much future—and not much past, for that matter—we have to get over the notion we carry from the Old Testament on down that we are super beings created in God's image to have dominion over everything else—over "nature." We have to feel our own evolutionary roots, and know that we belong to life in the same way as do the other animals and the plants and stones. . . . The real nature poem will not exclude man and deal only with animals and plants and stones; it will be a poem in which we men re-feel in ourselves our own animal and plant and stone life, our own deep connection with all other beings, a connection deeper than personality.[26]

This is not a rehashing of a tired Transcendentalism, or a dreamy refusal of the obvious fact that life is never quite as well-connected as language, or the controversial claim of some hipped-out biological visionary. It is not controversial in the least. It is merely a reminder of the basic tenets of ecological science (which have their analogues in modern physics). *Nightmares* acknowledges Christian man's historical denial of these facts, not in order to overcome history, but to remind us that the web of life, although strong, is not invulnerable; obviously, we can put an end to human life on earth.

Kinnell does not set out to put things right. His poem, rather, verbally re-enacts a vision out of which things might be put right. It is not a compensation for history, but a protest against it, a possible stay against our vanishing.[27] Historical events *may* abrogate this vision, and if the poem considers this possibility, well, we haven't quite yet destroyed ourselves. And even if we do, we cannot undo the communal life that once was; "no matter what fire we invent to destroy us," Kinnell writes in his next book, "ours will have been the brightest world ever existing" ("The Last Hiding Places of Snow").

## CHAPTER 5

# The Brightest World:
## *Mortal Acts, Mortal Words*

I

Cosmic in scope, obsessive in execution, *The Book of Nightmares* clearly drew forth from Kinnell everything he at the time had to give. We cannot easily imagine the "blued flesh" of the final page stirring again, uttering yet another volley of words. Had Kinnell written himself into the corner he had flirted with at the end of *Flower Herding on Mount Monadnock?* "I thought of that poem [*Nightmares*] as one in which I could say everything that I knew or felt. . . . I didn't want to let that poem go. I felt I could spend the rest of my life writing it—revising and perfecting it. So I held on to it. Eventually I had to force myself to get rid of it, though I knew I would feel an unsettling emptiness for a long time afterward" (*WDS* 31). The urge to revise and perfect, the alchemical obsessiveness—paradoxically, *Nightmares* sets out explicitly to renounce these very drives, to subvert the compositional energies that produced it. Kinnell "didn't want to let that poem go," but the poem pointedly enjoins him to do just that; his self-commandment, "Listen Kinnell . . . let go" (15), initiates the struggle, and his final surrender culminates it, "as he obeys the necessity and falls . . ." (75). Cary Nelson concludes that "the verbal apotheosis of *The Book of Nightmares* is also its failure" (96), but we might as easily say that its completion—its *cessation*—is its success.

Still, the question remains: what was left to say? One might have asked this after any of Kinnell's volumes, since they each articulate more or less the same vision, but *Nightmares* so obviously tried to "say everything" that he "knew or felt" that before his next volume of poems appeared one might have wondered if the vision had been extended to its limit. The publication of *Mortal Acts, Mortal Words* in 1980, nine years after *Nightmares,* demonstrates that it had not; or if it had reached the limit, there was yet ample unexplored territory behind the front lines. Kinnell backs away from the edge, but what *Mortal Acts* forgoes in struggle and urgency, it at least partly recoups in steadiness and becalmed power. It is at once more interested in the ordinary than his previous writings and more frankly mystical.

"It would be nice," Kinnell muses, "if in a single poem one could resolve a given problem forever—come to terms with it once and for all. But each poem comes out of its own moment" (*WDS* 28). "If love had not smiled we would never grieve" ("The Feast"), "The soul . . . wishes to be whole / and therefore dark" ("The Old Moon")—these are very early lines, from *First Poems,* but they stake out positions which Kinnell repeatedly reformulates. He inverts the first, for example, in *Nightmares,* where it is "the wound itself, / which lets us know and love," and reconstitutes this reversal in *Mortal Acts:* "It is written in our hearts, the emptiness is all. / That is how we have learned, the embrace is all" ("Goodbye"). Like Yeats, his early master, Kinnell spends his career working the same set of insights, but, predicated on changing experience, these are refashioned at every point. In "The Book of Ephraim" James Merrill quotes Heinrich Zimmer: "The powers have to be consulted directly—again, again and again. Our primary task is to learn, not so much what they are said to have said, as how to approach them, evoke fresh speech from them, and understand that speech" ("Q"). "The duty and pleasure of art is to invent a thousand and one ways of telling the same story," Helen Vendler tells us: "Nobody wants a new lyric subject. We want the old subjects done over."[1]

Although Kinnell knew he "would feel an unsettling emptiness for a long time" after letting go of *Nightmares,* he also knew, as he writes in *Mortal Acts,* that

>                    that enormous emptiness
> carved out of such tiny beings as we are
> asks to be filled; the need
> for the new love *is* faithfulness to the old.
>                                        ("Wait")

The need for the new poem is even more certainly such faithfulness. "Wait" implicitly addresses the unusually long interim between *Nightmares* and *Mortal Acts*. Time itself sustained him:

> Wait, for now.
> Distrust everything if you have to.
> But trust the hours. Haven't they
> carried you everywhere, up to now?

I exist in time, therefore I am. And if I am, I shall be restored. Kinnell's old subjects are "Personal events," "Hair," and "Pain"; they all "will become interesting again," although, blandly generalized, they are not so interesting at the moment. The world itself will revivify you, if you *attend* to it; "Only wait a little and listen" and you will hear

> music of hair,
> music of pain,
> music of looms weaving all our loves again.

*Mortal Acts* is a collection of poems, not a single work like *Nightmares*. But, to a lesser degree, it retains a tendency to bind itself together, to cohere by the centripetal force of its interlocking words. We *hear* this unity before we apprehend it any other way. Throughout the book, Kinnell returns to versions of what he calls in "There Are Things I Tell to No One" the "one sound," the "singing / of mortal lives" which incorporates all timbres of emotion, the spectrum of human sound from laughter to groaning; as in *Nightmares*, he "wants to make the opposite terms of polarities coalesce" (Nelson 77–78). Earlier in that poem, for instance, we learn that "the supreme cry / of joy, the cry of orgasm, also has a ghastliness to it." In "The Choir" Kinnell realizes that "Even sad music / requires an absolute happiness" as he hears children "strain together in quintal harmony / to sing Joy and Death well." The "Ah!" they say "for God" echoes in the disgruntled "*baaah* of sheep" the tennis players utter in "On the Tennis Court at Night" and, more pointedly, in "Crying" (a poem about laughing), where not until you "cry / until your pillow is soaked!" can you "throw open your window / and, 'Ha ha! ha ha!'", can you sing "'Happiness / was hiding in the last tear! / I wept it! Ha ha.'" "I want to be, ah me! aa," the poet exclaims in "Lava" ("aa," a variety of lava, is pronounced ắ˙ắ, a note explains), "a mass of rubble" which "a person without shoes / has to do deep knee-bends across, / groaning 'aaaah! aaaah!' at each step"; at the end of this poem a stone cries out "aaaaaah" twice more, once "in commiseration" and once "in envy." Kinnell tells his "broken heart brother" to "sing, even if you cry" ("Brother of My Heart") and remembers "nights when we would sing and cry" ("In the Bamboo Hut"), but later recalls a song that "old Amos sang, / or rather laughed forth" ("Memory of Wilmington").

Sighing, groaning, crying, laughing, and singing thus "gather into one sound," analogous to the "humming" of "omphalos blood" which sustains Maud before her birth (5) and its "whine" which carries the old tramp out of life (37). And we might add po-etry to the list, for throughout his career Kinnell has figured his work as music (the first poem in his first major book is "First Song"; *Nightmares* is "a concert of one"). The restorative power of the "music of grace" ("There Are Things") is also that of his own art. Those "who can sing" can "heal themselves" ("The Still Time"). In "Brother of My Heart" Kinnell asks fellow poet Eth-eridge Knight to

> sing to us
> here, in this place that loses its brothers,
> in this emptiness only the singing sometimes almost fills.

Knight's singing may issue from tears, but "the bravery / of the crying turns it into the true song." Indeed, like music and the "one sound," bravery is a big bone in *Mortal Acts*' skeletal structure. Kinnell's writing has always been an effort to face death's finality without resorting to the stories we make up for consolation. "The most difficult thing for the human being is the knowledge that he will die," he observes, and thus "we develop, one after another, some manner of accounting for death, or of turning it aside, or of making it more tolerable" (*WDS* 97). (Kinnell does imagine a whole into which each individual will return, the "one sound," but identity doesn't survive this merger.) Not until *Mortal Acts*, how-ever, does he address the sheer *courage* necessary to refuse conso-lation. Indeed, reformulating the Christian exchange of salvation (in heaven) for faith, Kinnell posits an exchange of salvation (on earth) for the courage to embrace "time and ruin" ("The Rainbow"). There is no original sin in his ontology, only "original fear" ("The Sadness of Brothers"). It is not a transgression to eat the apple, "brightening its bitter knowledge above us"; rather, it "only needs to be tasted without fear / to be the philosophers' stone and golden fruit of the risen world" ("The Apple").

Tasted "without fear," the apple of knowledge gives back a "risen world," over which a "music of grace" flows. But the risen world, in addition to its aural character, also evidences a visual one. The apple is *"brightening* its bitter knowledge" (my emphasis): throughout *Mortal Acts*, epiphanies materialize in moments of light. This departs sharply from Kinnell's previous way of representing his identification with the world: in *First Poems*, the soul is "Made of flesh and light, / And wishes to be whole, / And therefore dark" ("The Old Moon"); in *Flower Herding*, the poet knows "half my life belongs to the wild darkness" ("Middle of the Way"); in *Nightmares*, he follows Rilke's affirmation of death as "our reverted, our unilluminated, side of life." In "Dear Stranger," Kinnell begins to wonder, "Can it ever be true—/ . . . one light / made of everyone's darkness together?" (30). But only as *Nightmares* concludes can he assert that "Lastness / *is* brightness. It is the brightness / gathered up of all that went before" (73–74) (just as, in "There Are Things," the spaces "gather into one sound . . . the singing / of mortal lives").

This sacred brightness shines throughout *Mortal Acts*, where spiritual enlightenment is for once literally illuminating. "Lastness / *is* brightness," for example, in "There Are Things," where the "music of grace / . . . flows / through our bodies" and

> lets us live
> these days lighted by their vanity
> worshipping—as the other animals do,
> who live and die in the spirit
> of the end—that backward-spreading
> brightness.

Death itself, that is, isn't dark, but shiny. Thus, *"the black dust / we become"* is a *"souvenir / which glitters already in the bones of your hand,"* lovers try "to increase what light may shine / in their ashes" ("Flying Home"), and the apples in "The Apple Tree" "fail into brightness." The "glitter / on common things that inexplicably

shine" ("The Still Time") sometimes emanates from sadness or deprivation, as in "Flying Home" where "tears stream down across
the stars, / tears fallen on the actual earth / where their shining is
what we call spirit." More often, since crying and laughing are
manifestations of the same "one sound," the light expresses completion or possession, as in "52 Oswald Street":

> Then, when the full moonlight
> would touch our sleeping bodies,
> we liked to think it filled
> us with what we imagined was
> *fullness*—actual bright matter
> drifted down from the moon's
> regions, so that when we woke
> we would be shining.

But, in every case, the light shines forth the glory of the perishable
world:

> no matter what fire we invent to destroy us,
> ours will have been the brightest world ever existing . . .
>               ("The Last Hiding Places")

At least in this book, however, a conflagration seems remote; the
fire of Kinnell's early imagery has transmuted into water. Illumination, rather than flashing like lightning, instead comes on gradually here, with a perceptible, continuous, liquid motion—it flows,
spreads, gathers, and streams. Indeed, more things than light move
like waves in the volume; this liquid motion (like the earlier fire
imagery) often suggests either the dissolution of the individual
"back into all things" ("The Milk Bottle") or the resultant wash of
feeling for life. In "The Milk Bottle" a sea anemone sucks at the
poet's finger: "it may mean to kill" or, rather, "to eat / and flow,"
for like us it seems "to thrill / to altered existences." The "one
sound" in "There Are Things" is "the singing / of mortal lives"
which are

> waves of spent existence
> which flow toward, and toward, and on which we flow
> and grow drowsy and become fearless again.

Earlier in that poem, the "music of grace . . . flows / through our bodies" and, in "The Milk Bottle" again, Kinnell writes that "first dreams . . . flow from me in waves." The past and the present, indeed, keep flowing toward each other; "Ahead of us the meantime is overflowing" ("The Milk Bottle") even as "we die / of the return-streaming of everything we have lived" ("The Apple Tree"). Brightness, of course, backward-spreads, but "darkness flows / across a disappearing patch of green-painted asphalt" also, in "On the Tennis Court at Night," and "all of us little / thinkers" in "Flying Home" are "smearing the darkness / of expectation across experience."

The poems in *Mortal Acts* do more than merely talk about flowing and streaming. The break and snap of the previous work—the saw-toothed lineation scissoring apart syntactic units, the febrile abutment of long and short lines—has for the most part been smoothed over. Long and short lines still mix, but the hard edges have been eroded. Often, indeed, the poems seem about to crystallize into blank verse. Yet, because Kinnell still thinks in extremely long sentences and still relies heavily on strings of enjambed lines, we are kept moving. The poems themselves "flow toward and toward" as they gather and release like waves, the long, loosely structured sentences spreading down the page like the brightness of the world streaming over our lives.

Typically, a single one of these sentences will string together past, present, and future. Like light, time is an almost palpable presence in *Mortal Acts*, gathering up behind and flowing forward. The present and the future, thus, imply the past; Kinnell's efforts "to reach a new place" in his poetry (PPW 113) repeatedly lead, in *Mortal Acts*, to the old places, to the subject and substance of memory. Virtually half of the poems contain versions of the words "remember" or "memory," and many of the others in this most autobiographical of Kinnell's books take up the subject almost as directly.

Like Wordsworth, Kinnell starts with an interest in memory as a subject, is led by this general interest into the specifics of what lingers in his own mind, and thus arrives at a dual focus: Memory and memories. And, like Wordsworth, he recognizes memory's power to evoke an early or original state of completion or grace and thereby replenish the present. Wordsworth is nourished by his "spots of time," which, although "scatter'd everywhere" about our lives, "in our childhood even / Perhaps are most conspicuous."[2] "Life with me," he writes, "As far as memory can look back, is full / Of this beneficent influence." In "Saint Francis and the Sow" Kinnell supposes that "sometimes it is necessary / to reteach a thing its loveliness," to "retell it in words and in touch," as Saint Francis does for the sow, who begins "remembering all down her thick length . . . the long, perfect loveliness of sow." Sexual completion itself appears as a return, so that "When lovers embrace, / sometimes their arms seem only / to be remembering the other" ("The Apple"). In "52 Oswald Street" Kinnell recalls his childhood fantasy, "Then," that *"fullness"* would drift down from the moon and enter the sleeping bodies of his sisters and himself; "Now," looking back, they "taste / the lost fullness."

Wordsworth's spots of time are instantaneous and piercing. He is, as M. H. Abrams puts it, "a poet of the revelatory and luminous Moment, of the 'gentle shock of mild surprize,' of 'flashes, as it were,' of 'objects recognis'd / In flashes,' of outer 'gleams like the flashing of a shield,' as well as of 'attendant gleams / Of soul-illumination.'"[3] When he launches into a recollected incident in *The Prelude,* Wordsworth gives himself over to it, keeping to the narrative and reserving his commentary until after. Idea and example alternate. Kinnell, in contrast, foregrounds the present as he regards the past, narrating and interpreting simultaneously. Memories come on for him drained even of their "gentle shock"; like the streaming of the poems down the page, the past spreads over consciousness rather than piercing it, flows into the mind rather than flashing. Kinnell's memories, indeed, don't occur here as charged, isolated spots of time; rather, they remain more diffuse, uncrystallized, as they meander in and out of present consciousness. Memory doesn't lift special moments of revelation out of the temporal flow, but rather, like sex, it plunges us in, makes us feel the tug of the current all the more strongly; "Memory, which affirms time," ("Pont Neuf at Nightfall") cannot rise above it. Memory is only as replenishing, then, as time itself, but that will suffice: "Distrust everything if you have to," Kinnell advises in "Wait," "But trust the hours. Haven't they / carried you everywhere, up to now?" If remembering can clarify the simultaneous privation and possession which is anybody's lot, can help us "taste / the lost fullness" even as it lets us "know how far our hearts have crumbled," nevertheless "where a girl and a boy give themselves / into time," it is "memory, which affirms time," which "lights their moment / all the way to the end of memory."

If by "the end of memory" we understand "the end of time," then perhaps memory *can,* after all, point beyond the temporal stream, not by rescuing from it transcendental spots of time, but, homeopathically, by submerging us more fully. Through time, time is conquered. Or rather, in the doubleness of Kinnell's vision, time and eternity *both* stake valid claims—indeed, have come to depend on one another.

The "one sound" and courage, memory and light and liquid flow—all these contribute to the poetic matrix of *Mortal Acts, Mortal Words.* If this matrix does not bear a solitary giant of an only child like *The Book of Nightmares,* nevertheless its multiple litter is unusually close-knit; poems written at about the same stage of a poet's life will naturally show resemblance, but few volumes are so much of a piece. Indeed, a more complete delineation of the poetic matrix of *Mortal Acts* would trace many other figures of thought—falling and rising, fullness and emptiness, heaven, blooming, dreaming, arches and arching, the wind, and especially the setting of the poems in border zones (dusk or dawn, the shore, a tide pool, a doorway, a bridge, an airplane, an equinox) suggestive of the thin membrane between life and death, time and eternity:

> and at the gates of the world, therefore, between
> holy ground
> and ground of almost all its holiness gone, I loiter.
> ("The Last Hiding Places of Snow")

II

Against this backdrop, Kinnell groups the poems in four sections. The first bears out his 1975 prediction that "whatever my poetry will be, it will no doubt come out of this involvement in the ordinary" (*WDS* 85). His previous work seemed always at the edge—between light and dark, human and animal, consciousness and unconsciousness—and if the newer poems also inhabit borders, they patrol these liminal spaces more calmly, the poet "loitering" rather than straining, as if the far side were in its way as familiar as the near. Little is "ordinary" in *Body Rags* or *Nightmares*, but even as *Mortal Acts* reaches into the eternal, it leaves room for Fergus's pajamas, a fishless fishing trip, a game of tennis.

*Nightmares* ends with Fergus's birth, and *Mortal Acts* begins with "Fergus Falling." When the boy climbed a tree, "probably to get out / of the shadow" of his father, and above the treetops saw a pond which in its "oldness" embodies the local history, "he became heavier suddenly / in his bones / the way fledglings do just before they fly, / and the soft pine cracked. . . ." Fergus falls out of the tree into the knowledge of history and time. Just as in *Nightmares* his father "took him up in my hands and bent / over" when he was born, here both parents "bent over him" on the ground at this second birth, into language and self-consciousness; before blacking out, his response to his vision is to rehearse it in speech: "'Galway, Ines, I saw a pond!'" (Fergus, in fact, has something to say—indeed, is quoted—in each of the first three poems.)

Although Fergus's rise and fall suggests the onrush of time, the poem balances this with a sense of continuity. The Whitmanesque lines in which Kinnell associates Bruce Pond with the local history harp on transience, as independent clauses rush into one another separated only by commas, and as the characters in them are evoked and then summarily dismissed by the refrain "he's gone" or "they're gone." The last of these lines, however, inverts the refrain: "pond where an old fisherman in a rowboat sits, drowning hooked worms, when he goes he's replaced and is never gone." Kinnell, moreover, returns to this fisherman at the poem's conclusion, where the timeless presence he embodies counters the sense of temporal progression implicit in the shift to present tense; "Yes—a pond," the father affirms the son's vision,

> where even now an old fisherman only the pinetops can see
> sits in the dry gray wood of his rowboat, waiting for pickerel.

Kinnell is more willing to take what consolation he can from the timelessness evinced in this image, but the absolute perishability of identity remains unquestioned. Those who are "gone" are specific people—Clarence Akley, Milton Norway, Gus Newland—while the one who "is never gone" remains nameless, just "an old fisherman."

"Brother of My Heart" focuses more squarely on this discreteness of the self. Its three stanzas, functioning roughly as the three parts of a syllogism, also illustrate that, despite the discursiveness of *Mortal Acts,* the writing is carefully crafted. Stanza 1 establishes as the syllogistic "major premise" that human identity happens once and once only:

> Brother of my heart,
> don't you know there's only one
> walking into the light, only one,
> before this light
> flashes out, before this bravest knight
> crashes his black bones into the earth?

The second person modulates here into the third as "you" becomes "this bravest knight," and this flashing-out of "you" enacts the objectification of death itself; what is present becomes absent, talked *about,* not talked *to.* This deathly transfiguration also occurs as the same letters that comprise the live "heart" at the end of line 1 by the stanza's end permute into inanimate "earth." The stanza's movement, thus, dramatizes the "premise." And since death reduces the differences of identity to physical sameness, all the verbal samenesses—word repetition ("only one," "light"), assonance (long *o* in l. 2, short *a* in l. 6), consonance (*r* in l. 1), alliteration (the *b*'s in ll. 4–6), isocolon ("before this light"/"before this bravest knight"), rhyme (initial—flashes/crashes; end—light/knight; and rich—only one/only one), and syllabic agnominatio (cras*hes his*)—make the stanza also *sound* as though it were about the reductiveness of death.

Having asserted in stanza 1 his "major premise" that the identity which distinguishes us in this life is erased by death, in stanza 2 Kinnell proceeds, logically, to his "minor premise," to what comes after death. Nothing does. Or at least we live as humans once only. If anything succeeds human life on earth, it's worm life *in* earth, as if the Karmic spiral spun only in reverse. Again, the stanza traces a descendental movement from life to death or sub-life: "you" (talked to) becomes "those" (talked about); first there's laughing,

then grubbing; the world of humans becomes the world of worms.
Just as stanza 1 leaves us with bones crashed into earth, this stanza
leaves us just lying there. Its structure also helps suggest the logical, syllogistic framework: first it makes a claim ("You will not
come back") and then it substantiates it ("because . . .").

The third stanza completes the pseudo-syllogism. Having first
announced the ephemerality of the self (major premise), then dis-
patched with afterlife and human reincarnation (minor premise),
Kinnell draws his conclusion: "Therefore, as you are, this once /
sing." (The rhetorical question of stanza 1—a debater's device—
and the logical "because" prepare for the starkly rational tone of
"therefore.") In lines that echo the end of the first of the *Duino
Elegies*—

> Is the story in vain, how once, in the mourning for Linos,
> venturing earliest music pierced barren numbness, and how,
> in the horrified space an almost deified youth
> suddenly quitted for ever, emptiness first
> felt the vibration that now charms us and comforts and helps?

—Kinnell counters emptiness with song:

> sing to us
> here, in this place that loses its brothers,
> in this emptiness only the singing sometimes almost fills.

For the first time in the poem, death doesn't quite have the last
word, and thus finally "you" remains "you." There is no descen-
dentalism or closing down (no bones, worms, or moles); rather
the stanza opens out, starting with short, constricted phrases seg-
mented by commas and relaxing into longer, unbroken utterances
("the bravery / of the crying turns it into the true song") that build
up to the final line, where we catch Kinnell in the very act of singing to fill the emptiness. The line's length (it's the poem's longest)
and flow suggest the filling, and its dense, relentless sibilance sounds
the singing. Like the poem itself, the line begins on emptiness and
moves, via singing, toward conditional fulfillment.

Part 2 of *Mortal Acts* consists mostly of small, sometimes amus-
ing poems, built around a single effect. At the heart of "The Gray
Heron," for example, is the descendental regression we saw in
"Brother of My Heart," the drift from subject to object, from ani-

mal to mineral. "'The most universal endeavor of all living substance,'" Kinnell elsewhere quotes Freud, is "'to return to the
quiescence of the inorganic world'" (PPW 123); and here he dramatizes the return, if not the endeavor. The poet watches the heron, it
stalks away, and when he tries to find it, he discovers in its place

> a three-foot-long lizard
> in ill-fitting skin
> and with linear mouth
> expressive of the even temper
> of the mineral kingdom.

The bird has been transfigured into the lizard, associated with the
inanimate "mineral kingdom," whose head "was much like / a
fieldstone with an eye"; the heron's "body and green / legs wobbled
in wide arcs / from side to side," but this animate, curved motion
gets flattened into the "linear mouth / expressive of the even temper." The poet, too, is caught in what Kinnell called in *First Poems*
the "downward drift" ("Islands of Night"). At first he is the ob-
serving subject, watching the heron, but soon the tables turn and
he becomes also the observed object; the lizard's head was like

> a fieldstone with an eye
> in it, which was watching me
> to see if I would go
> or change into something else.

In the short course of the poem, that is, he already *has* changed
"into something else" and, given the operating downward drift,
will soon change into something else yet again.

In "Lava" Kinnell again addresses the drift from the animal
kingdom to the mineral. Indeed, although it is a kookier poem
than the even-tempered, laconic "Gray Heron," it is more forth-
right about the implications of its subject. The "drift" openly appears now less as an imposed, external force than as that Freudian
wish "to return to the quiescence of the inorganic world": "I want
to be pahoehoe," (like "aa," a kind of dried lava) the poet admits,
"but even more, / I want to be, ah me! aa, / a mass of rubble." This
wish, however, is actually two contrasting wishes, for Kinnell loads
the two kinds of lava with two opposite meanings. Pahoehoe is

> swirled, gracefully lined,
> folded, frozen where I flowed,
> a clear brazened surface
> one can cross barefooted

—its smoothness is related to the "linear mouth" and "even temper" of the lizard. Aa, on the other hand, is a jagged "mass of rubble . . . which a person without shoes / has to do deep knee-bends across, / groaning 'aaaah! aaaah!' at each step." More intricate and disorderly than the simpler pahoehoe, yielding up more sensation, it is more suggestive of an animal state than a mineral one, more like life than death. The contrast remains imperfect, because *both* lavas figure *both* organic and inorganic states of being, motion and stillness; if the poet were pahoehoe, he would paradoxically be "frozen [stillness] where I flowed [motion]," and if aa, would be "still / tumbling [motion] after I've stopped [stillness]."

Nevertheless, the poem emphasizes the deathly aspects of one lava and the lively side of the other. The "dismal shore" the poet approaches—one of the volume's recurrent images for the border between life and death—is "all made, I know, of pahoehoe." He does not want to go gentle into that linear, even-tempered, dismal shore, does not "want to call, 'ahoy! ahoy!' / and sail meekly in. Unh-unh." Rather,

> I want to turn and look back
> at that glittering, black aa
> where we loved in the bright moon,
> where all our atoms broke and lived,
> where even now two kneecaps gasp,
> "ah! ah!" to a heiau's stone floor,
> to which the stone answers,
> "aaaaaah," in commiseration
> with bones that find the way very long
> and "aaaaaah" in envy of yet unbroken bones.

"Glittering," "bright," "gasp," "ah!"—the passage incorporates the book's key words and, as it does so, yokes opposites together: the aa is "glittering" and "black"; the atoms "broke and lived"; the kneecaps gasp two "ah!"'s, one for pleasure (making love) and one for pain (doing it on the rubble). This antithetical doubling was prefigured in the dual condition on the lavas (simultaneously moving and motionless), in their contrasting physical qualities (smooth/prickly), and in the doubling of sounds in their names. The crescendo of unified oppositions reaches its climax in two final meanings of "aaaaaah." To feel "commiseration / with bones that find the way very long" is to yearn for the quiescence of the mineral kingdom. Kinnell is more candid about what he calls in "There Are Things" "these wishes . . . to die," less troubled by the "downward drift," but the last "aaaaaah" is sighed "in envy of yet unbroken bones," in affirmation of life in all its abrasiveness.

In Part 3 of *Mortal Acts* Kinnell for the first time writes directly of his family history. Indeed, one aspect of the mellowing of his vision is that he is now no longer *merely* the unattached, unhoused wanderer, a trimmed-off edge of the social fabric. He has not renounced his marginality but rather recontextualized it in light of some details of his early family life. Or a few of them, anyway. Kinnell does not rely on the continuous sweep of autobiographical detail, as Merrill and Lowell do, although this doesn't mean his work is thereby less personal. "The basic subject of modern poetry is the self," Kinnell observes, "and whether one deals with it through autobiography or some other way isn't that important. The materials that provide the language of the poem are the things that interest you most at that point."[4]

The "materials that provide the language" of the poems in part 3, the volume's most sustained exploration of memory, derive from the Kinnell family circle. "The Sadness of Brothers," in particular, is built on a series of familial recollections. An imaginary reunion with his dead brother leads Kinnell to recall some events in Derry's life and the occasion of his premature death. This triggers earlier memories of his childhood in Pawtucket, Rhode Island, of the "well-wandered Scotsman" of a father and the "Irish mother," but these past scenes are not suffused with nostalgia. Rather, they bristle with disharmony, are haunted by an unsatisfied hunger for something or somewhere else. We get a more detailed account of what R. W. Flint called the "Kinnell family romance" which, Flint writes, "was obliquely summed up" in the early poem, "Conversation at Tea" (*FP*):[5]

> Each year I lived I watched the fissure
> Between what was and what I wished for
> Widen, until there was nothing left
> But the gulf of emptiness.
> Most men have not seen the world divide,
> Or seen, it did not open wide,
> Or wide, they clung to the safer side.
> But I have felt the sundering like a blade.

The apparently bitterly frustrated father "disgorged / divine capitalist law / out of his starved craw." As he "peered through pupils / screwed down very tiny, like a hunter's," he must have seemed openly hostile, and his very presence in the family, or in the world itself, seemed tenuous, as he now appears to Kinnell

> in the light of last days, jiggling
> his knees as he used to do—
> *get out of here*, I knew
> they were telling him, *get out of here, Scotty—*
> control he couldn't control
> thwarting his desires down
> into knees which could only jiggle.

Kinnell remembers his mother here, not as hostile, but as contributing nevertheless to the "fissure"; if he and his brother are now "friends to reality," this is in spite of the mother who "willed / the bourgeois illusion all of us dreamed / we lived." She "used to sit up / crying for the lost Ireland / of no American sons" and was thus also perhaps a tenuous parental presence to those sons who, themselves only precariously rooted in the family, "would slip out at night" and "stagger home / near dawn, snarl to reproaches, silence to tears."

"But no, that's fear's reading," and there is another way to see those years. Even as the family seems to be disintegrating before our eyes, the inevitable connections are reaffirmed. Kinnell may have "felt the sundering like a blade" but recognizes his father in both his brother and himself. Indeed, the whole family appears almost as a single organism on

Mortal Acts, Mortal Words

those Sunday mornings when six of us
hugged sideways in the double bed—
when father turned we all turned . . .

"The Sadness of Brothers" ends with Kinnell's return to the imaginary meeting with his brother, a reunion that now represents a reconciliation with the past in general. The "embrace in the doorway" (the line between life and death, present and past) marks a new peace, an at-least-provisional family reunion.

Ambivalence and eventual affirmation also characterize "The Last Hiding Places of Snow," the longest of three poems in which the "materials that provide the language" come from Kinnell's response to his mother's death. This is less a poem built on memories, like "The Sadness of Brothers," than an exploration of the workings of memory, a meditation on a single autobiographical event. Typically, Kinnell is physically isolated here, on the edge once more; he haunts the lonely spots where you find the undisturbed remnants of the title, he wakes "at night / in some room far from everyone." This outsidership, a career-long tendency, results from what Kinnell recognizes as the difficulty of human relationships. About "The Call Across the Valley of Not-Knowing"— where the *achievement* of love is apparently the main event—he once remarked, "I don't think I went far enough into the subject of love and the failure of love," almost as if the one subject automatically implied the other.[6] The genesis of this outsidership is, I think, implicitly addressed in "The Last Hiding Places." Earlier in his career, Kinnell had written of the circumstances of his birth—

I weighed eleven pounds
At birth, having stayed on
Two extra weeks in the womb.
Tempted by room and fresh air
I came out big as a policeman
Blue-faced, with narrow red eyes.
It was eight days before the doctor
Would scare my mother with me
　　　　　("Flower Herding on Mount Monadnock")

—and, by juxtaposition, linked this to his adult sense of "nothingness":

> Turning and craning in the vines
> I can make out through the leaves
> The old, shimmering nothingness, the sky.

In "The Last Hiding Places," he returns to the subject of his extended intra-uterine stay, but now the connection to later feelings of emptiness is spelled out:

> My mother did not want me to be born;
> afterwards, all her life, she needed me to return.
> When this more-than-love flowed toward me, it brought
>   darkness;
> she wanted me as burial earth wants—to heap itself gently
>   upon but also to annihilate—
> and I knew, whenever I felt longings to go back,
> that is what wanting to die is. That is why
>
> dread lives in me,
> dread which comes when what gives life beckons toward death,
> dread which throws through me
> waves
> of utter strangeness, which wash the entire world empty.

If love contains within it an annihilating "more-than-love," no wonder human relations are hard.[7] Outsidership is safer. If "waves / of utter strangeness, which wash the entire world empty," keep flowing through you, you must refill the world again each time, must re-establish contact over and over. You must keep writing poems.

The natural world functions in "The Last Hiding Places" as refuge but also as model and catalyst for social reconnection. The poet starts with the moment of his mother's death, her "groans made / of all the goodbyes ever spoken," but suddenly switches to "a place in the woods / where you can hear / such sounds." Kinnell instinctively turns to the natural world to integrate both the terrible groan of death and the call of love, and the woods provide the images with which he can accommodate these sounds in language: the mother's dying sounds are like those coming from the trees, "a breeze, that's all"; "passing this place, / I have imagined I heard / my old mother calling, thinking out loud her / mother-love toward me," Kinnell writes,

> But when I've stopped and listened,
> all I've heard was
> what may once have been speech
> or groans, now
> shredded to a hiss from passing
> through the whole valley of spruce needles.

By the poem's end, the woods have taught him (or writing about them has) that mother *is*, after all, mysteriously there. A fantasy about her girlhood leads him to a renewed gratitude for the earth itself—"the brightest world ever existing"—which in turn renders her accessible to him in the landscape. The presence he feels in the falling snow is now inseparable from the love he has achieved for his absent mother:

> Every so often, when I look
> at the dark sky, I know she remains
> among the old endless blue lightedness
> of stars; or finding myself out in a field
> in November, when a strange
> starry perhaps first snowfall blows
> down across the darkening air, lightly,
> I know she is there, where snow
> falls   flakes   down   fragile   softly
> falling until I can't see the world
> any longer, only its stilled shapes.

The ambivalence toward his mother's love remains, for the softly falling snow is but a transmutation of the "burial earth" to which she was earlier compared. Snow, like earth, "heap[s] itself gently upon," and, like the earth, it "annihilate[s]" what it covers, until the poet "can't see the world / any longer." But by the end he can acknowledge his ambivalence and at the same time confirm his attachment to the presence embodied in both his mother and the world he has come to discover, or rediscover, is "the brightest world ever existing":

> Even now when I wake at night
> in some room far from everyone,
> the darkness sometimes
> lightens a little, and then,

> because of nothing,
> in spite of nothing,
> in an imaginary daybreak, I see her,
> and for that moment I am still her son
> and I am in the holy land
> and twice in the holy land, remembered
> within her, and remembered in the memory
> her old body slowly executes into the earth.

Many of the poems in part 4 grow from Kinnell's epiphanic vision of "the brightest world." These "semi-oracular" poems, as Flint calls them, keep verging on the mystical, but theirs is a mysticism rooted in—circumscribed by—the terrestrial, ordinary world of "time and ruin." Kinnell evokes the things of the world almost as if—already half a ghost, inhabiting the border zone of his own life—he regarded them in his final moments, as if his own wishes to die had highlighted his sense of the deathward tilt of all things, which in turn, death being the mother of beauty, draws forth from him a flood of gratefulness, the "Tenderness toward Existence" that *The Book of Nightmares* tells us is "the dream / of all poems." Repeatedly imagining the final moment, Kinnell is astonished by the familiar, moved to the brink of silence: "I sat in the last light and listened, there among rocks, / tin cans, feathers, ashes, old stars. This. This" ("Memory of Wilmington").

"The Rainbow" elaborates a key image from "The Last Hiding Places of Snow" in which Kinnell imagines his mother as a girl, swinging:

> Now she wears rhythmically into the air
> of morning
> the rainbow's curve, but upside down
> so that angels may see
> beloved dross promising heaven.

She is "innocent of groans, beyond any / future, far past the past: into a pure present," but soon "The vision breaks, / the child suddenly grows old, she dies . . ." "The Rainbow" begins with a similar breaking of a spell; if the poet's heart leaps up when he beholds a rainbow, it is forthwith tugged back to the material world:

> The rainbow appears above us
> for its minute, then vanishes, as though
> we had wished it, making us
> turn more carefully to what we can
> touch and feel, things and creatures
> we know we haven't dreamed.

The rainbow itself, otherworldly, has only the substance of a dream, but the upside-down rainbow curve inscribed by the swinging girl does point to "beloved dross promising heaven." Kinnell here follows, and perhaps extends, Rilke. The world of things "we haven't dreamed," of "dross," proves not merely astonishing to the angels, as in the *Elegies,* but it betokens heaven itself; it *is* heaven itself, "the brightest world ever existing."

"The ultimate defect of all heavens with immortality beyond the grave," Norman O. Brown writes, "is that in them there is no death; by this token such visions betray their connection with repression of life" (108). At the conclusion of "The Rainbow," a right-side-up rainbow appears, but it is a "misery-arc" whose very existence is a final breath, and although it rises for a moment, its final drift is downward. The very brightest moment is the very last: everyman's

> carcass expels
> defeated desire in one final curve
> of groaning breath, the misery-arc
> farewelling hands have polished
> before each face, a last outrush
> which rises through the iridescence
> of spent tears, across a momentarily
> heavenly sky, then dies
> toward those invisible fires,
> the other, unfulfilled galaxies,
> to win them over, too, into time and ruin.

The curve of iridescence promises an earthly heaven without Brown's "ultimate defect." Indeed, it is by its *pen*ultimate "defects"—dross, "time and ruin"—that this heaven allows the unrepressed fulfillment of life. This interdependence of life and death, in fact, is figured by the poem's structure. A single sentence, it keeps unbroken the syntactic flow that carries us on from fetal existence in

> the crater
> we floated in, in the first life,

to birth, when

> the world-ending inkling
> of what pain would be for all
> of our natural going—a blow so well-struck
> space simply breaks—befell us,
> and we fell, scanning about,
> the cleverest of us, for a lover,

to our passing out of the world on

> the day the carcass expels
> defeated desire in one final curve
> of groaning breath . . .

As always, death is a return. The poem seems slowly to recall its rhythmic origins in the iamb and finally expels itself in a concluding line of near perfect blank verse—"to win them over, too, into time and ruin."

"The Milk Bottle," too, hovers just off an iambic base and comes to rest finally on a line of almost pure blank verse ("streams and sparkles over everything") whose steady rise and fall suggests the wavelike flow of time, the immersion in which is the action of the poem. Earlier, the flow also describes the passing from life to death or from one state of being to another, but at that point the poet is only "mildly" implicated:

> A sea anemone
> sucks at my finger, mildly, I can just
> feel it, though it may mean to kill—no,
> it would probably say, to eat
> and flow, for all these creatures
> even half made of stone seem to thrill
> to altered existences.

He still resists the flow. Although he imagines that "any time / would be OK / to go, to vanish back into all things," he still wishes he could

> separate out
> time from happiness, remove
> the molecules scattered
> throughout our flesh that remember, skim them off,
> throw them at non-conscious things,
> who may even crave them . . .

But the poet's whimsical desire to toss away memory—to banish his awareness of time—is summarily dashed. Just as he considers the filtering out of memory, memory itself intrudes:

> It's funny,
> I imagine I can actually remember one certain
> quart of milk which has just finished clinking
> against three of its brethren
> in the milkman's great hand and stands,
> freeing itself from itself, on the rotting
> doorstep in Pawtucket circa 1932.

Again, it is "memory, which affirms time." Kinnell's recollection triggers a renewed consideration of ephemerality and permanence, a Heraclitean prophesy:

> The old milk bottle will shatter no one knows when
> in the decay of its music, the sea eagle
> will cry itself back down into the sea
> the sea's creatures transfigure over and over.

Sudden, short sentences then squeeze attention into the present, plucked moment: "Look. Everything has changed." But it is a present made bright, pressed against by time past and, now, time future:

> Ahead of us the meantime is overflowing.
> Around us its own almost-invisibility
> streams and sparkles over everything.

The sparkling meantime also streams over the present in the beginning of "There Are Things I Tell to No One," the longest of the "semi-oracular" pieces and the nerve center for many of the themes and images that interlace *Mortal Acts, Mortal Words*. Like that of most others in the volume, the rhetorical stance of this poem is discursive, as the poet talks to us about things rather than straining to appear to present experience directly: "here is what I think" rather than "here." Yet, just as ordinary things shine with sacredness, the opening discursiveness builds to the bardic pronouncement of the lyrical conclusion.

The suffusion of brightness over the world lies at the heart of "There Are Things." Kinnell first speaks of "God" as "a music of grace / that we hear, sometimes, playing to us / from the other side of happiness." This music, however, transubstantiates into the "backward-spreading / brightness" that lights our days when we live "as the other animals do, / who live and die in the spirit / of the end." "It is not the consciousness of death but the flight from death that distinguishes men from the animals," Brown claims (100), but Kinnell wants us to overcome this particular distinction (as indeed does Brown), to be like "the free animal" who, Rilke writes in "The Eighth Elegy,"

> has its decease perpetually behind it
> and God in front, and when it moves, it moves
> into eternity, like running springs.

Opening toward death, or the whole which encompasses life and death, implies a re-arising of a fuller sexuality. "If death is a part of life," Brown explains, "if there is a death instinct as well as a life (or sexual) instinct, man is in flight from his own death just as he is in flight from his own sexuality" (101–2). In Kinnell's poem the music thus "speaks in notes struck / or caressed or blown or plucked / off our own bodies"; our physical beings are (literally) instrumental in the production and reception of "grace," and sex is thereby revealed in its sacred aspect. Even if his "last temples" are rotted down by the spirochete, Eros remains "the last god."

"There Are Things" moves toward the momentary reconciliation of the life instinct and the death instinct. Kinnell acknowledges both equally in the last section, where he has learned to speak of "these wishes to live / and to die / in gratefulness, if in no other virtue." For awhile, anyway, these wishes keep free of the "dread" and "permanent remorse" they stir up in "The Last Hiding Places":

> For when the music sounds,
> sometimes, late at night, its faint
> clear breath blowing
> through the thinning walls of the darkness,
> I do not feel sad, I do not miss the future or need to be
>     comforted.

Kinnell has heard this music (identified here as a "music of grace"—one name, he implies, for "God") throughout his career, as for example in "Freedom, New Hampshire": "In bed at night there was music if you listened, / Of an old surf breaking far away in the blood." However, that early poem, an elegy for his brother, seethes with "permanent remorse." "It is true," even the younger Kinnell senses, "That only flesh dies, and spirit flowers without stop / For men, cows, dung, for all dead things; and it is good, yes— / But . . ." How that "but" gives the lie to any consoling vision of unity! Spirit may flower without stop, but his brother "remains dead, / And the few who loved him know this until they die." And that's that.

Existence and extinction don't butt heads quite so violently in "There Are Things." Kinnell doesn't renounce his fierce attachment to particular flesh or his fear of dissolution—"Yes, I want to live forever. / I am like everyone"—but he knows more surely now that true loyalty to life demands a reconciliation of Eros and Thanatos, a willingness to dissolve back into the ground of being:

> But when I hear
> that breath coming through the walls,
>
> . . . . . . . . . . . .
>
> then it is not so difficult
> to go out, to turn and face
> the spaces which gather into one sound, I know now, the
>     singing
> of mortal lives, waves of spent existence
> which flow toward, and toward, and on which we flow
> and grow drowsy and become fearless again.

Kinnell knows that such a willingness must remain tentative, momentary, partly fictionalized. "Keats in one of his last letters," he observes, "says something like this: 'Here I've been writing all these poems about the longing for death, and now that I'm dying, I'm shrieking worse than any farmer.'"[8] But a willingness to "cease upon the midnight with no pain" needn't be inevitably false. Kinnell admires how Rilke can imagine death as "friendly," can suppose that the "early-departed" are fulfilled by their leaving the world, can feel that (as Kinnell paraphrases it) "it is nothing to pass into cosmic life"—and yet "it doesn't mean Rilke died thinking that." Unlike Whitman in "When Lilacs Last in the Dooryard Bloom'd," according to Kinnell, "Rilke is convincing, even though one feels that it's just a momentary understanding. It's not something that you can bear with you. In fact, you would probably evaporate if you could."

Kinnell is in no danger of evaporating. He can tell us that "I do not feel sad, I do not miss the future or need to be comforted," that "it is not so difficult / to go out," but these understandings, however believable, remain momentary. They enliven, but cannot ultimately override, the outrage over the flashing-out of identity which he felt in "Freedom, New Hamphire" and which has driven his poetry ever since. "We don't have to worry about being too consoling," he knows, "because the reality is so inconsolable."

Stephen Yenser finds the conclusion of "There Are Things" "one of the volume's loveliest testimonies to unicity,"[9] although Flint warns that it "should be avoided by anyone allergic to uplift" (57). To those who don't sneeze at uplift, *Mortal Acts* does offer Kinnell's most sustained vision of the wholeness of which life and death are complementary parts. Eternity and time, continuity and discreteness keep feeding into each other, and if at any one point the claims of one predominate, eventually they are drawn together. "[H]e's gone," Kinnell intones about Clarence Akley, Milton Norway, and Gus Newland, in "Fergus Falling," but at the same time and in the same sentence, the old fisherman is "never gone." In "Les Invalides," natural process announces decay, but it is a process caught up in the flow of time, itself unceasing; keeping this balance, lines start with eternity ("always"), lengthen out toward the ephemeral ("dusk deepening"), and point ahead to the next recurrence of the oscillation:

Always at boules it's the creaking grace, the slow amble,
    the stillness,
always it's the dusk deepening,
always it's the plane trees casting down their leaves,
always it's the past blowing its terrors behind distracted eyes.

Stillness and process likewise play seesaw in "The Apple Tree"—in the apples "that still grow full, / that still fail into brightness"—while "Lava" intertwines time and eternity more paradoxically, as the poet wants to be, like lava, "frozen where I flowed" and "still tumbling after I've stopped." Or again, in "The Last Hiding Places of Snow" Kinnell knows that "we may go" but that his mother's annointing love "remains, / telling of goodness of being, of permanence."

Kinnell has always held in tension isolation and belonging, division and wholeness—two sticks rubbed together to start the fire of his poems. But to a greater extent they now play *with* rather than against each other. "Freud postulates an ultimate duality grounded in life itself," according to Brown (79), who then reinterprets the relationship between the life and death instincts as one of dialectic unity, not unresolved dualism. Kinnell's work has always held out the theory of this dialectical position (hence Richard Howard's emphasis on the link with Heraclitus, who, Brown notes, "asserted the ultimate unity of opposites, including life and death" [83]); but in actual practice the poems often churn with conflict, are often pulled in opposite directions on their rocky road to tentative resolution. Only with *Mortal Acts* does duality yield readily to dialectic. *Nightmares,* Yenser explains, "attests to what he once observed in Whitman, 'the double thought of death,' the simultaneous fear and desire for it. As Whitman grew older, Kinnell thinks, 'he was able to transfigure both the fear and the desire into a willingness to die and an even purer wish to live,' and something of the same change has taken place in his work" (127). Indeed, the willingness may *be* the wish, the dark and light sides of the same moon.

One can chart an equivalent change in the very construction of Kinnell's verse. His trademark has long been the extended, grammatically observant sentence which incorporates into it the jagged fragments of highly irregular lines. *Mortal Acts* maintains, and sometimes increases, the sentence length, but as I suggested earlier, the pieces now are frequently sanded down, now smoothly flow into one another like the waves to which they often refer. Where once the lines seemed to fight each other off, now they gather together into "one sound." Where the verse once often floundered and staggered toward resolution, now it frequently floods and sweeps.

In the final poem of *Mortal Acts* Kinnell has it both ways. "Flying Home" inscribes yet one more of the volume's descents to earth, as it follows Kinnell's jet ride from mid-flight to touchdown. As in "The Rainbow" and many other poems in this and previous books, "uplift" spends itself in a falling arc. The "Home" of the title is "the life down there, the doorway each will soon enter"— domestic, quotidian, earthly life, the "ordinary" sphere of "things and creatures / we know we haven't dreamed" ("The Rainbow") in which part of *Mortal Acts* immerses itself. Kinnell spends much of the poem thinking about love for his wife. Yet by this point in the book "Home" is also the universe back into which we will soon enough vanish, the shore where the waves "on which we flow / and grow drowsy and become fearless again" will break; "the doorway each will soon enter" leads also to an altered existence. The "clouds of glory" that Wordsworth sees us trailing as "we come / From God, who is our home" are refashioned by Kinnell into the "sudden, tiny, white puffs" which the jet's tires give off as they "*know* the home ground." Conflating the two homes, "Flying Home" evokes the dialectic whole for which Brown argues and to which Rilke and Whitman in different ways testify. It recognizes the complementarity, or the identity, of the pure wish to live and the willingness to die. Between two worlds, Kinnell wants both: "at the very same moment"—and the feeling may last for only that moment—

> I feel regret at leaving
> and happiness to be flying home.

# Epilogue
# Both of Time's Names: *The Past*

I

"Tell me a story," Robert Penn Warren sweetly commands at the end of *Audubon*. "Make it a story of great distances, and starlight" and whatever else—no matter: "The name of the story will be Time, / But you must not pronounce its name." You must not, that is, concede the nightmare message of any narrative: no matter how it ends, it ends. Better to let the message of sameness go unspoken (we must hear it anyway, just as Warren must pronounce the name in the act of warning us not to), better to elaborate on difference, on the movement that distinguishes the narrative, rather than the destination that would reduce it to all others. Warren has loosed the familiar paradox: time is the name of both the telling of the story and of its end; Audubon's gold watch, Calvin Bedient observes, is "a reminder of both opportunity and mortality."[1] We must not pronounce *one* of the story's names (which anyway is pronouncing us[2]), but we must speak the other. The result: "A story of deep delight."

If Kinnell's deep delight has always been measured by deep sadness, it is because he has always spoken both of time's names. *The Past* (1985) suggests how this departure from Warren has defined both the possibilities of his poetry and its limits. In *Mortal Acts, Mortal Words* Kinnell moved simultaneously toward the quotidian and the mystical; like Whitman he was "Both in and out of the game and watching and wondering at it" (SM 4). The recent volume locates the poet more often out of the game than in—out *looking* in—and the remove allows Kinnell his idiosyncratic slant on the world (the book's possibilities) even as it sometimes blurs the outline of what he can see (its limits).

This remove isn't new in Kinnell's writing, but *The Past* seems to define it more clearly than the previous work, to play out more starkly its double consequence. This results from his attention to both of time's names. If this too is not a new preoccupation, the doubleness at the heart of Kinnell's work (self/world, one/all, light/dark, motion/stillness, life/death, intricacy/simplicity) is now expressed mainly in its temporal aspect (time/time), as the title of the volume suggests. A line in the first poem describes his posture and preoccupation in many of the others: "Here I sat on a boulder by the winter-steaming river and put my head in my hands and considered time—which is next to nothing, merely what vanishes, and yet can make one's elbows nearly pierce one's thighs" ("The Road Between Here and There"). Time is "next to nothing, merely what vanishes," but also everything, the unvanishing medium in which we ponder it; the winter-steaming river flows on, the boulder remains fixed. The poem ends considering "all the spaces along the road between here and there—which the young know are infinite and all the others know are not."

Because Kinnell is one of those others, he supposes that when the spaces "get used up, that's it"; but I don't think this discredits what the young "know." Time's tug will finally cancel the release of eternity, but both have their place in *The Past*, and often the balance seems about even. "All the elsewheres, so far away . . . fade," the poet muses in "Lake Memphramagog," loafing in a boat that "lies very still in the Memphramagog water, and it's still." The last phrase of "The Frog Pond" drastically complicates the meaning of the final passage: the pond has vanished, but Kinnell will return to the spot

> and will think of smallest children
> grown up and of true love broken
> and will sit up abruptly and swat
> the hard-biting deer fly on his head,
> crushing it into his hair, as he has done before.

Even as the last lines of "The Shroud" anticipate the end of the planet's story, they imply an endlessly postponed funeral:

What sheet or shroud large enough
to hold the whole earth
are these seamstresses' chalks
and golden needles
stitching at so restlessly?
When will it ever be finished?

When two lovers in "The Waking" hear a clock ticking, "The feeling . . . that time passes, / comes over them," but the syntactic flow of this sentence, its unwinding in time, is resisted by a long interjection (elided above) in which the poet thinks, "perhaps it is only a feeling." Kinnell sees these lovers simultaneously going out into the New York streets (in the present) and lounging by a river bank (in memory), and he knows that "Something in them—the past—belongs / to the away-going water, and must flow away / into time to come forever." "Fire in Luna Park" pictures a "natural world, / where all are born, all suffer, and many scream / and no one is healed but gathered and used again," while in "December Day in Honolulu," the "wail of a cat in heat" seems to say

> *This one or that one dies but never the singer: whether in Honolulu in its humid mornings or in New York in its unbreathable dusk or in Sheffield now dark but for chimney sparks dying into the crowded heaven, one singer falls but the next steps into the empty place and sings . . .*

"On the Oregon Coast" considers the deaths of James Wright and Richard Hugo, but the final image calls finality into question: "The log gets up yet again, goes rolling and bouncing down the beach, plunges as though for good into the water."

In this preoccupation with the simultaneity of motion and stillness, *The Past* elaborates on an element of *Mortal Acts:* the possibility of being, like either of two kinds of lava, "frozen where I flowed" or "a mass of rubble still / tumbling after I've stopped" ("Lava"). But sitting on the boulder, nearly piercing his thighs with his elbows as he speaks time's two names, Kinnell also continues the meditation of *The Book of Nightmares* on the distinction between and identity of endings and beginnings. Just as Maud's birth in section 1 and the old man's death in section 5 oppose and are versions of each other and as in "Lastness" "the dead lie, / empty, filled, at the beginning," when Hugo and Wright die they go "back to the end" ("On the Oregon Coast"). Wright's "last, saddest poems" embody the "chant of the beginning, / older than any poem" and, "as when first light blooms / clouds of night," they "give us *mourning's* morning," in "Last Holy Fragrance," a fragrance which is "first perfume or last stink, the same smell." In "That Silent Evening" Kinnell recalls a time "when the past just managed / to overlap the future," and in "The Seekonk Woods" he experiences "Knowledge beforehand of the end."

But in 1985 to know the end beforehand is to see the end of knowing. If time appears to be a closed circuit, Kinnell in *The Past* also understands that we've created a world where the dead may not rise incorruptible, where the circuit can be smashed, where the ground of human consciousness in which past and future take meaning is at risk. In Nagasaki, the poet watches some school-children in front of a museum commemorating the bomb:

> The children go away. By nature they do. And by memory,
> in scorched uniforms, holding tiny crushed lunch tins.
> All the ecstasy-groans of each night call them back, satori
> their ghostliness back into the ashes, in the momentary shrines,
> the thankfulness of arms, from which they will go
> again and again, until the day flashes and no one lives
> to look back and say, a flash, a white flash sparkled.
>
> ("The Fundamental Project of Technology")

When will the "shroud large enough / to hold the whole earth . . . ever be finished?" Kinnell asks in "The Shroud," the "ever" implying it *won't* be finished. But considering the question in light of a white flash changes the tone; if in one sense the question is rhetorical, in another it is deadly literal. Time may have two names now, but Kinnell foresees the possibility that soon there will be nothing left to name.

## II

It is the combination of Kinnell's intense attachment to and wary distance from the world that brings time's two names into focus and that enables him to broach the subject of its end. I've suggested that while in *Mortal Acts* he is, like Whitman, both in and out of the game (or, we could add, like Eliot in "The Dry Salvages," "in and out of time"), *The Past* locates him outside (the game, time) looking in. He is also, however, outside *speaking* in, or outside *making poetry* in. It has never been plainer that his art is the search of an inveterate outsider for the world. Writing (or reciting) is love.

Partly, this is a historical matter. Michel Foucault proposes that in "the modern age, literature is that which compensates for (and not that which confirms) the signifying function of language"—compensates for, that is, the *separation* implied by language since the seventeenth century, the absolute gulf between signifier and signified, word and thing, self and world. In literature since the nineteenth century, then, we see language "finding its way back from the representative or signifying function . . . to this raw being that had been forgotten since the sixteenth century."[3] The parallel journey is that of the self making its way back by means of language to the "raw being" from which it came: for Kinnell the journey is biographical as well as epistemic. In "Last Holy Fragrance" he describes the young James Wright watching a river flow,

> humming and lulling first beginnings
> that would heal not only his dumb-born self
> but also the solitaries mute until death
> who sprawl cast-down stupid on sidewalks.

But this vision of the poetic impulse ("humming and lulling") healing the dumb-born and the solitary is as much a re-telling of his own past as a sympathetic engagement with Wright's: Kinnell has described *himself* as a silent child who thought that when he finally did speak it would be in poetry. "It will be a long time before anyone comes / who can lull the words" like Wright, he mourns, who can "hum and coax them" so that they "press up against" the world, "shape themselves by" it, "know, true-love, and idolize" it; but the elegy for Wright's unlulled words is also a celebration of how his own still-lulled ones keep on discovering and loving the world, healing his dumb-born self.

This discovery usually involves a *recovery* (a return to Foucault's "raw being"), as in "The Waking," where "The true word, if it exists, exists *inside* the tongue / and from there must make *every*

word, even consciousness, / even all of forgetting, remember." But
if endings and beginnings overlap, then a recovery of the past is
also an exploration of the future; "in a poem you wish to reach a
new place," Kinnell thinks (PPW 113), but his work conceives of
time in such a way that you can wish also to reach an old place.
The point is not whether poetry faces you forward or back or—
Janus-like—both, but that it carries you closer to the world, compensates for self and loss, "sings past even the sadness / that begins
it" ("Last Holy Fragrance"):

> Words, in the mouth of our mouths,
> and in our tongues touching their words as silently,
> are almost ready, already, to bandage the one
> whom the *scritch scritch scritch,* meaning *if how when*
> we will lose each other, scratches scratches scratches
> from this moment to that.
>
> ("That Silent Evening")

Kinnell clings to language, then, as to life itself—or, rather, even
more desperately than to life: "I will come back from the living
and enter / death everlasting: consciousness defeated. / But I will
not offer, no, I'll never / burn my words. Wishful phrases!" But as
these lines perhaps hint, that poetry recovers the world gives pause
as well as cause for celebration. Doesn't the world, after all, have
its own designs on us, want to annihilate as well as compensate for
self, to enfold us in "death everlasting" as it gathers us into its
arms? Is not kinship in *The Past* still terrible? Nowhere is Kinnell
more characteristically American than when he opposes identity
and community, when like the transcendentalists he sees the existence of other people as a menace to the self. Nowhere is his work
more important than when he calls this opposition into question
or seeks out the world despite what, given the transcendental tendency, he perceives it to cost.

If Kinnell is sometimes less in and out of the game than outside
looking in, he is also sometimes merely outside, his back imperially
turned to the game:

> I want to lie out
> on my back under the thousand stars and think

my way up among them, through them,
and a little distance past them, and attain
a moment of nearly absolute ignorance,
if I can, if human mentality lets us.
("The Seekonk Woods")

But such purely Adamic moments are rare, and even this one is
more the expression of a desire than the achievement of it. Fair
enough to harbor the impulse (and admirable to express it so that
it may be examined), and anyway the final condition ("if human
mentality lets us") compromises the whole thing. The passage,
moreover, reveals only one of *two* desires at that point in the poem.
Just preceding it, Kinnell is turned over:

I want to crawl face down in the fields
and graze on the wild strawberries, my clothes
stained pink, even for seven years
if I must, if they exist.

Again, the last phrase compromises. Kinnell faces both toward and
away from the world, but either way feels a tug from behind.

Despite the impulse toward "absolute ignorance," Kinnell usually faces toward the world and searches his way in its direction.
But his journey home is seldom as merry as the sow piglet's (in
"The Sow Piglet's Escapes") who escaped, let herself be captured,
and—though she "wriggled hard"—cried "*wee wee wee*, all the
way home," punning out her tragically gay affirmation: *yes yes yes*
as she heads for the slaughter. Because poet, unlike piglet, realizes
that "in Sheffield the *dolce vita* / leads to the Lyndonville butcher,"
he considers both the sweetness of the journey and the bitterness of
its destination (though he always lets himself be captured). The
world thus continues to baffle as well as to beckon—sometimes in
the same gesture. In "Middle of the Night" Kinnell remembers
when "Kenny Hardman and George Sykes / called 'Gaw-way-ay!'
at the back / of the house. If I didn't come out / they would call
until nightfall." But even in the act of crying out his name, the
world puts him off: the phonetic leap from "Gaw-way-ay!" to
"Galway!" is no shorter than the one from "Gaw-way-ay! to "Go
way!" or "Go away!"

Indeed, although this poem is ostensibly about affirmation, its secret name is withdrawal. When Kinnell hears his friends calling his name, he thinks:

> If I didn't come out
> they would call until nightfall,
> like summer insects. Or like
> the pay phone at the abandoned
> filling station, which sometimes
> rang, off and on, an entire day.

No one answers the phone—does anyone answer Kenny Hardman and George Sykes? The poem doesn't tell us, but we do know that the poet's first response isn't "Kenny! George!" but "If I didn't come out. . . ." Even if you do affirm, the act turns itself inside out, for "the word 'yes' said too many times" makes up "The final yawn before one sleeps." Kinnell remembers a moment when his whole body was saying "yes": "The shocking dark / of her eyes blew alive in me / the affirmative fire." But who is this woman, indentified earlier only as "she"? All we know of her is that she reminds Kinnell of a turtle (just as Kenny and George are compared to insects). Like the scene itself, she is bereft of social context. Affirmation blows alive, apparently, only when the scene is kept at a distance (in memory, the social dimension filtered out). And anyway, even as the affirmative fire is lighting, they are withdrawing from each other ("On the landing / she turned and looked back"). Just as we don't know exactly whether his friends' cries are answered, we don't see what happens when affirmation is blown alive. Does Kinnell approach the woman? All we know for sure, as the poem concludes, is that "It would have hurt / to walk away, just as it would bewilder / a mouth making the last yawn to say 'no.'" When the fire is lit, that is, the poet doesn't let it spread, doesn't affirm the affirmation by writing "I ran toward her as fast as my legs would carry me." Rather, the first thing he considers is walking away. This "would have hurt," but perhaps no more than walking toward her. It might bewilder the mouth to say it, but the last word of this poem is "no."

The next two poems in the volume, however, end on "yes," and in them affirmation sounds perhaps louder than withdrawal (though they still sound simultaneously). Although in "Conception" a man is literally withdrawing from a woman after making love, his "cock / shrugging its way out of her," the poem concludes with an assertion of community as she says "'Yes, I am two now, / and with thee, three.'" And, as we've seen, in the final scene of "The Sow Piglet's Escapes" the pig squeals her triple pun of community (*we*), affirmation (*oui*) and delight (*whee*): *wee wee wee.*

This affirmation, though, seldom actually points to *social* community. "'Don't lose / all touch with humankind,'" Kinnell in "The Past" recalls his (nameless) "friend / and mentor" warning him in a letter, as if this were a serious possibility (one that "The Past" itself, with its miles-from-anywhere, unpeopled setting, does not dispel—indeed, even the warning does not arrive in person). The namelessness of the woman in "Middle of the Night" is typical. The other people who do stir with life in *The Past* are mainly dead poets (though even here it is sometimes hard to tell where Wright or Hugo leaves off and Kinnell begins), and in the volume's kookiest lines Muriel Rukeyser is glimpsed in a moment of pure (if obscure) personality: the mailman has brought Kinnell, in Hawaii, first "a letter from Providence lamenting the 'siege against poets,'" then "Richard Hugo's memoir of James Wright," and

> Last, around the time of stars in Sheffield, a package holding
> four glass doorknobs packed in a *New York Times* of a year
> ago, which Muriel Rukeyser had sea-mailed to me, to fulfill if
> not explain those mysterious words she used to whisper
> whenever we met: "Galway, I have your doorknobs."
>
> ("December Day in Honolulu")

Kinnell's vision is seldom social in this manner, but it is strongly idiosyncratic and fresh. But if his distance from the world can help him find new angles of approach, it can also, as I've suggested, sometimes blur the outlines of what he can see. In and out of the game, Whitman can (in SM 33) soar over the terrain and still delineate it in stunning and copious detail, an avalanche of observation. The world, though, can pose no threat to one who imagines "No guard can shut me off, no law prevent me," who sees the "dead resuscitate" (SM 33). A poet more attuned to what laws tragically prevent him may not always see the world so eagerly and thoroughly. If it baffles as well as beckons, you may not want the world to come always into sharp focus. If part of you seeks "absolute ignorance," the experience of vision will remain problematic.

"First Day of the Future" defines Kinnell's ambivalent position, outside looking in, and it illustrates the possibilities and limitations of that position. The poem locates him not in what it calls the "permanent present" but at the remove suggested by the title, not in the game, but out. But after working so hard to achieve the remove, the poet wants back:

> Even though I burned the ashes of its flag again and again
> and set fire to the ticket that might have conscripted me into its
> ranks forever,
> even though I squandered all my talents composing my
> emigration papers,
> I think I want to go back now and live again in the present
> time, back there

He glances "back there" at the world then and—still keeping his distance—describes what he sees, back there

> where someone milks a cow and jets of intensest nourishment
> go squawking into a pail,
> where someone is hammering, a bit of steel at the end of a stick
> hitting a bit of steel, in the archaic stillness of an afternoon.

These descriptions typify Kinnell's remove from, and mixed attraction to, the world; they are full of feeling and alive, but queer. This is hammering observed for the first time, from the point of view of absolute ignorance, as if a Martian had with fascination happened upon a carpenter. As the poem ends, Kinnell hasn't yet returned and is left more or less stranded in the future, where he "must take care. For here / one has to keep facing the right way, or one sees one dies, and one dies." But which is "the right way"? Toward the world? Death, that way. Away? No life there. Kinnell's predicament should keep provoking him into poetry for some time to come.

"I'm not sure I'm going to like it living here in the future," "First Day of the Future" concludes: "I don't think I can keep on doing it indefinitely." Kinnell's strongest impulse is back toward the present, I think, and he prays:

Whatever happens. Whatever
*what is* is is what
I want. Only that. But that.
                    ("Prayer")

To pray for something, though, is to acknowledge seriously incomplete possession of it; Being is desperately insisted upon—"
*is* is is"—but it is easier to feel unambiguous desire for existence
conceived in this general form, only the rough beckoning outlines
visible, not the details that might baffle. Kinnell ends *The Past* in
an apparent rush toward the world, but, as the last two words echo
"Prayer," it is a world posed in this tamer, generic aspect: "Behind,
/ the world made of wishes goes dark. Ahead, / if not tomorrow
then never, shines only what is" ("The Seekonk Woods").

In working (and sometimes working through) its ambivalence,
*The Past* is courageous and human—even as (or because) "los[ing] /
all touch with humankind" remains a possibility. Calvin Bedient
praises Robert Penn Warren as "a poet who has found the right
relation (right for him and in general seemingly right) between
struggle and submission, glory and truth, nobility and self-knowl-
edge, joy and pain, quest and common sense" (21). If Kinnell has
not yet settled permanently on his own "right relation," it is at least
partly because, ignoring Warren's admonition, he resolves to speak
both of time's names to its face. This leaves him on sometimes sacred, sometimes shaky ground: he is less a poet of right relation
than a poet of the *search* for right relation.

In "The Road Between Here and There" a fortune teller considers Kinnell's hand: "'What is still possible is inspired work, faithfulness to a few, and a last love, which, being last, will be like looking up and seeing the parachute dissolving in a shower of gold.'"
No matter what combination of fear and desire will inspire his future work, clearly the palm that cradles the pen holds out the
promise that as the lifeline frays he will sing out *yes yes yes* all the
way home. The fortune teller saw Kinnell's end in a shower of gold,
not in the sparkle of a white flash, and if she is good at her work,
we can look forward to hearing the love story of his dying fall. A
poet who knows that the earth on which he will crash down is itself desperately contingent will earn every *yes* he can manage
to sing.

# Notes

## Introduction

1. Norman O. Brown analyzes the psychoanalytic basis for understanding life and death as complementary parts of an encompassing unity in *Life Against Death* (Middletown, Conn.: Wesleyan University Press, 1959). References to this work appear in the text.

2. Galway Kinnell, interview with the author, 31 March 1984.

3. William Blake, "The Marriage of Heaven and Hell."

4. Charles Altieri, *Enlarging the Temple: New Directions in American Poetry during the 1960's* (Lewisburgh, Pa.: Bucknell University Press, 1979), p. 37. Further references appear in the text.

5. Quoted in Altieri, p. 49.

6. Robert Peters, *The Great American Poetry Bake-Off* (Metuchen, N.J., and London: The Scarecrow Press, 1979), p. 26. The caricature gleefully continues: "seedy, his body scarred in various stages of healing, as he prepares to tuck his guts back into the cavity so as to free his hands for pushing that rock back up that interminable Monodnockian mountain."

7. Robert Pinsky, *The Situation of Poetry: Contemporary Poetry and Its Traditions* (Princeton: Princeton University Press, 1976), pp. 47–61. Further references appear in the text. Pinsky does not oppose Keats to Wordsworth and Coleridge, as I do, and in fact proposes that "Ode to a Nightingale" *exemplifies* one of the "essential Romantic conflicts" (47). My argument is developed in part 3 of my third chapter.

8. Richard Howard, *Alone With America,* enlarged edition (New York: Atheneum, 1980), p. 309. Further references appear in the text.

9. This view—that nature is wild and that poetry shouldn't try to tame it with formal regularity but rather should partake of its wildness—illuminates much modern poetry, especially Kinnell's own. But it overlooks the fact that, wild as nature may be in one sense, it also contains within it nearly perfect symmetries and minutely ordered systems. Kinnell's sense of meaning is founded on an appreciation of the natural

human body, but although it dies, for a while doesn't one side of the body usually rhyme with the other, isn't its heartbeat metrically regular, and aren't its internal workings astonishingly patterned? Thus, formally regular modern poems like Theodore Roethke's "I Knew a Woman," James Merrill's "Samos," and W. H. Auden's "Lullaby" partake of natural order even as they steadfastly confront "the thing which dies" without smelling nostalgic. Each uses that counterpoint for different ends, but none wants to tame chaos, really, and none resorts to the easy consolation that Kinnell sees in *In Memoriam*. Kinnell himself in his earlier years wrote some good rhymed poems, and in his later work the seven-sectioned poems (*The Book of Nightmares*, especially) use a very loose but obsessively repeated structural pattern to confront what does not last.

10. This misprint is corrected in a slightly revised version of the essay, which appears in *Walt Whitman: The Measure of His Song*, ed. Dan Campion, Ed Folsom, and Jim Perlman (Minneapolis: Holy Cow! Press, 1981).

11. Randall Jarrell, *Poetry and the Age* (New York: Ecco Press, 1953), p. 121.

12. Kinnell, interview with the author.

13. Suzanne Juhasz, *The Undiscovered Continent: Emily Dickinson and the Space of the Mind* (Bloomington: Indiana University Press, 1983), p. 4. Further references appear in the text. References to Dickinson's poetry in the text are to *The Poems of Emily Dickinson*, ed. Thomas H. Johnson (Cambridge, Mass.: The Belknap Press of Harvard University Press, 1955).

## Chapter 1

1. Gerard Manley Hopkins, "That Nature Is a Heraclitean Fire and of the Comfort of the Resurrection," in *Poems and Prose of Gerard Manley Hopkins*, ed. W. H. Garder (Baltimore, Md.: Penguin Books, 1963).

2. Ralph Mills, "A Reading of Galway Kinnell," *Iowa Review* 1 (1970): 67. The essay appears on pages 66–86 and is continued (Part 2) in *Iowa Review* 1 (1970): 102–21. Subsequent references are included in the text, where the page number will indicate which part is being quoted. Both essays also appear in Mills's *Cry of the Human: Essays on Contemporary American Poetry* (Urbana: University of Illinois Press, 1975).

3. Donald Davie, "Slogging for the Absolute," *Parnassus* 3 (1974): 9–22, quotation on 22. Further references appear in the text.

4. Altieri, *Enlarging the Temple*, especially chapter 1.

5. Glauco Cambon, *Recent American Poetry* (Minneapolis: University of Minnesota Press, 1961), p. 36. Further references appear in the text.

6. Kinnell, quoted by Mills, in *Poet's Choice,* ed. Paul Engle and Joseph Langland (New York: Dial Press, 1962), p. 257.

7. James Merrill, "Mandala," in *Braving the Elements* (New York: Atheneum, 1979).

8. Philip L. Gerber and Robert J. Gemmett, eds., "Deeper Than Personality: A Conversation with Galway Kinnell," *Iowa Review* 1 (1970): 129. The interviewers are Gregory Fitzgerald and William Heyen.


## Chapter 2

1. Thomas Kinsella, "The Divided Mind," in *Irish Poets in English,* ed. Séan Lucy (Cork: The Mercier Press, 1973), p. 215.

2. Seamus Heaney, "Digging," in *Poems: 1965–1975* (New York: Farrar, Straus and Giroux, 1980), pp. 3–4, and idem., *Preoccupations: Selected Prose, 1968–1978* (London: Faber and Faber, 1980), p. 41.

3. Robert Lowell, "91 Revere Street," in *Life Studies* (New York: Noonday Press, 1964), p. 45.

4. Yves Bonnefoy, *On the Motion and Immobility of Douve,* trans. Galway Kinnell (Athens: Ohio University Press, 1968). Further references appear in the text, cited by page number.

5. Jean-Paul Sartre, *The Flies,* in *No Exit and Three Other Plays,* trans. Stuart Gilbert (New York: Vintage, 1955), act 3.

6. Anthony Rudolph, *Selected Poems* (London: Jonathan Cape, 1968), p. 27. Further references appear in the text.

7. Sarah Lawall, Preface to Yves Bonnefoy, *Words in Stone,* trans. Susanna Lang (Amherst: University of Massachusetts Press, 1976), p. xiv. Further references to Lawall's preface appear in the text.

8. Pablo Neruda, "Toward an Impure Poetry," in *Five Decades: A Selection (Poems: 1925–1970),* trans. and ed. Ben Belitt (New York: Grove Press, 1974), p. xxi.

9. Yves Bonnefoy, "Shakespeare and the French Poet," *Encounter* 18, no. 6 (1962): 38–43, quote on 41. Further references appear in the text.

10. Charles Molesworth, "The Rank Flavor of Blood: Galway Kinnell and American Poetry in the 1960's," *Western Humanities Review* 27 (1973): 225–39, quote on 229. Further references appear in the text. This article is collected in Molesworth's book, *The Fierce Embrace: A Study of Contemporary American Poetry* (Columbia: University of Missouri Press, 1979).

11. William Wordsworth, Prospectus for "The Recluse," quoted in M. H. Abrams, *Natural Supernaturalism: Tradition and Revolution in Romantic Literature* (New York: Norton, 1971), p. 466.

12. Ekbert Faas, *Toward a New American Poetics: Essays and Interviews* (Santa Barbara: Black Sparrow Press, 1978), p. 208.

13. Jane Taylor, "The Poetry of Galway Kinnell," *Prospective* 15: 189–200, quote on 198.

14. Susan Wheeler, "An Interview with Galway Kinnell," *New England Review* 3, no. i: 115.

15. Cary Nelson, *Our Last First Poets: Vision and History in Contemporary American Poetry* (Urbana: University of Illinois Press, 1981), p. 65. Further references appear in the text.

16. Robert Pinsky formulates Keats's dilemma in terms of these two key words, taken from "Ode to a Nightingale" (*The Situation of Poetry*, p. 55). I elaborate on this issue in part 3 of my third chapter.

17. My basic text for the discussion of "Spindrift" is the version that appeared originally in *Flower Herding on Mount Monadnock,* not the version reprinted in *The Avenue Bearing the Initial of Christ into the New World.* A discussion of the significant emendations appears in the text.

18. Although Kinnell sees poetry's task as "breaking out of the enclosed ego" (PPD 64), he also thinks "the basic subject of modern poetry is the self" (interview with the author); Merrill—playfully, but more or less seriously—once remarked to me that "the self is as small as a raisin."

## Chapter 3

1. Ekbert Faas, *Ted Hughes: The Unaccommodated Universe* (Santa Barbara: Black Sparrow Press, 1980), p. 207. The quotation appears in an interview Faas conducted with Hughes. Further citations from Hughes's remarks are included in the text.

2. Kinnell, "Author's Note" to *First Poems: 1946–1954* in *The Avenue Bearing the Initial of Christ into the New World,* p. 3. This note was written in 1970.

3. Calvin Bedient, *Eight Contemporary Poets* (London: Oxford University Press, 1974), p. 95. Further references appear in the text.

4. W. B. Yeats, *The Letters of W. B. Yeats,* ed. Allan Wade (London: Rupert Hart-Davis, 1954; New York: Macmillan, 1955), p. 583.

5. This comparison to Disney cartoons is offered by David Lodge in *Critical Quarterly* (Spring 1971), as noted by Bedient, *Eight Contemporary Poets,* p. 113.

6. Galway Kinnell, *Black Light,* p. 62. References in the text are to the North Point Press edition (San Francisco: 1980). I cite this version because the differences are slight and it is more widely available.

7. Albert Camus, *The Stranger,* trans. Stuart Gilbert (New York: Alfred A. Knopf, 1972), pp. 151–52. Further references appear in the text.

8. Galway Kinnell, Introduction to *The Poems of François Villon,* trans. Galway Kinnell (New York: Signet, 1965), p. 7. Kinnell has also published another translation of Villon: *The Poems of François Villon* (Boston: Houghton Mifflin, 1977). I cite the introductions of both editions in my text; Arabic numerals refer to the 1965 edition, Roman to the 1977. The quoted lines are from the later edition.

9. Kinnell, in Thomas Gardner, "An Interview with Galway Kinnell," *Contemporary Literature* 20: 423–33, quote on 431.

10. Andrew Taylor, "The Poetry of Galway Kinnell," *Meajin Quarterly* 36: 228–41, quote on 229. Further references appear in the text.

11. W. B. Yeats, *Mythologies* (London and New York: Macmillan, 1959), p. 331.

12. Barbara Herrnstein Smith, *Poetic Closure: A Study of How Poems End* (Chicago: University of Chicago Press, 1968), p. 244.

13. This paragraph quotes from my article, "Singing Amid Uncertainty: Yeats's Closing Questions," in *Yeats Annual No. 2,* ed. Richard J. Finneran (London: Macmillan, 1983), pp. 35–45.

14. Henry David Thoreau, *Walden,* ed. J. Lyndon Shenley (Princeton: Princeton University Press, 1971), pp. 216–17. Further references appear in the text.

15. Helen Vendler, *Part of Nature, Part of Us: Modern American Poets* (Cambridge, Mass.: Harvard University Press, 1980), p. 110.

16. Samuel Taylor Coleridge, "On Poesy or Art," in *Criticism: The Major Texts,* ed. Walter Jackson Bate (New York: Harcourt Brace Jovanovich, 1952, 1970 [enlarged]), p. 396. Further citations are to this page.

17. Kinnell, in "The Weight That a Poem Can Carry: An Interview with Galway Kinnell," by Wayne Dodd and Stanley Plumly, *The Ohio Review* 14, no. 1 (1972): 35.

18. Stephen Spender, "Rilke and Eliot," in *Rilke: The Alchemy of Alienation,* ed. Frank Baron, Ernst S. Dick, and Warren R. Maurer (Lawrence: The Regents Press of Kansas, 1980), p. 49. Further references appear in the text.

19. Kinnell, in Gerber and Gemmett, "Deeper than Personality," p. 127.

20. Kinnell, in "The Weight That a Poem Can Carry": 37.

21. William Heyen quoted in Gerber and Gemmett, "Deeper than Personality," p. 127.

## Chapter 4

1. Stanley Kunitz, "The Life of Poetry," *Antaeus* 37 (1980): 149–53, quote on 153. Compare Kunitz with a passage Michel Foucault—in *The Order of Things* (New York: Random House, 1973)—quotes from G. Porta, *Magie Naturelle* (Fr. trans., Rouen, 1650, p. 22): "As with respect to its vegetation the plant stands convenient to the brute beast, so through feeling does the brutish animal to man, who is conformable to the rest of the stars by his intelligence; these links proceed so strictly that they appear as a rope stretched from the first cause as far as the lowest and smallest of things, by a reciprocal and continuous connection; in such wise that the superior virtue, spreading its beams, reaches so far that if we touch one extremity of that cord it will make tremble and move all the rest" (19). The idea that Being is continuous is an old one. Foucault analyzes how until the end of the sixteenth century the concept of similitude "made possible knowledge of things visible and invisible, and controlled the art of representing them" (17). In this sense, my argument in this chapter is that *Nightmares* tries to recover an old way of knowing—or to integrate it with newer ways. (My discussion of alchemy and *Nightmares*, especially, implies this point.) Some new ways of knowing, of course, need no such integration, are already reformulations of old ways. On page 125 of *The Tao of Physics* (New York: Bantam Books, 1977) Fritjof Capro quotes atomic physicist Werner Heisenberg: "The world thus appears as a complicated tissue of events, in which connections of different kinds alternate or overlap or combine and thereby determine the texture of the whole" (*Physics and Philosophy* [New York: Harper Torch Books, 1958], p. 107).

2. Samuel Taylor Coleridge, *Notebooks*, quoted by Geoffrey Hartman in *Saving the Text* (Baltimore: Johns Hopkins University Press, 1981), p. 14. Yeats defines "subjective men" as those "who must spin a web out of their own bowels" in *The Autobiography of William Butler Yeats* (New York: Macmillan, 1965), p. 128.

3. Rainer Maria Rilke, *Duino Elegies*, trans. J. B. Leishman and Stephen Spender (New York: Norton, 1939 [The Norton Library Edition, 1963]) p. 21. Further references appear in the text. I use this edition because it is the one Kinnell admires most and the one he quotes.

4. Leishman, in Rilke, *Duino Elegies*, p. 93.

5. Elizabeth Sewell, *The Human Metaphor* (Notre Dame, Ind.: University of Notre Dame Press, 1964), p. 157.

6. Robert Langbaum, "Galway Kinnell's *The Book of Nightmares*," in *The American Poetry Review* (March/April 1979): 30–31. Further references appear in the text.

7. T. S. Eliot, *Four Quartets* (London: Faber and Faber, 1959), p. 58. Further references appear in the text.

8. C. G. Jung, *Psychology and Alchemy*, 2nd ed. (Princeton: Princeton University Press, 1958), p. 23. Subsequent references to this work appear in the text. In my discussion of alchemy, I also cite the following works: H. Stanley Redgrove, *Alchemy: Ancient and Modern* (London: William Rider and Son, 1922); Arthur John Hopkins, *Alchemy: Child of Greek Philosophy* (New York: Columbia University Press, 1934); E. J. Holmyard, *Alchemy* (Penguin Books, 1957); John Read, *The Alchemist in Life, Literature and Art* (London: Thomas Nelson and Sons, 1947); M. M. Pattison Muir, *The Story of Alchemy and the Beginnings of Chemistry* (New York: D. Appleton and Company, 1903).

9. Kinnell, in "Craft Interview with Galway Kinnell," *New York Quarterly* 8 (1971): 11–19, quote on 16, reprinted in *The Craft of Poetry*, ed. William Packard (Garden City, N.J.: Doubleday and Company, 1974).

10. Kinnell, in "The Weight That a Poem Can Carry": 30.

11. Langbaum also notes this connection in "Galway Kinnell's *The Book of Nightmares*": 30.

12. Gardner, "An Interview with Galway Kinnell": 429.

13. Kinnell, in "The Weight That a Poem Can Carry": 30.

14. Kinnell goes on about hens: "Though not very personable, hens have an unusual psychic dimension, due, I like to think, to the suppression of their capacity to fly. When you hold their heads under their wings they slump into a coma. You might think they think it is the night, except they do the same thing if you turn them on their backs and stroke their throats. They'll lie there for several minutes, apparently in a trance. Maybe the throat is their Achilles' heel, emotionally speaking, and they've fainted from too much. But they also fall out if you face them toward infinity—if you draw a straight line in the earth and hold them down with their beaks touching it. There are doubtless other mysteries in the hen."

15. Kinnell, in "The Weight That a Poem Can Carry": 30.

16. Ibid.: 34.

17. Gerber and Gemmett, "Deeper Than Personality": 131.

18. Kinnell, interview with the author.

19. Robert Peters points out that the title of section 6 is a papoose name.

20. The "ten thousand things" is a reference to Lao Tse, *Tao Te-Ching*, 5: "Heaven and earth are ruthless; / They see the ten thousand things as dummies" (trans. Gia-Fu Feng and Jane English [New York: Vintage Books, 1972]). In place of "dummies," other translations have "straw dogs"; a footnote about this phrase in the translation by D. C. Lau (Penguin Books, 1963) seems pertinent to Kinnell's allusion: "In the *T'ien yun*

chapter in the *Chang Tzu* it is said that straw dogs were treated with the greatest deference before they were used as an offering, only to be discarded and trampled upon as soon as they had served their purpose" (61).

21. Gardner, "An Interview with Galway Kinnell": 427. The prose quotations in the rest of this paragraph and the next are cited from this interview.

22. Ibid.: 428–29.

23. Miners would take a canary down into the mine. Odorless poison gas would kill the songbird sooner than the men, so a cessation of the trilling would serve as a warning.

24. Marjorie Perloff, "Poetry Chronicle: 1970–71," *Contemporary Literature* 14 (1973): 97–131, quote on 124.

25. Alan Helms, "Two Poets," *Partisan Review* 44 (1977): 287–95, quote on 291.

26. Kinnell, in "Craft Interview with Galway Kinnell": 16.

27. I take this phrase from the title of a book of conversations: Allen R. Grossman, *Against Our Vanishing: Winter Conversations with Allen Grossman*, conducted and edited by Mark Halliday (Boston: Rowen Tree Press, 1981).

## Chapter 5

1. Helen Vendler, "Making It New," *New York Review of Books* 31, no. 10 (June 14, 1984): 32–35, quote on 32.

2. William Wordsworth, *The Prelude* XI, 258–79.

3. Abrams, *Natural Supernaturalism*, p. 387. Abrams quotes *The Prelude* V, 407; VII, 469; V, 628–29; I, 614; and (1850) VI, 513–14.

4. Kinnell, interview with the author.

5. R. W. Flint, "At Home in the Seventies," *Parnassus* 8 (1980): 51–62, quote on 52. Further reference appears in the text.

6. Kinnell, interview with the author.

7. Whitman writes, "To touch my person to someone else's is about as much as I can stand" (SM 27).

8. Kinnell, interview with the author. Kinnell's comments in this paragraph and the next also are cited from this interview.

9. Stephen Yenser, "Recent Poetry: Five Poets," *The Yale Review* 70 (1980): 105–28, quote on 127. Further references appear in the text.

## Epilogue

1. Calvin Bedient, *In the Heart's Last Kingdom: Robert Penn Warren's Major Poetry* (Cambridge, Mass: Harvard University Press, 1984), p. 147. Further references appear in the text.

2. I am thinking of a sentence in Robert Hass's "Songs to Survive the Summer," a poem in his volume *Praise* (New York: Ecco Press, 1979): "We are the song / death takes its own time / singing."

3. Michel Foucault, *The Order of Things* (New York: Random House, 1973), p. 44.

# Index

# Index

Index

## Note on the Author

Lee Zimmerman holds degrees from the University of
California, Los Angeles, and teaches in the Department
of English at Hofstra University. *Intricate and Simple
Things: The Poetry of Galway Kinnell* is his first book.